THEN CAME HISPANGELICALS

by

Rudolph D. González, Ph.D.

Then Came the Hispangelicals

Published by Deep River Books
Sisters, Oregon
www.deepriverbooks.com

ISBN – 13: 9781632695161
Library of Congress: 2019913766

Printed in the USA
2019—First Edition

28 27 26 25 24 23 22 21 20 19 10 9 8 7 6 5 4 3 2 1

Dedication

To my beloved parents
Mr. and Mrs. Rodolfo and Irene González
The first Hispanics I ever knew, and Hispangelicals by God's grace

Contents

INTRODUCTION: Then Came the Hispangelicals. 7

CHAPTER ONE: Then Came History. 27

CHAPTER TWO: Then Came Philosophy 49

CHAPTER THREE: Then Came Culture. 73

CHAPTER FOUR: Then Came Syncretism 93

CHAPTER FIVE: Then Came the Ahistorical Hispangelical. 117

CHAPTER SIX: Then Came the Hispanic Mind 145

CHAPTER SEVEN: Then Came the Hispangelical's Challenge 189

CHAPTER EIGHT: Then Came Evangelism and Discipleship. 221

CONCLUSION: What Comes Now? 243

Selected Bibliography. 253

Introduction

Then Came the Hispangelicals

Though there are more contemporary uses of the phrase "Then came . . .," my first recollection of it stems back to a television program that lasted for only the 1969–1970 season. *Then Came Bronson* was the show's title and featured Jim Bronson, a roving journalist, who toured the countryside riding a Harley Davidson in search of himself. Ironically, those whose lives crossed his path seemed to find the answer to their questions, but he never did and remained a seeker. In retrospect, this program, though short-lived, probably did as much as anything else to get corporate types out of their offices on weekends to tour the scenic roads of America on Goldwings and Electra Glides. Back in the day, however, the first inclination would have been to see this lone biker as a rebel. But, Jim Bronson wasn't a "one-percenter."[1] He may not have always been understood, and he did tend to mumble, but you knew Bronson was a friend who tried to leave people better off than he found them.

"Then Came the Hispangelicals" is a phrase I borrow, along with a term I coin, to speak of a kind of Christian believer who, like Jim

[1] The term "one percenter" refers to an alleged comment made by a spokesman for the American Motorcyclist Association (hereafter AMA), wherein he stated that 99 percent of motorcycle riders were law-abiding citizens. His comment implied the last one percent belonged to "outlaw" clubs not sanctioned by the AMA.

Bronson, was unanticipated upon his arrival. After all, it wasn't so long ago that to speak of Hispanics and their religious background was to pigeonhole them as Roman Catholics, and rightly so.[2] The unwavering commitment of Western Latinos to Roman Catholicism was rock solid for over 450 years. In fact, even though Protestants attempted to evangelize Latin America beginning in the mid-1800s, almost a century later they were still no more than a mere fraction of a percent of the total Spanish and Portuguese-speaking population.[3] If we were to think of the time Latin Americans have existed on this planet as one hour—sixty minutes—the length of time Hispanics have significantly embraced Protestantism would take in only the last six to seven minutes. Despite modest interest in Protestantism, Latin America was overwhelmingly Roman Catholic, but then came something unexpected: Hispanics began to connect with evangelicalism in unprecedented ways!

To be precise, while Protestant and evangelical churches had made some converts, sometime beginning in the mid-twentieth century, Latinos began to embrace Pentecostal and later charismatic forms of evangelicalism, a stunning development to say the least.[4] Today, Philip Jenkins, professor of history and religious studies at Penn State University, notes that even though mainline Protestantism had a one-hundred-year jump

---

[2] I acknowledge that the terms "Hispanic" and "Latino" are not universally accepted by all Spanish-speaking peoples. A recent Pew Hispanic Center Poll, "'When Labels Don't Fit': Hispanics and Their Views of Identity" (http://www.pewhispanic.org/files/2012/04/Hispanic-Identity.pdf, accessed September, 16, 2012), found that a majority of people prefer to be identified by their country of origin (e.g., Cuban, Mexican, Colombian, etc.). In this study, I use Hispanic and Latino interchangeably to speak generally of people from predominantly Spanish and Portuguese-speaking countries from throughout Latin America and those living in the United States.

[3] Philip Jenkins, *The Next Christendom: The Coming of Global Christianity* (Oxford: Oxford University Press, 2002), 61. Jenkins notes that in 1940 there were fewer than one million Protestants throughout Latin America.

[4] David Stoll, *Is Latin America Turning Protestant?* (Berkeley: University of California Press, 1990), 27. Stoll argues that Roman Catholic charismatic renewal encouraged Latin American interest in Pentecostalism. Today there are Protestant charismatics, allowing us to use the terms Pentecostal and Charismatic interchangeably as descriptors of the varieties of faith groups that subscribe to such "spirit-filled" teachings.

on outreach to Spanish-speaking countries, Pentecostal and charismatic believers outnumber all other Protestant Hispanics by far. Of the more the 150 million Latin American Protestants today, Jenkins figures that 80 to 90 percent are either Pentecostal or charismatic—a number that continues to increase at a fair clip.[5] This affinity for Pentecostalism is not limited to Latin America either. Though Hispangelicals can be found in all Protestant denominations in the United States, a significant majority finds the Pentecostal church appealing.[6] Non-Pentecostal evangelical churches have found this to be so patently true that they incorporate Pentecostal musical influences to draw the Hispanic family to their churches.[7]

Personally, I can attest to the rise of Pentecostal-style praise and worship in my own Baptist denomination. In the early 1970s one could already hear *coros*, popular worship choruses, being sung even while the use of the hymnal was still evident, but things were changing quickly. In the 1980s and thereafter, the popularity of the more emotive *cantos de alabanza* became a driving force that pushed traditional hymn-singing onto the proverbial curb. Yes, there are holdout churches where the hymnal is still used, but they are rare. Today, you can still see hymnbooks in the pews and, to be fair, many churches have left the piano or organ in their place. However, such mainstays

---

[5] Jenkins, *The Next Christendom*, 63. A 2005 Pew Forum Survey found 156 million Pentecostals, or Charismatics in Latin America, while according to the World Christian Database, 73 percent of all Protestants in Latin America are Pentecostal or charismatic. See http://www.christianpost.com/news/pentecostal-impact-growing-in-latin-america-23067/#KjvoYC1KkzRs6sZo.99 (accessed September 25, 2016).

[6] Jon Garrido, The Jon Garrido News Network, January 12, 2010, Hispanic8.com. Garrido reports that 85 percent of all US Hispanic Protestants identify themselves as Pentecostals, approximately 6.2 million people.

[7] The Pew Hispanic Research Center released a report in 2007 entitled *Changing Faiths: Latinos and the Transformation of American Religion*, asserting "religious expressions associated with the Pentecostal and charismatic movements are a key attribute of worship for Hispanics in all the major religious traditions—far more so than among non-Latinos." See http://www.pewhispanic.org/2007/04/25/changing-faiths-latinos-and-the-transformation-of-american-religion (accessed September 5, 2016). See also Stoll, *Is Latin America Turning Protestant?*, 4.

of congregational singing continue as little more than artifacts of a bygone era. This is not to say we don't sing an occasional hymn, but even when we do it is usually a stanza or a piece of one coupled to some contemporary praise song. Many have noted and raised concern about charismatic influences on theological grounds, but its popularity has not abated.[8] Its continued growth is a *de facto* admission that Pentecostalism, or perhaps neo-Pentecostalism,[9] will continue to be a major draw for Latinos in the United States and throughout Latin America who embrace evangelicalism in the years to come.[10]

Then Came the Wakeup Call

Clearly, Hispangelicals are on the increase, and one has to wonder if the broader evangelical community has given this serious thought. Douglas Sweeney, associate professor of church history at Trinity Evangelical

[8] Pentecostal and charismatic praise and worship regularly calls for bodily expression, inviting people to twirl in place, or to offer a sacrifice of praise, which means having freedom for personal expression. In non-Pentecostal congregations, while some venture to raise their hands, the more demonstrative elements are rarely, if ever, practiced. Most non-Pentecostal Hispangelicals contend that worship is a "spiritual experience," implying that bodily involvement is not essential to the worship of God. Pentecostals, however, consider such demonstrations as evidences of being Spirit-filled and thus Spirit-led. As one Pentecostal insists, "In the Pentecostal Church, I feel more freedom to perform what the Lord wants me to do." Clearly, the non-Pentecostal Hispangelical church has failed fully to consider the problems of theology and conscience that charismatic praise and worship music can pose, particularly when it champions a message that cuts across the grain of strong theological convictions.

[9] Hiram Almirudis, *Episodios de mi vida y la Iglesia de Dios que yo conocí,* (Leon Valley, TX: Self-published, 2013). See especially the chapter, "Las Razones de un Viejo," 19–43. I acknowledge Dr. Almirudis, a prominent Hispanic Pentecostal preacher and theologian, for his analysis of the evolution of a new type of Pentecostalism, or neo-Pentecostalism as he labels the movement. Here, I speak generally of Pentecostalism with the understanding that Almirudis and others of that tradition might want to distinguish contemporary Pentecostalism as a development, which has deviated in considerable fashion from historic Pentecostalism.

[10] Daniel A. Rodriguez, *A Future for the Latino Church* (Downers Grove, IL: InterVarsity Press, 2011), 42–43. Rodriguez acknowledges the growing presence of "English-dominant" Latinos. While Latino membership in Protestantism is diverse, it represents a relatively low percentage of the overall denomination's membership. Still, non-Pentecostal/Charismatic denominations continue to target this growing demographic in North America.

Divinity School, acknowledges that Hispanics are pouring in by the millions, and admits frankly, "Anglo-Americans are largely unaware of the massive scale of this development."[11] Here, I would add that if Hispanics are to be the next chapter in evangelicalism, as Sweeney also foresees, it behooves the evangelical church to think about its implications. Philip Jenkins ponders what the Latino growth within evangelicalism might mean. In earlier times, Jenkins remembers that Americans tended to treat Hispanic cultures as "shrinking islands of language and faith within the new U.S. borders," seeing them as little more than "quaint tourist attractions." Jenkins has changed his mind, seeing those islands as bridgeheads for the advancement of the Hispanic within the evangelical community.[12] I would agree that all Protestant and evangelical churches are seeing increased numbers of Hispanics but add that if Pentecostal inclinations continue within the Latino community, evangelicalism won't just grow in numbers but may change significantly in theological focus.

Whatever the case, given the growing numbers of Hispanic believers across all sectors of evangelicalism, should evangelicals not try to understand who they are—along with their goals, their dreams, their aspirations, and their serious challenges? The evangelical church may naively assume that the "born-again" experience brings Latino believers seamlessly into the fold, but the issue is somewhat more complicated. We can liken Hispangelicals to the rings or circles of the Olympic symbol with areas of overlap, but also significant areas that remain distinct. There may be things with which the Hispangelical identifies by virtue of being heir to a common Judeo-Christian worldview. Yet, so much of what it

---

[11] Douglas A. Sweeney, *The American Evangelical Story* (Grand Rapids, MI: Baker Academic, 2005), 182. Sweeney identifies Hispanics and to a lesser extent Asians as the major groups for Evangelical growth. See also Jenkins, *The Next Christendom,* 2–6; Jenkins also acknowledges that "the era of Western Christianity" is passing, yet this momentous development goes largely ignored by the European and Euro-American Christian world.

[12] Jenkins, *The Next Christendom*, 101.

means to be Hispanic was forged in a history that, to put it bluntly, was and is strikingly unique to the Hispanic experience.

Equally important is the fact that whereas the average North American evangelical lives out his or her faith in a nominally welcoming Protestant-evangelical environment, the Latino believer continues to have deep roots with a people that cherishes its ancient traditions, beliefs, and cultural expressions, many of which are antithetical to the tenets of their newfound faith. So, just how does a Hispangelical navigate these two quite different worlds? To illustrate the challenge many Hispangelicals face, we turn to an enduring desire of Latinos, especially Mexicans, there for those who have eyes to see it, yet it goes largely undetected on the American radar screen.

Then Came La Reconquista

Most Hispanics living in the United States—which is to say, Hispanics largely of Mexican extraction or heritage—know all too well what future opportunities await, and many are anxious to take full advantage of them. If we should ask for specifics, perhaps a short overview of the potential Hispanic impact on the United States[13] will help.[14]

With rare exception, those who study Latino trends in the United States foresee the day when Hispanics will likely inherit the land, culturally speaking. In his sober look into the future, George Friedman, founder of the think tank Stratfor, has argued in his *The Next 100 Years*

[13] This is not to infer that the whole of the non-Hispanic US population is of Anglo extraction. For the typical Hispanic, however, one is "Anglo" if their predominant language is English regardless whether they have German, Polish, Italian, Greek, Irish, etc. ancestry.

[14] It would be easy to talk about the Hispanic impact on North America and assume the reader understands this to mean the United States and Canada. This view is so imbedded even missionary sending agencies divide North and South America along language lines thus including Mexico and the Caribbean in the "southern" mix. The reader should note that North America is a continent composed of twenty-three sovereign countries, numerous possessions and territories, including Greenland, Canada, the USA, Mexico, six Central American countries, and all sovereign countries in the Caribbean.

that Mexico may well extend its cultural dominion over the lands sold to the United States under the 1848 Treaty of Hidalgo.[15] There is no doubt that with the election of Donald Trump to the presidency of the United States, such ambitious hopes may lose momentum or suffer a setback, but they are not dashed. As most Hispanics know, US administrations come and go, but these deeply held desires to re-enshrine the Latino ethos have been more than a century and a half in the making and, besides, the economic needs of the United States all but assures it will happen.

The migration of Latinos, both legal and illegal, to the US can fluctuate according to political administrations, but one thing is certain: The United States needs the influx of millions of immigrants to replenish the labor force necessary to sustain her economic engine.[16] While this country will welcome immigrants from around the world, a vast majority will come from Mexico and Central America, and the dynamic they present is different than other foreign workers. Due largely to the geographical proximity of their mother country, the cultural borderland of Mexico will, in effect, shift north-by-northwest, according to Friedman, encompassing large segments of the western United States. With well over 100 million Hispanics expected to live in the contiguous forty-eight states by 2060, Friedman projects that most will be predominantly of Mexican extraction.[17] This leads him to predict a possible scenario where Mexico "will have solved its final phase of population growth by extending its non-political boundaries into the Mexican Cessation" driven by US economic needs.[18] Thus, Friedman foresees a bargain of sorts wherein millions of low-skilled Mexican and Central American

---

[15] George Friedman, *The Next 100 Years: A Forecast for the 21st Century* (New York: Anchor Books, 2009), 82–87.

[16] Ibid., 132.

[17] US Census Bureau, "Projections of the Size and Composition of the U.S. Population: 2014 to 2060" June 14, 2015, http://www.census.gov/content/dam/Census/library/publications/demo/p25-1143.pdf (accessed September 3, 2016). According to the US Census Bureau, Hispanics in the US will swell to more than 119 million by 2060.

[18] Friedman, *The Next 100 Years*, 227.

workers supply the muscle necessary for labor but, in exchange, the United States pulls back, acquiescing to Latino labor force demands.

Friedman's analysis is not without its critics, and he wrote before the recent flow of caravans from Central America materialized, but his broad point is hard to discount, especially when Latino voices have been saying as much in their own way. Back in 1992, Xavier Hermosillo, a Sacramento talk show host, expressed the same future, yet without Friedman's analytical skills. Hermosillo put it quite openly when he said, "We [Latinos] will take over house-by-house, block-by-block. We may not overcome, but we will overwhelm."[19] Jorge Ramos, the Hispanic rock star of Spanish-language journalism, agrees with Hermosillo, but uses the language of determined sustained conquest.[20] "Latinos are culturally reconquering lands," he notes.[21] Ramos is a man who deals in words, so we have to believe that he chose this concept deliberately. For anyone of pure Spanish heritage, the *reconquista* is bound to evoke great pride and emotion, but does it ring equally true for the Hispanics? Alas, it doesn't matter, for *reconquista* is a useful slogan to marshal the ignorant masses.[22] Thus, in the same way that Spanish monarchs drove the Muslim Moors out of the peninsula in AD 1492, retaking Granada and reestablishing the primacy of their Roman Catholic religion, Mexicans, Mexican-Americans, and Central Americans who are also heirs of the Mesoamerican legacy look forward to reinstating, by hook or crook, Latino culture throughout vast segments of the United States.

While those in media like Ramos and Hermosillo have made their affections known, academicians have also joined in this struggle. Ilan Stavans, Lewis-Sebring Professor in Latin American Studies at Amherst

[19] William Buchanan, "We Shall Overwhelm: Deciphering Bureau of Labor Statistics Data on Hispanic Workers," The Social Contract, http://www.thesocialcontract.com/pdf/twenty-two/tsc_20_2_ w_buchanan.pdf (accessed July 26, 2016).

[20] Jorge Ramos, "Biography," https://www.jorgeramos.com/en/biography (accessed August 14, 2017).

[21] Jorge Ramos, *The Latino Wave* (New York: Harper Collins Publishers/Rayo, 2004), 185.

[22] Read the Conclusion of this book, where Ramos and the issue of *Reconquista* is taken up again.

College and a Jew of Mexican ancestry, quips ironically about Moctezuma's Revenge. In his study of Hispanic society in the United States, *The Hispanic Condition*, Stavans delves into the Hispanic psyche in North America. Ominously, his chapter on those of Mexican descent is entitled, "At War with Anglos."[23] Addressing his son, Stavans is confident that Hispanics, "shall infiltrate the enemy; we shall populate its urban centers, marry its daughters and establish the kingdom of Aztlán. They are here to reclaim what we were deprived of; to take revenge. This isn't a political battle . . . but a cosmic enterprise to set things right."[24] Stavans is certainly provocative in his language, but is it only that? Speaking as a Latino, I have sensed over my considerable adult lifespan the ever-growing expectation that Hispanics should not necessarily seek to adjust to the North American experience. Especially through Spanish-language media, Mexicans and Mexican-Americans are encouraged to become one with the future waves of immigrants—to establish an overwhelming presence that will change the United States as we know it. The thought of this may shock many, finding it totally incredible, but then again you may have noticed that this is already happening, and with considerable help from political allies.

In an April 23, 2017 *Meet the Press* interview with host Chuck Todd, House Minority Leader Nancy Pelosi, a Democrat from California, was asked to react to a proposed continuing resolution where funding was being included to begin the building of a wall along the US-Mexico border. Minority leader Pelosi, who is an opponent of President Trump's wall, called its construction "immoral, expensive, and unwise," but then she proved Hermosillo's and Ramos' *bona fides*. "You have to understand," Pelosi instructed her host, "this part of the country, there is a community with the border going through it."[25] Did you catch it? For Pelosi, who speaks for a large segment of the country, the border

---

[23] Ilan Stavans, "At War with Anglos," in *The Hispanic Condition: The Power of a People* (New York: Rayo, 2001), 61–106.

[24] Ibid., 246.

[25] NBC, *Meet the Press,* April 23, 2017.

between the southern US and northern Mexico is really an inconvenient obstruction, for it runs through a more enduring "country" and "community" that, in her mind, incorporates both the southern US border states and northern Mexico.

And Representative Pelosi is not alone. Many politicians have begun to speak of their constituents indiscriminately not to refer specifically to voting citizens, but to include the undocumented who live among them.[26] In this same vein, the regents of the University of California system recently enacted Policy 2019, which recognizes the undocumented as legal residents for the purpose of making them eligible to receive resident in-state college tuition.[27] The fact is, there are countless instances where American founding principles are being sidestepped, giving way to idiosyncrasies and demands, fueling this pan-Hispanic dream of a culturally unified Latino land.

We are repeatedly reminded that ignorance is no excuse for having violated a law, and something similar can be said here—for ignorance of this deeply held dream does not mean it doesn't exist. Believe it: For many, American claims on the southwest part of the United States are illegitimate. These lands, they believe, have always really belonged to Mexico. Of course, when Ramos, Stavans, or others speak of such things, they are not calling for a military campaign. However, that does not mean there is no real struggle. But through it all, many are confident of victory. And in this struggle, they are convinced that the ups and downs of history will work to their favor, bringing to life again a vital spiritual dimension.

For Victor Zamudio-Taylor, co-curator of the Los Angeles County Museum of Art's exhibit "The Road to Aztlán: Art from a Mythic Homeland," this movement has more than just cultural implications. "Aztlán," notes Zamudio-Taylor, "symbolizes the persistence of

---

[26] Luis Gomez, a Democrat representative from Illinois' 4th congressional district, regularly speaks of the undocumented in his district as his "constituents."

[27] University of California Residence Policy and Guidelines, "Policy 2019," http://ucop.edu/general-counsel/_files/ed-affairs/uc-residence-policy.pdf (accessed June 21, 2017).

tradition, language, and spiritual beliefs."[28] Thus, the idea of a cultural reclamation of this land is tied to the recovery of a "state of mind" of what it means to be a Mexican, *un Hispano,* a Chicano.[29] Stavans eagerly adds his enthusiastic voice, looking forward to establishing "the kingdom of Aztlán."[30] President Barack Obama may have said on October 30, 2008 that he was at the threshold of "fundamentally transforming the United States of America," but I doubt whether he ever imagined that it would be the gargantuan wave of Latinos that may have the greatest power to shape the cultural and spiritual landscape of the US moving forward, displacing the concept of America as a melting pot.[31]

Yes, many Hispanics look forward to a day when the border between Mexico and the United States will be practically irrelevant. For many, the border that cuts below Texas, New Mexico, Arizona, and California is a wound that has festered for too long, and it must heal.

Then Came the Pros and Cons

Not surprisingly, some Anglo commentators have seen the writing on the wall and have expressed alarm. In 2005, for example, Dr. Daneen G. Peterson posted on her website her concern about "American culture and language being ripped from American control."[32] In a sense, Peterson's alarm is ill-founded, based on the false assumption that Hispanics

[28] See "La voz de Aztlán," http://www.aztlan.net (accessed October 5, 2016).

[29] The appeal of "Aztlán" of the pre-Columbian Aztecs is used to encourage Chicano activism. In *World War Z,* Max Brooks notes the collapse of the Mexican government in the wake of the "undead" epidemic, yet resurrecting as the nation of Aztlán. See http://zombie.wikia.com/wiki/World_War_Z (accessed May 12, 2016).

[30] Stavans, "At War with Anglos," 61–106.

[31] Ramos, *The Latino Wave,* 187. See also, Stavans, *The Hispanic Condition,* 205–206.

[32] Daneen Peterson, "Stop the North American Union," http://www.stopthenorthamericanunion. com/InsanityReigns.html (accessed July 26, 2016). See also Ramos, *The Latino Wave,* 184, for other concerns.

are somehow foreign.[33] News flash!: Latinos are more native to Florida and the western part of the US than those who cut across the prairies in wagon trains in the 1800s. Spanish was spoken and Latino culture existed for 250 years before US Marines ever charged "the halls of Montezuma,"[34] or Zachary Taylor ever secured title and deed to the western lands. Like the saguaro, which has dotted the Arizona desert for centuries, the Latino is indigenous to the US. If people have never bothered to realize that Hispanic culture thrived within the lower forty-eight, it compounds the problem to cast Hispanics as aliens simply because of their cultural and language differences. Whatever ancestry runs through our blood—whether Mexican, Anglo, Irish, German, or Cuban—if the United States of America is our place of birth, or naturalization, we are citizens.

Still, while some do see the growing Hispanic presence with considerable alarm, others are very much encouraged by it. Rev. Samuel Rodriguez, president of the National Hispanic Christian Leadership Conference, testified before the United States Senate Subcommittee on Immigration in 2009. In his prepared remarks, Rodriguez assured the committee that Hispanic illegal immigrants are "God-fearing, hard-working, family loving children of God who reflect the values of our founding fathers and embrace the tenets of the American Constitution, the Declaration of Independence, and the Bill of Rights."[35] There should be no doubt that, by wide margins, most illegal immigrants who hail from countries to our south are honest, hard-working people who have risked life and limb in the hope of securing a better future for them and their families back home. That said, Rodriguez's statement

---

[33] Daily Mail, "More Than a Third of Americans Think Hispanics Are Illegal Immigrants . . . and Films and T.V. Are to Blame," September 12, 2012, http://www.dailymail.co.uk/news/article-2202444/More-THIRD-Americans-think-Hispanics-illegal-immigrants--films-TV-blame.html#ixzz26MW2WI7m (accessed September 13, 2016).

[34] The actual name is "Moctezuma," but it has been popularized into "Montezuma."

[35] See US Government Publishing Office, "Comprehensive Immigration Reform: Faith-Based Perspectives," https://www.govinfo.gov/content/pkg/CHRG-111shrg56073/html/CHRG-111shrg56073.htm (accessed May 3, 2019).

is astounding. Would he have the United States Senate believe that undocumented Latinos embrace the founding principles of this country? If Charles W. Anderson, Hawkins Professor of Political Science at the University of Wisconsin at Madison, holds any weight, Latin America has been a living museum of every political philosophy since its earliest beginnings.[36] Latin America is a conflict society, as Kalman Silvert has long noted. Most undocumented Hispanics don't come to the US because they revere its founding principles. As Howard J. Wiarda, Leonard Horwitz professor of Iberian and Latin American Studies at the University of Massachusetts, notes, US founding principles are not seen as fundamental to Latin American social structures.[37] Indeed, regardless of time or country—the latest examples being Venezuela and Honduras—Latin American history proves its political schizophrenia over and over again.

All things considered, as the ethnic profile of North America continues to take on a more Hispanic and Mestizo complexion, the founding ideals that were formative for the North American state will be seriously tested. Latinos bring with them other values and religious convictions, which they are not likely to check at the increasingly US/Mexico non-border.

Then Came the Crossroad

Each one of the issues I have briefly noted begs the question, "Where do Hispangelicals stand?" Here, I am not saying that Hispangelicals should have to answer for their personal views on illegal immigration, or the fate of "dreamers," or the practice of illegals coming with the intent purpose of giving birth to so-called "anchor babies," or illegals receiving federal subsidies, or sanctuary cities, or federal deportation policy, or

[36] See Charles W. Anderson, *Politics and Economic Change in Latin America: The Governing of Restless Nations* (Princeton, NJ: D. van Nostrand, 1967).

[37] Howard J. Wiarda, *The Soul of Latin America: The Cultural and Political Tradition* (New Haven, CT: Yale University Press, 2001), 136–137.

chain migration, or any number of other things that pertain to political realities in this country. In the United States, we deal with our differences at the ballot box.

Rather, I am asking if the Hispangelical is up to the challenge his own community poses. The Aztlán mythology is dynamic and can manifest itself in unexpected ways. In recent times, for example, the *Santa Muerte* cult, which is tied to the veneration of *Mictecacihuatl*, an Aztec goddess of death, has grown tremendously.[38] Once the "tailored" religion of drug traffickers and criminals, this religion has gone public, attracting millions of followers from poor, homosexual, and disenfranchised peoples. Is it not dumbfounding that people are turning to a matron saint of death as their only hope? The Latino world is in desperate straits politically, economically, but more so spiritually. So, it begs the question: Since evangelicalism is a faith orientation, does the Hispangelical have a real alternative to share with their beleaguered *gente*? Many Hispangelicals may simply steer clear, thanking God they have been saved from such lunacy, but is that the thing to do? If the Hispangelical defers, "how will they hear without a preacher?" (Rom. 10:14).

For my part, I am convinced that silence does nothing less than squander the moment. That said, silence is sometimes the better part of wisdom, especially if the Hispangelical is not at all clear as to the "light," the "darkness," and the "gray" areas of their own cultural heritage. This much is certain, the Hispangelical has a huge learning curve for the evangelical gospel has only recently begun to make inroads into the Latino community and its ramifications for the Latino world have not been fully discovered, much less understood. As the Hispangelical

---

[38] Duncan Tucker, "Santa Muerte: The Rise of Mexico's 'Death Saint'," BBC News, November 1, 2017, https://www.bbc.com/news/world-latin-america-41804243 (accessed August 30, 2018).

continues to be shaped by a renewed mind in Christ (Rom. 12:1–3), he will doubtless come to the same conclusion that hounded the apostle Paul when he thought of his kinsmen. Paul notes:

> Brethren, my heart's desire and my prayer to God for them is for their salvation. For I testify about them that they have a zeal for God, but not in accordance with knowledge. (Rom. 10:1–2)

Is the Hispangelical so wrapped up in his own salvation, he has forgotten where God found him? The Hispangelical should know the absurdity of a *Reconquista* mentality, the pipedream of an Aztlán spirituality, the insanity of a *Santa Muerte* cult—indeed, the foolishness of so many things that entrap Latinos. Knowing such things are the product of desperation, does the Latino evangelical have the insight to present the gospel authentically to his own?

Then Came the Hispangelicals

As we have briefly noted, there are differences of opinion as to whether Latinos in general present a benefit or a risk to the United States moving forward. But what are evangelicals saying about the recent influx of Hispanic believers into the churches? On this issue there is general enthusiasm, and anyone with a heart for evangelism would certainly applaud the harvest. That said, evangelical leaders need to ponder this increase thoughtfully. Luis Lugo, director of the Pew Forum on Religion and Public Life, speaks as a would-be prophet:

> Leaders in every denomination have to recognize that this is their destiny; just look at the recent census projections. We got a postcard from the future, and it told us that in the not-too-distant future, this country is going to be minority white.

> So, the future of many religious traditions in this country will depend upon the second-generation Latinos.[39]

If Lugo is accurate in his assessment of the Hispanic evangelical presence for the future, it does no good to pin wild and unfounded hopes upon a group of believers that is still acquiring its "sea legs" in many respects.[40] Simply to assume that by virtue of their numbers Hispangelicals may rescue evangelicalism is faulty thinking at its best, and for good reason.

Then Came the Conflicted Hispanic Mind

When Ilan Stavans considers what makes Latinos unique, he chooses a baffling set of depictions. Latinos, he says, are "a collision of selves and idiosyncrasies, a labyrinth with corridors of reason and madness, enlightenment and obscurantism," and "an encounter with chaos."[41] I, of course, would not go so far as to maintain that Hispanics are the only people in the world prone to irrationality, but I also do not believe Stavans said what he said merely for shock value. There is a reason *Don Quixote de la Mancha* by Cervantes is as revered in Latin American contexts as Shakespeare is among Anglophiles. For Stavans, Quixote personifies the Latino who is "incapable of distinguishing between reality and dreams."[42] In all this, Stavans insists that the Hispanic personality has still not developed into a demonstrable form—and why?

Multiple identities make up the Latino collective, causing Stavans ultimately to ask, "Can the United States incorporate in its multifarious

---

[39] Beliefnet News, "Why Are U.S. Hispanic Catholics Joining Pentecostal, Evangelical Churches?" (2011), http://blog.beliefnet.com/news/2011/10/why-are-u-s-hispanics-choosing-to-leave-the-catholic-church.php (accessed September 6, 2016).

[40] Ron Boehme, "The Fourth Wave," Youth with a Mission (http://www.usrenewal.org/the-fourth-wave (accessed July 10, 2016). Boehme, a leading founder of *Youth with a Mission* (YWAM), is so optimistic that he ponders whether Hispanic Evangelicals could contribute to saving the Western way of life.

[41] Stavans, *The Hispanic Condition,* 32, 109, 113.

[42] Ibid., 109.

metabolism such a display of irrationality—an ancestral legacy of which it is impossible to dispossess Hispanics?"[43] Reluctantly, I agree with Stavans' broader assessment, but here I focus on the church and ask, "Can the evangelical community incorporate into its metabolism the Hispangelical who brings with them an ancestral legacy of which it is impossible to strip away from Hispanics?"

In recent history, we have seen the emerging church movement and neo-evangelicalism come on the scene, suggesting that evangelicalism may be splintering.[44] Some might see the arrival of Hispanic evangelicals as evidence of more of the same, just another group staking its particular niche at the cost of weakening the whole. But I rather agree with Sweeney who notes, evangelicals "have always shared a strong centripetal faith."[45] Being an evangelical still means something, and Hispangelicals who are drawn to communal life embrace that same conviction. But this does not mean they will be mere passive recipients of a tradition. Whether this happens consciously, or perhaps not, the Hispangelical will contribute in a way that is both consistent with their reality as Hispanics and as followers of the risen Christ.

Then Came the Hispangelicals

My reasons for writing this book are straightforward. First, I hope *Hispangelicals* will serve as a primer, providing some insight into the Hispanic mind and condition. This might seem unnecessary to some, for the country is inundated by Hispanics from throughout Latin America. For many, their prolific presence would equate with familiarity, but

---

[43] Ibid., 152.

[44] Millard J. Erickson, *The Evangelical Left* (Grand Rapids, MI: Baker Books, 1997), 28–31. Erickson notes that the emergence of a post-conservative evangelical strain identifying a number of contemporary scholars who even then (1997) were advancing a theology that broke away from traditional evangelical conservatism on eleven key points.

[45] Sweeney, *The American Evangelical Story*, 183, passim.

this does not necessarily follow. Many have ill-conceived perceptions, learned through popular channels—and often, some Hispanics—parrot a convenient caricature. In all of this, one thing that is sorely lacking is a deeper, more historically attuned perspective.

And so, *Then Came the Hispangelicals* devotes the first four chapters as follows:

- Chapter One offers an analysis of a phenomenon of redundancy in Latino history.
- Chapter Two surveys Greek, Roman, and European philosophies that shaped Hispanic colonial and post-colonial life.
- Chapter Three studies how the baroque worldview contributed to the formation of Latino culture.
- Chapter Four investigates the phenomenon of religious syncretism in Latin America, giving rise to popular Latin American religions.

With each of these four chapters, the aim is to describe and illustrate a vital component that arguable fashioned the Latino mind and way.

The following chapter, Chapter Five, develops what I identify as the "ahistorical" Hispangelical, setting forth a theory that it was the Latin American colonial experience that inadvertently created the environment that would allow the emergence of the Hispangelical. Chapter Six is important, for it draws from the previous five chapters and assesses the Hispanic mind from an evangelical, Christ-centered perspective. The next chapter, Chapter Seven, is pivotal, turning to Hispangelicals specifically offering a profile of the Hispangelical mind and suggesting the challenges Latino evangelicals face both with respect to their native culture and to the evangelical church. The final chapter, Chapter Eight, addresses the challenges for effective evangelism and discipleship in the Latino context, offering a number of strategies that have proven effective in reaching Hispanics with the gospel.

The Conclusion provides a rationale and defense for the book's methodology, and one other thing: my personal hope for how the Hispangelical can make the greatest contribution moving forward.

To be clear, my aim in each chapter is not to offer an exhaustive study on any one subject, for each could command a book-length treatment of its own. Rather, in each chapter, I focus on the subject attempting to show how it was critical to the creation of the Hispanic *persona*, adding personal anecdotal experiences to illustrate the points being made. Were there and are there other factors that have influenced the Latino? Of course. And if this book succeeds, then the reader will be motivated to deepen their understanding of Hispanics all the more.

Another reason for writing this book is to offer some observations concerning the nexus between the Hispangelical mind and evangelicalism. Evangelicalism, when first conceived, came forth from a Protestant root, but Hispanics derive from a very different worldview. In my estimation, I do not believe that this significant divide has received proper attention and reflection. How then should the Hispangelical, who now lives within both worlds, think? Even more, if the message of the gospel holds true—and it does—how does the Hispangelical evaluate his own worldview roots? What is the makeup of a healthy "renewed" mind (Rom. 12:2; Eph. 4:3; Col. 3:10; Titus 3:5) within a Latino context? In all of this, my hope is to spark a conversation among Hispanic evangelicals, and indeed, within evangelicalism at large.

Additionally, I hope to challenge evangelicals to think deeply and seriously about the new Hispangelical arrivals (new by historical measures). This I believe is vital, for I also agree that they are poised to make a big difference within evangelicalism at large. That being said, it is in the interest of those who have carried the evangelical baton for so long, to know, to teach, but also to learn from Hispangelicals, who are already grabbing for the baton.

Finally, I hope to offer concrete strategies for pressing the claims of the gospel upon native and foreign-born Latinos. While we are all charged with the task of evangelism and discipleship, Hispangelicals have a unique role to play. They, perhaps more than anyone else, should be faced with having to answer the same question God asked Job. Do Hispangelicals know. . .

> Where is the way to the dwelling of light? And darkness, where is its place, that you may take it to its territory, and that you may discern the paths to its home? (Job 38:19–20)

As earlier stated, like any other person who comes to faith in Christ, Hispangelicals need to discern the light from the darkness of their own circumstance, for we are not simply Hispanics any more. The apostle Paul declares, "For God, who said, 'Light shall shine out of darkness,' is the One who has shown in our hearts to give the light of the knowledge of the glory of God in the face of Christ" (2 Cor. 4:6; cf. Eph. 5:8). We are Hispanics who have seen the true light of the gospel in Christ Jesus, and that light allows us to see with greater clarity what we must discard and what we can continue to embrace.

Then Came Bronson, the television show, came and went, but we should not expect nor desire for the Hispangelical to follow suit. In virtually every one of his letters, the apostle Paul appeals to the church's knowledge of him (e.g., 1 Cor. 11:2; 2 Cor. 1:12–15; Gal. 4:12–20; 1 Thess. 2:1–4). Far from seeking personal glory, Paul longed to be known in honest transparency (2 Cor. 4:1–2). Paul's heart should be ours, to be open letters, willing to read something of each other's life and faith without prejudice (2 Cor. 3:3). Given the demographic shift within evangelicalism today, knowing the Hispangelical on their own terms is integral to evangelical self-knowledge, for we are all permanent members of the body of Christ.

CHAPTER ONE

Then Came History

Is not the pretense of any other starting-point the pretense of jumping off one's own shadow? How could we possibly escape from the cultural history of our race?

Austen Farrer
Faith and Speculation[46]

Introduction

Some years ago, before the Obama administration reversed long-standing US policy concerning Cuba, I was invited to do some teaching to pastors for the Western Cuba Baptist Convention. During my stay, I visited the home of a pastor in Havana, and the television happened to be turned on. To my surprise, there he was—Che Guevara, addressing fellow revolutionaries concerning the glories of Marxist socialism. My first thought was that it was probably a movie with footage of *El Che* rallying the party faithful, but I was wrong. State-run media was broadcasting the original speech that dated to sometime in the early 1960s, before Guevara headed off on his ill-fated attempt to foment revolution in Bolivia.

[46] Austin Farrer, *Faith and Speculation: An Essay in Philosophical Theology* (Edinburgh: T. & T. Clark Ltd., 1967), 1.

My hosts were hardly sympathetic to Marxism, so I asked why they were watching that particular program. The pastor's wife responded with a grin, which she made sure I noticed, and proceeded to turn the dial. Immediately, I knew why. Every station was running the same speech! The revolution, my hosts informed me, had to remain alive in spite of the Soviet collapse. The authorities did this by playing reruns of old speeches given by Castro, Guevara, Cienfuegos, and others, endlessly.

So, why have the TV on? Well, the pastor's wife informed me, normal broadcasting did come on—eventually. The whole thing made me chuckle, but then I had a thought: We in the US don't even give this kind of air time to sitting presidents. In fact, that brief exposure to Cuban broadcasting caused me to think of the contrast with the United States. Is it conceivable that all network channels, including cable and PBS stations, would ever give American statesmen the time to speak without commercial interruption, and to air the same speech over and over again for years?

I concede that, in Cuba, the regime's control of mass media has much to do with what is puts on the public airwaves. However, in the United States, our voracious appetite for fresh news would never stomach anything like that. C-SPAN aside, even the annual State of the Union address is immediately shredded by the rival party and becomes yesterday's news within hours. It is a testament to something deep-seated in the Latino people, not an exclusive Marxist trait by any means, that dated words can be rebroadcast so unapologetically half a century later.

In the United States, we revere the words of our leaders, those who inspire us to achieve, who console the nation during trying times, or who challenge us to acts of selflessness.[47] But as inspirational as our

[47] Some of the most enduring American speeches include Franklin D. Roosevelt's "The only thing we have to fear is fear itself," 1933; John Fitzgerald Kennedy's 1961 inaugural address with its statement, "Ask not what your country can do for you; ask what you can do for your country"; Ronald Reagan's 1987, "Mr. Gorbachev, tear down this wall" challenge delivered to the Soviet Premier on the steps of Brandenburg Gate; Martin Luther King's "I Have a Dream" speech given August of 1963, which fueled the advancement of civil rights in the US. It is telling, however, that there is no acclaimed speech delivered by a Latino which rises to similar prominence in the US.

political orators can be, we don't air their speeches completely without edits or commercial interruption. In this respect, Hispanics are strikingly different. They reveal a strong fondness for repetitive memory, and it can manifest itself in many ways.

Note a recent example that bled across Mexico into the United States. In 2008, we may remember, Latinos throughout the United States protested immigration policy, and they used a well-worn script to make their point. The images of the Mexican flag, the Virgin of Guadalupe, along with other banners, were hoisted for news cameras to capture and air. In doing so, American-born Latinos, along with many native and undocumented Mexicans, were tapping into primal images that dated back before the founding of Mexico. It was no new strategy to recruit the matron Virgin of Mexico, some say all of Latin America, to add spiritual *gravitas* to their cause. Fully two hundred years earlier, Hidalgo and Morelos, both Roman Catholic friars, inspired the Mexican peasantry to press for liberation from colonial control, and they did so with images of the Virgin of Guadalupe spearheading the effort. We should not fail to note that the exact image of *La Morenita,* as she is affectionately called, was at that time already three hundred years old and fully etched into Hispanic hearts and minds. The image of 1810 was identical to the image of 2008, or of 2018, but there is more.

It was practically a given that when California farm workers—mostly Latinos, led by Cesar Chavez—marched in their historic boycotts across the Southwest, they would also raise images of the Virgin of Guadalupe. You see, it is in the playbook of the Latino mind to latch on to earlier struggles as if they are happening right then and there. Interestingly enough, the fact that grapes were at the center of both struggles made the association all the more preordained.

In 1810, it began with Catholic Priest Father Miguel Hidalgo y Costilla, credited with giving the initial *grito*, the shout for Mexican independence. When Hidalgo tried to help the poor by showing them how to grow grapes to better their lives, colonial authorities responded by monopolizing the grape industry, endangering the local farmers' livelihood. Grapes were at the heart of the movement for Mexican independence. And, in the early 1960s, the National Farm Workers Association, founded by Chavez, boycotted California grape growers in an effort to gain concessions that would improve the working conditions of migrant workers.[48]

Aside from the legitimacy of both struggles, 150 years apart, my point is simply to illustrate the way Hispanics tend to respond to their crisis situations. While the grievance may have its current aspects, there is almost always an association to something ancient. For most Latinos, few things in life, good or bad, are ever interpreted completely independent of their history. But don't just take my word; go to the Internet and look for images of Juan Diego (1521), Hidalgo y Costilla (1810), Mexican revolutionaries (1917), the Cristero rebellion (1926–29), Cesar Chavez boycotts (1962), immigration protests in the US (2008), or of any other historical moment of Mexican importance, and you will see that faces change and time continues, but there remains one constant. The Virgin of Guadalupe, who dates to the beginning of Latin American history, is ever present because she was there at the start when fair-skinned conquerors raped native concubines, giving birth to Hispanics and Mestizos. And so, centuries later, the Virgin Mother is called upon to witness it all. By blessing the march, the boycott, the armed conflict, and the celebration with her presence, she immortalizes history for all later generations.[49]

Yes, some things about Latin American history are perpetually relevant. This continual recycling can be heard conceptually and seen visually across time through countless situations.[50] Certainly not everyone

[48] W. Dirk Raat, ed., *Mexico: From Independence to Revolution, 1810–1910* (Lincoln: University of Nebraska Press, 1982), 23.

[49] David Carrasco, *Religions of Mesoamerica* (San Francisco: Harper & Row, 1990), 137. Note Carrasco on the Virgin of Guadalupe.

[50] Jenkins, *The Next Christendom,* 117. Jenkins notes that the veneration of the Virgin Mary is especially poignant for Mexicans. In Mexican folklore, the Virgin of Guadalupe is the mother of all border crossers.

with a Hispanic surname will identify with this mode of being, but it is a broadly held attitude, and especially by those who live, have lived, or have been significantly exposed to Latin American life.

The North American experience is different. The "Wild, Wild West," for example, is not a fictional creation from Hollywood. That rough-and-tumble world truly existed in the western states and territories during the mid to late 1800s. But, we would all agree that it is relegated to history today. What relics remain of that era are housed in museums scattered across the western United States and in private collections. No one gets from here to there on horseback wearing pistols, chaps, boots, and spurs, at least not as a regular way of life. Today's cowboy is more likely to drive a pickup truck with the appropriate gun rack, and a ball and hitch to haul his horses, cattle, or hay. In the United States, we relive the past by viewing Westerns at the Cineplex or on TV, going to a rodeo, or spending a weekend at a dude ranch. But in Latin America, all it takes is just a little acclimation before it sinks in that, despite the trappings of modern life, there is an underlying modality of living that seems arrested in time. This mode of being is lived out vibrantly even in Latin America's most modern and cosmopolitan cities.

Put someone in Times Square wearing apparel of a typical cowboy from the 1870s, and most people will think "urban cowboy." Go to the *Zócalo* at the heart of Mexico City, or along *Avenida Libertador* in Caracas, Venezuela, *or* the *Plaza de la República* in Buenos Aires, Argentina, place a person there wearing the typical attire of a nineteenth-century *vaquero* or *gaucho,* and most people will think him to be someone from the countryside. Where we suspend disbelief for the price of an admission ticket, Latin Americans have found a way to suspend time itself. In Latin America, the past regularly invades the present, and the two often exist side by side.

So, what are we to make of this mindset? Evangelicals are better served if they have some sense of how Latin Americans process their past. As William Baird notes, "Failure to know one's history is a failure to understand one's identity."[51] History is integral to understanding Hispanic identity, for they tend to see life through a mental framework, five hundred years in the making.[52]

Liberated for Monarchy, Dictatorship, and Despotism

Consider Agustín Cosme Damián de Iturbide y Arámburu (1783–1824).[53] In my opinion, this liberator prefigures the Latino mentality perfectly. Iturbide was the military leader who successfully led Mexico to gain its independence from Spanish rule in 1821. Initially, like General George Washington, Iturbide became the first president, signaling that Mexico might move to put in place a democratic representative government. But within a year, despite having banished the Spanish crown, he was more than willing to try one on for size. Iturbide took it upon himself to place the first imperial Mexican crown on his head.

Emperor Agustin I, as he was titled, reigned briefly from May 1822 to March the following year—a mere ten months. The tides of government were anything but peaceful during those early years,[54] and it didn't help that under Iturbide's rule Mexico lost the land that today constitutes most of Central America. Tragically, Mexico's liberator-turned-emperor was sentenced to death and executed by firing squad in July of 1824.

---

[51] William Baird, *History of New Testament Research,* Vol. 1 (Minneapolis: Fortress Press, 1992), xxii.

[52] This work does not argue that Latinos are unique in their view of history. The question of whether history is progressive, or repetitive has long been the subject of philosophical study. See G. W. Trompf, *The Idea of Historical Recurrence in Western Thought, from Antiquity to the Reformation* (Berkeley: University of California Press, 1979); Gordon Graham, "Recurrence," in *The Shape of the Past* (New York: Oxford University Press, 1997).

[53] The point is that the names themselves evoke a fondness for the family's long history.

[54] E. Bradford Burns and July A. Charlip, "The Age of Anarchy in Mexico: Heads of State, 1822–1855," in *Latin America: A Concise Interpretive History*, seventh edition (Upper Saddle River, NJ: Prentice Hall, 2002), 89. Burns and Charlip count thirty-eight heads of state during a thirty-three-year period.

One could conclude that with the execution of Emperor Agustin I, Mexico was turning away from despotic rule, but that would be premature. Iturbide was just the first in a line of tyrants that would entertain visions of grandeur.[55] In his "Ode to Napoleon Bonaparte,"[56] British poet Lord Byron epitomizes the failed and exiled French dictator, thinking it inconceivable that anyone would ever want to emulate the man, but then again, he didn't understand the Hispanic mind. With a total tin ear to the lessons, which could be drawn from Napoleon's Waterloo and banishment,[57] Generalissimo Antonio de Padua María Severino López de Santa Ana y Pérez de Lebrón (1794–1876) fancied himself his successor, the Napoleon of the West. It is truly ironic that the very year Bonaparte died, in 1821, the world would see the birth of the Mexican nation. Mexico was at a propitious moment in history to lead the Spanish speaking hemisphere by example, and she did, looking to past history for the same troubled political model. Not surprisingly, Mexico endured the establishment of a second empire under the French emperor Ferdinand Maximilian Joseph (1832–1867), whose life, as fate would have it, also ended violently. And toward the end of the nineteenth century, Mexico was ruled by Don Porfirio Díaz, a soldier turned president, who ruled like a dictator for more than three decades (1884–1911), setting the country on the path to bloody revolution upon his departure.

Is this what Mexico expected when they took the path of independence? To be fair, Mexico did have its shining stars, men like Francisco Madero (1873–1913), and especially Don Benito Juarez (1806–1872), a duly elected president who curbed the power of the Catholic church and made some necessary land reforms. But as we know, a star here and there does not a firmament fill. By and large, Mexico's earliest leaders

---

[55] For despotic rule in Mexico see John Charles Chasteen, *Born in Blood & Fire: A Concise History of Latin America* (New York: W.W. Norton & Company, 2006), 126–130.

[56] William Stanley Braithwaite, ed. *The Book of Georgian Versè* (New York: Brentano's, 1909).

[57] Napoleon Bonaparte died on May 5, 1821 at age fifty-one, at Saint Helena island, of the British Empire.

were incapable of seeing a future for their newly minted country that was anything but the continuation of the past.

This characteristic trait was not limited to Mexico. Argentina gained her liberation from Spain in 1825, but Juan Manuel de Rosas, a revolutionary hero, resisted writing a constitution to become the dictator of the new country from 1829 until 1852. Depending on who interprets the facts, Rosas was either a despot who craved complete and unfettered power, or a true servant of the state who nevertheless needed to exercise authority to manage the chaos of the times.[58] Either way, it was authoritarian rule not unlike the monarchial rule that had been thrown off, that was given a new lease under the *Caudillos* of the nineteenth century.

This knee-jerk turn to autocratic rule, noted Chilean Jose Victoranio Lastaria, appeared almost immediately after driving the Spanish out of Central America and the Southern Hemisphere. As Lastaria saw it, the mindset was entrenched into the training and hearts of leaders and people alike.[59] Simón Bolívar also recognized the problem.[60] Bolívar is credited with bringing about the liberation and birth of Venezuela, Colombia, Ecuador, Peru, and Bolivia. But for all his success in freeing his homeland from Spanish control, was he able to break free from a colonial way of thinking? It is well-known that Bolivar agreed with Jean-Jacques Rousseau, who noted that, for Latin America, liberty was always a succulent morsel, "but one difficult to digest."[61] I believe that Latin America's early leaders personify the chronic struggle that many Hispanics would reveal in their own peculiar circumstances, hanging on

---

[58] Félix Luna, *Grandes protagonistas de la historia argentina: Juan Manuel de Rosas* (Buenos Aires: Grupo Editorial Planeta, 2004).

[59] Jose Victoranio Lastaria, *Recuerdos Literarios* (Santiago Chile: Servat, 1885).

[60] Bolívar's full name: Simón José Antonio de la Santísima Trinidad Bolívar y Palacios Ponte y Blanco (July 24, 1783–December 17, 1830). Bolívar was aided by Gr. José de San Martín, who secured the liberation of Ecuador.

[61] Cited from Simón Bolívar's address to the Second National Congress, Angostura, Colombia, 1819.

to a way of thinking that had stamped Latino cultures over the span of three centuries.[62]

The Colonial Legacy

Did this fondness for the past happen *ex nihilo*, or were there real-life factors that contributed to its development? Consider Latino names. We have purposefully noted Iturbide and Santa Ana's full names to underscore a trait, but one that is by no means limited to dictators. Pablo Picasso's full name was Pablo Diego José Francisco de Paula Juan Nepomuceno María de los Remedios Cipriano de la Santísima Trinidad Ruiz y Picasso; this is not an isolated case. Many Hispanics, past and present, and from all walks of life, would seem to rival royalty, tracing their name back to antiquity. We should not think it burdensome for Latinos embrace their genealogy joyfully, cherishing the rich, sometimes painful trajectory of their ancestral legacy.

From another perspective, consider Latin American colonial history, which reveals that the Spanish never had an interest in establishing colonies that might one day become sovereign states.[63] Of course, the same can be said of Great Britain's attitude toward her colonial holdings. However, despite the self-interest of English and Spanish colonizers, the two colonies they founded experienced very different conditions. The English colony had the advantage of having begun much later in history than the Latin American colonies. As such, whereas the Spanish colony had been founded in the fifteenth century still steeped in medieval life, the British colony began in the early seventeenth century, as enlightened thinking was well under way.

---

[62] Some key writers and statesmen of the nineteenth century who wrote favorably of US democracy included Benito Juarez, José Vasconcelos, Domingo Faustino Sarmiento, Simón Bolívar, Jose Luis Romero, Alejandro Korn, Juan Bautista Alberdi, Francisco Bilbao, and Jose Victoriano Lastaria. All of these were renowned for their espousal of the liberal democratic doctrines sweeping across Europe and Anglo America.

[63] Kinsbruner, *Independence in Spanish America,* 126; Burns and Charlip, *Latin America: A Concise Interpretive History,* 94, 142–45.

Moreover, England never isolated her colonies from learning and hearing of what was happening elsewhere. The British may not have been willing to grant their colonies proper representation before the court of King George, but the colonies were never kept ignorant of world events. In this sense, the American colonies were "worldly minded." Their minds were filled with ideas that in short time would allow them to pen the founding principles of modern democracy. But Spain thought differently. For their part, the Iberians never permitted their colony to understand their place in the context of the larger world. Yes, the elite *peninsulares* and *criollos*,[64] who had been educated in European universities, could speak of the latest trends and happenings abroad, but it was often pretentious conversation that rarely spilled into the streets. For the vast sea of Latino humanity, there was never any sustained effort to educate the illiterate masses. Whereas the American colonies knew their history, European history, and even Latin American history, the only history Latin America knew was Spain's history and their interpretation of it. Sadly, the average Latino was rarely exposed to ideas and events that were moving the Western world forward into a future, in many ways, distinct from its past.

Religiously, the two colonies were very different. The Pilgrims were not merely the offspring of the Protestant Reformation; in critical ways, they embraced the ideals of the Radical Reformation. As such, most of the earliest settlers came across the Atlantic wanting to throw off state-sponsored religion. In Latin America, the state and the Roman Catholic Church ruled as one for centuries. The same can be true of the Scriptures. The Catholic Church in the Latin colony had exclusive access to the Bible, protecting her spiritual dominance over the people. But in Protestant America, people regularly read from their Geneva and King James Bibles, insuring the democratization of church leadership and the priesthood of the believer.

---

[64] *Peninsulares*, Spanish-born colonial citizens; *criollos*, people born in Latin America to Spanish parents.

The things we have briefly noted are broadly known. However, there is one significant factor that is not always understood, and it has to do with geography. Sometimes less is more and, in the case of the British colony, the compact size of the thirteen colonies certainly helped them achieve independence. When they got around to airing their grievances to the British court, and later to declaring independence, they did it in unison. It was surely messy, but the American colonies communicated with each other, and when it absolutely mattered, stood together as one.

In Latin America, there was little effort ever made to weave the region into one cohesive people. The geographical immensity of the region kept this from ever being a real possibility. Through the centuries, Spain and Portugal had carved roads and founded cities and ports to facilitate the shipment of raw materials to Europe, but it was never their intent to engage in creating societies that could one day stand on their own. And so, the Spanish colony wasn't just kept from knowing of the sweeping changes that were happening throughout Europe; they were kept from knowing themselves. The possibility that the Latin American people could ever gather in something resembling a Continental Congress to consider their hemispheric or even regional interests was near impossible.

It goes without saying that the various factors that I have briefly noted are worthy of greater treatment. Studying any of them will lead us to an inevitable point. Although the Latino elite knew of forward-leaning ideologies, the masses could conceive of nothing other than the continuation of the same, for they were never given the tools to think differently. Is it any wonder that the one-time activist and seventh president of Argentina, Domingo Faustino Sarmiento (1811–1888), considered the Spanish legacy nothing less than a disease? José María Luis Mora Lamadrid (1794–1850) was a Mexican priest, historian and lawyer, and one of the earliest proponents for the separation of church and state. Mora believed that Mexico needed to undertake an intellectual revolution, believing that the entrenched colonial attitudes and customs of the nation had to be repudiated in total.[65] Nothing of the sort ever happened—not in Mexico, not anywhere in the Spanish-speaking countries.

The Latin American countries that emerged between 1806 and 1825 could not have foreseen this, but while vanquishing the Spanish, the Iberians left a parting gift that kept on giving. Some might quarrel that this is all history, but what goes around comes around in Latin America, and it does so endlessly. That fact gave Latin America its eternal stamp of being; it filters through the ages, sometimes more or less pronounced. It shows up across Latino cultures, manifesting itself subtly or forcefully in so many individual lives. Stavans, a student of contemporary Latino culture, is not off the mark when he admits to an "ancestral legacy of which it is impossible to dispossess Hispanics."[66] That ancestral legacy is rooted in history.

The Hispanic Condition, in Their Own Words

We could continue showing examples of this predisposition—of the past intruding into the present continually—but it is enough to note that few would deny it exists. What more often happens is that some will insist that Hispanics should simply get over it and move on, as if it didn't matter. However, is it even possible—or desirable—to ignore this character trait? As the preeminent philosopher of Mexico, Leopoldo Zea, noted, "Spain continued alive, influencing every action of the Hispanic American,"[67] reminding us that "history" is part of man's circumstance: it gives him a configuration and a profile, thus making him

---

[65] Jose Luis Mora, *Obras Sueltas de Jose Luis Mora, Ciudadano mejicano: Revista Politica* (Sydney: Wentworth Press, 2018). See also Charles A. Hale, *Mexican Liberalism in the Age of Mora, 1821–1853* (New Haven, CT: Yale University Press, 1968).

[66] Stavans, *The Hispanic Condition,* 152.

[67] Leopoldo Zea, *The Latin-American Mind.* trans. James H. Abbott and Lowell Dunham (Norman: University of Oklahoma Press, 1963), 9.

capable of some endeavors and incapable of others. Hence, we must take our history into account; because it is there that we can find the source of our abilities and inabilities. We cannot continue to ignore our past and our experience, because without knowing them we cannot claim to be mature. Maturity, age, is experience. He who ignores his history lacks experience and he who lacks experience cannot be a mature, responsible man.[68]

In the Bible, the elderly are venerated and respected for the wisdom and maturity that age itself bestows upon them, and the young are admonished to learn from them (Lev. 19:32; Job 12:12; 1 Tim. 5:17; Titus 2:2). But does age always guarantee maturity? Ironically, Latin America's iconic colonial semblance would seem to signal the existence of a tried and tested people who have surely learned the harsh lessons of time. Moreover, her youthful population must surely be reaping the benefits of her maturity.[69] Alas, a number of thoughtful Latin American thinkers have pondered the Latino experience and offered insights that question whether Latinos have fully come to grips with their history, and thus matured for having experienced it.

Leopoldo Zea

For Leopoldo Zea, to whom we have already turned, this constant backward glance reveals a problematic mindset that the Hispanic wrestles

[68] Leopoldo Zea, *Essays on Philosophy and History,* published in *Latin American Philosophy,* Jorge J. E. Garcia, ed. (Buffalo, NY: Prometheus Books, 1986), 227.

[69] Tanvi Misra, "The U.S. Hispanic Population Is Disproportionately Young," Citylab, April 20, 2016, https:// www.citylab.com/life/2016/04/six-out-of-ten-latinos-are-millennials-or-younger-pew-research-centerstudy /479010 (accessed December 18, 2016); "Latin America & the Caribbean: Youth Facts," Youthpolicy.org, http://www. youthpolicy.org/mappings/regionalyouthscenes/latinamerica/facts (accessed December 18, 2016).

with endlessly.[70] Zea advances the thesis that the Latino considers his colonial experience to be foreign to who he is, and therefore is destined to relive it endlessly.[71] Zea couches the issue within Wilhelm Hegel's dialectical framework for assimilating history and making it one's own. To the degree that Latin America refuses to see their past as theirs, moving on to a new synthesis that allows for development, truly new history becomes impossible to realize. In Zea's opinion, the dialectical process has been arrested throughout the region—Latin America remains at a standstill.

For Zea, this pause has serious ramifications, for unreconciled history haunts the person as an ever-present reality. Their history cannot be considered with any objectivity, for:

> The Conquest and the colonization remains alive in his mind, and about them revolve, after all is said and done, all of his discussions. Sometimes we see him defending the rights of the conquered, at other times defending the conquerors; at times justifying the colonies, at other times justifying independence. He always takes the same point of view, in spite of disguising it with different ideological labels or different terminology. The problem of the dependence and independence of the Hispanic American is always evident.[72]

---

[70] Leopoldo Zea (born Leopoldo Zea Aguilar, June 30, 1912–June 8, 2004) was a Mexican philosopher, associated with the National Autonomous University of Mexico (UNAM) beginning in 1943. In 1947 Zea founded the faculty of philosophy and gave lectures on "History of Ideas in America." In 1954, he was appointed to a full-time position as a researcher at the Philosophical Studies Center of UNAM. In 1966, Zea became director of the faculty, holding this position until 1970. During his time as director, Zea founded the Latin American Studies College (in 1966) and later founded the Coordination and Propagation Center of the UNAM Latin American Studies (1978). Zea received multiple awards including the *Premio Nacional de Ciencias y Artes* in 1980, the *Premio Interamericano de Cultura* "Gabriela Mistral" and the Medalla Belisario Domínguez (of the Senate of Mexico) in 2000. Zea was honored by the UNAM as the oldest professor to work continually until his death.

[71] Zea, *The Latin-American Mind*, 44–51.

[72] Ibid., 5–6.

Things are different north of modern-day Mexico. In North America, her colonial past is history, even if some pick up slogans from that period. The political Tea Party, for example, echoes back to 1773 in name, but its issues were early twenty-first-century. But throughout the Latin American countries, people live a chronic problem that is truly baffling. The unresolved relationship many Latinos have with their national past keeps it from becoming something that can be handled and studied dispassionately. In fact, so long as Hispanics continue to see their past as something perpetrated against them, they will never get past it because, for better or worse, it is a history they need to own.

Leopoldo Zea observes that Hispanics throughout the hemisphere need to assimilate their past, the whole of it, so they can move forward into maturity. Short of that, their modern history is always really a constant repeat of the past. Zea may be right, in which case time could help ease the trauma of a region that continues to see itself as having been victimized, an attitude felt in many sectors of the Latino world. But, then again, there may be an intractability about it, and especially if the Latino we have labored to describe is hardwired by design.

Claudio Véliz

The Chilean-born historian and sociologist Claudio Véliz is one who thinks the Spanish-speaking Americas were purposefully "invented" for the history they have experienced.[73] The Spanish crown and pope of the late fifteenth century, according to Véliz, sought specifically to create a culture in the New World dedicated to upholding one shining truth in a world they perceived filled with error and heresy. In *The New World of*

[73] Claudio Véliz is a Chilean economic historian and sociologist, who has held numerous academic posts in various institutions of higher learning including La Trobe University (Australia), Harvard, and Boston University. Véliz was educated at the Mackay School (Valparaiso, Chile) and the Grange School (Santiago, Chile). Véliz completed a Bachelor of Science degree at the University of Florida, and subsequently completed a PhD in economic history at the London School of Economics.

the Gothic Fox, Véliz borrows Isaiah Berlin's "hedgehog and fox" metaphor[74] to speak of the vital differences between the two dominant cultures that crossed the Atlantic. And the two worlds they created could not be any more different than night and day.[75]

If the dominant cultural achievement of the British "foxes" was their ability to thrive on diversity and change—illustrated dramatically by the discoveries of the Enlightenment, and later the wealth-generating Industrial Revolution—the Iberian "hedgehogs" burrowed into their Latin American colony the tenets and attitude of the Counter Reformation. While the Anglo foxes were forward-looking, unafraid of obstacles they might encounter, the Spanish hedgehogs were defensive and reactionary, indoctrinated to preserve a way of life threatened to be blown away by the winds of change that were sweeping across the European landscape. Both cultures succeeded wildly in cementing their respective ideological visions.

Claudio Véliz paints a compelling picture of life in the Spanish colony, a life locked into one and only one way of expression. This, of course, leads to one inescapable question. Given that Latin America has moved past those early days, has she left the hedgehog behind? The easy answer might be to shout a resounding "Yes!" for you can see the evidences of a new and secular Latin America, and Hispanics at every turn.

---

[74] Isaiah Berlin, *The Hedgehog and the Fox* (London: Weidenfeld & Nicolson, 1953).

[75] Véliz, *The New World of the Gothic Fox* (Berkeley: University of California Press, 1994), 12–13. Note Véliz' description of the two attitudes. "Berlin noted that 'The fox knows many things, but the hedgehog knows one big thing.' The cryptic sentence conveys intimations about a profound difference between those thinkers and writers and human beings generally 'who relate everything to a single, central vision, one system less or more coherent or articulate, in terms of which they understand, think and feel—a single, universal, organizing principle in terms of which alone all that they are and say has significance,' and those who pursue many ends, often unrelated and even contradictory, connected, if at all, only in some *de facto* way, for some psychological or physiological cause, related by no moral or aesthetic principle; these last lead lives, perform acts, and entertain ideas that are centrifugal rather than centripetal, their thought is scattered or diffused, moving on many levels, seizing upon the essence of a vast variety of experiences and objects for what they are in themselves, without, consciously or unconsciously, seeking to fit them into, or exclude them from, any one unchanging, all-embracing, sometimes self-contradictory and incomplete, at times fanatical, unitary inner vision.' The former disposition corresponds to the hedgehogs, the latter to the foxes."

It is telling that though it happened 12 billion years ago, astronomy tells us that the noise of the Big Bang is still reverberating throughout the cosmos. In like manner, even if the social architects that set the hedgehog mentality in place belong to history, their legacy continues to echo through countless dreams and expectations, beliefs, suspicions, and presuppositions that feed Latino culture.

Ernesto Mayz Vallenilla

Venezuelan philosopher Ernesto Mayz Vallenilla offers his thoughts on this important discussion.[76] In his works that deal specifically with the question of the Latin American identity, Mayz Vallenilla coins a provocative phrase. The Hispanic, notes Mayz Vallenilla, is a "*no ser siempre todavia*"—rough translation: "an eternal not yet."[77] By this, he characterizes Hispanics as people with a quasi-absent past, a conflicted present, and an uncertain future. Mayz Vallenilla goes on to specify that when it comes to dealing with the cultural legacies of the Hispanic world—the past—Latinos live forever taking note that such legacies are neither fully absent nor fully present at any given moment. His observation is subtle and worth pondering. Mayz Vallenilla is not saying that Latin American history is both fully absent and yet fully present, quite the opposite. Rather, because history—whether it is a nation's or an individual's history—is never fully absent in the sense that it has been fully processed and filed away, its coattail trips up the Latino's present. Conversely, since

---

[76] Ernesto Mayz Vallenilla (born September 3, 1925) graduated from Universidad Central de Venezuela in 1950, where he also obtained his PhD in philosophy. He also studied in the universities of Göttingen, Freiburg, and München. Mayz Vallenilla was a professor at the Universidad Central de Venezuela and the rector-founder of Universidad Simón Bolívar, where he currently holds the UNESCO Chair of Philosophy. Mayz Vallenilla has been an active writer for more than fifty years. In 2001, the Argentinean Philosophical Society named Mayz Vallenilla the most outstanding Latin American philosopher of the twentieth century.

[77] Ernesto Mayz Vallenilla, *El Problema de América*, Cuadernos de Cultura Latinoamericana 93 (Mexico City: Universidad Nacional Autónoma Mexicana, 1994), 11–30. See http://ru.ffyl.unam.mx/jspui/bitstream/handle/10391/3037/93CCLat_1979_Mays_Vallenilla.pdf?sequence=1&isAllowed=y (accessed June 17, 2017).

history is also never ever fully present, its significance is always incomplete and thus unsure. Time is supposed to provide the opportunity to reflect on the past, and learn from it. But one cannot reflect on a history that is, in many ways, mystified by our conflicts and insecurities.

In light of this, Mayz Vallenilla proposes that the Latin American is consigned to live a puzzling existence, which may in the long run define them. Ultimately, Mayz Vallenilla puts the best positive face, asserting that the permanent way of being for the Hispanic is "never to truly be already." According to Mayz Vallenilla, Hispanics are prone:

- ***Never*** *to truly be already*, asserting a kind of fatalism that in the long run cannot be overcome. The Latino lives an ongoing and static reality.
- *Never* ***to truly be*** *already*, proposing the absence of genuine identity, possessing a personality not yet complete, but still in its development. By implication this also communicates the possible absence or, at the very least, the underdevelopment of faculties and abilities that come with maturity, however such might be defined.
- *Never to truly be* ***already***, suggesting an existence that, in spite of its challenges, nevertheless is, stressing a sense of urgency as something already pressing and not a condition that is still in the future.

In considering Mayz Vallenilla's statement, we are struck by what is lacking. There is no *telos*, no apparent end in sight, that brings fulfillment to the Latino personality. While Mayz Vallenilla never denies that Hispanics can hope for tomorrow, "never to truly be already" captures an essential trait, to live doleful on the cusp of a longed-for future that never quite arrives.

Zea, Véliz, Mayz Vallenilla

In their own way Zea, Véliz, and Mayz Vallenilla dare to touch the third rail of Latino identity. How are Hispanics to think about the five hundred years that have shaped them as a people? It is difficult to render an interpretation of the Latin American mind, for there is much in their collective history and experience to love and value. Yet, so much of it carries the fingerprint of colonialism, and therein lies the crux of the matter. Leopoldo Zea observes, "The past, if it is not completely assimilated, always makes itself felt as present. In each gesture, in every act carried out by the Hispanic American, the past becomes evident."[78] If true, one cannot talk about Latin American history without Hispanics taking it personally, as if referring to them specifically. This works whether one critiques some aspect of colonial rule, or praises its romantic legacy. For Zea, Latin American identity is tied to history, despite its progress in so many aspects of modern life.

One thing is certain: The cultural relics of Latin America's past are like museum pieces that have not been assigned their final significance; the informational placard in front of the exhibit is still being written.[79] This means the Hispanic is a project in the making, though his genesis is in the hundreds of years. For Leopoldo Zea, the project cannot continue until Hispanics come to terms with their troubled past and accept it for what it is, for better or worse. Claudio Véliz would remind us that so long as the foxes of the world push the envelope, the hedgehog mentality becomes more anachronistic and out of touch. Ernesto Mayz Vallenilla's views are self-evident. For all their progress, the world has yet to see what the mature Hispanic will be.

Conclusion

Is the Latin American condition unprecedented? We hardly think so. If truth be told, we could write a history of the world from the perspective

[78] Zea, *The Latin American Mind,* 10.

[79] Mayz Vallenilla, *El Problema de América*, 20, observes, of Latinos, "El americano siente que el hombre que hay en él (y que mora cabe un Mundo en torno esencialmente advenidero, antes de ser algo ya hecho o acabado, y de lo cual pudiera dar testimonio como acerca de la existencia de una obra o de una cosa concluida, es algo que 'se acerca,' que está llegando a ser, que aún no es, pero que inexorablemente llegará a ser."

of countries that continued the imprint of an early primal ideology. If such a history were to be written, doubtless we would discover many nations and cultures that labored hard to maintain something of their beginnings throughout their social evolution, the United States of America included.

Still, in considering the difference between the Hispanic and the Anglo mentality, I can't help but be drawn to two metaphors. For myself, the Pony Express symbolizes, as much as anything else, the American mind—the rider galloping at top speed, knowing there is a fresh horse just around the bend. The rider does not slow down to take in the scenery, for one thing matters: delivering the mail to its final destination. American culture is purpose-driven, intent to reach an end even if it is not clearly in sight. The race to the moon is a prime example of this mindset.

By contrast, the Hispanic is also mounted on a horse, or so it would seem—but upon closer inspection there is a difference. Unlike the Pony Express rider, the Hispanic rider is not pushing his steed forward at full gallop. The rider is content to mosey along, believing he is moving forward, but the things he sees along the way repeat themselves with predictable regularity. The Hispanic mind is like a carousel beaming with bright lights, vibrant colors, and lively music. It can be exciting, but also predictable. The *cholo* penchant for airbrushing on to the hood of their car the image of a pre-Columbian emperor *Moctezuma,* holding a damsel in his arms, illustrates this mindset. While we could conclude that both the Anglo and the Latino are riding a horse, the Hispanic, for all his apparent progress, seems to find himself right where he was not long before.

But what of the Hispangelical? As we might expect, believers do not cease to be who they are upon embracing the gospel. Faith in Christ does, however, force every believer to take stock of who they were then, and who they now are in him. The apostle Paul evaluated his ethnicity (Phil. 3:3–6). To our best understanding, he did not reject it, but placed it under the rule and Lordship of his Savior (Phil. 3:7–11). This, I believe, is the Hispangelical challenge: to embrace their history, but not be ruled by it; to learn from their history, but to know that the gospel allows their story to continue to be written. The Hispangelical will need to move beyond what their cultural matrix dictates, affirming with Paul:

> Not that I have already obtained *it* or have already become perfect, but I press on so that I may lay hold of that for which also I was laid hold of by Christ Jesus. Brethren, I do not regard myself as having laid hold of *it* yet; but one thing *I do*: forgetting what *lies* behind and reaching forward to what *lies* ahead, I press on toward the goal for the prize of the upward call of God in Christ Jesus (Phil. 3:12–14).

If Zea, Véliz, and Mayz Vallenilla speak truth, then the Latino is conscripted to the historical and social realities that have shaped them. But, if Scripture has the ultimate word, then spiritual regeneration is the only experience that deals decisively with the past, reconciling its conflicts and absurdities, and inviting us to become a genuine player in redemption history, bringing fullness and maturity to life.

CHAPTER TWO

Then Came Philosophy

A library, to modify the famous metaphor of Socrates, should be the delivery room for the birth of ideas—a place where history comes to life.

Norman Cousins
The Saturday Review[80]

Introduction

The history of the world is largely driven by ideas—thoughts that are spoken, or written, with such persuasion that people are driven to action. Some ideas are complex and are only truly grasped by relatively few among us; nevertheless, their impact can be powerful. This is probably true of modern theories of physics altering the way we understand the universe. Other ideas, however, are capable of holding the average intellect, making a tremendous difference. In 1867, Karl Marx published his *Das Kapital,* wherein he critiques the Western economic system and, specifically, the accumulation of wealth through the exploitation of labor. Marx's economic philosophy took Russia by storm,

[80] Norman Cousins, "Introduction: The Need for Continuity," *American Library Association Bulletin* (October 1954), 475.

blowing away the imperial czars and setting in place a Communist economic system that, in time, would reach as far as Eastern Europe, Cuba, Central America, and much of the Asian continent.

On April 19, 1775, a shot was fired that was "heard around the world," so wrote Ralph Waldo Emerson.[81] Whether the British fired first, or it was the American militia at Lexington, Massachusetts, is impossible to say with complete finality. What is certain is that the volley of musket balls fired on that fateful Wednesday stand for far more than the skirmish that began the American Revolution. World history is riddled with civil wars, revolutions, *coup d'etats*, struggles for liberation, but this one was different. It was a revolutionary set of principles that were heard around the world. These ideas, considered self-evident by those who drafted them (though no one had bothered to act on them until that time), were codified into the founding documents of the United States. And, if imitation is the highest form of flattery, who can deny the influence that the Declaration of Independence, the United States Constitution, and the Bill of Rights have had in guiding other countries to fashion their political futures?

Still, one wonders if those ideas that troubled absolute monarchies and tyrants in distant places were heard, and actually understod, by their colonial neighbors to the South. Whether Latin America had a yearning for such freedom at the latter end of the eighteenth century is moot. The Spanish colonies languished under Iberian control for at least three decades more. Sensing an opportunity during the first decade of the nineteenth century, the Latin colony began to make its break. It took time, and over the following decades most modern Latin American countries came into existence. But, were they inspired by the same principles defended at Lexington and secured six years later at Yorktown? It is no exaggeration to say that the freedom achieved was surely geopolitical, perhaps economic, but it was hardly philosophical. In the

---

[81] Ralph Waldo Emerson, "Concord Hymn," first sung on July 4, 1837 upon completion of the Monument for the Battle of Concord.

newly formed countries, old ideas about the nature of the person and their place in the world showed stubborn resilience, shaping, limiting whatever freedoms their revolutions had secured.

The philosophical roots of Latin America were different than the ideas that held sway in North America and, we will argue, intentionally so. If Anglo America championed the rights of the individual, such ideas had their genesis in the writings of Locke, Adams, Montesquieu, and others. But in that part of the hemisphere where Spanish and Portuguese were spoken, different ideas prevailed. Howard J. Wiarda, Leonard Horwitz professor of Iberian and Latin American Studies at the University of Massachusetts, Amherst, notes that in Latin America, "political culture has tended historically to emphasize the more conservative and nondemocratic features of Greek thought"[82]—shaping, as we shall see, the fabric of Latin American culture and social life.

Plato, Aristotle, and Their Non-Democratic Legacy

It may come as a shock to some, but Plato (and Socrates, if he truly existed) along with Aristotle were not necessarily the ardent defenders of democracy as we sometimes think. Though they certainly recognized the value of democratic pluralism, each of them, were they living today, could be charged with harboring ideas clearly subversive to modern representative government, checks and balances, and the coequality of its branches.

Plato is clear in his writings, for instance, that he had no confidence in the democracy practiced in his day. Because most people were members of a guild, either craftsmen or merchants, he saw them all as committed to promoting their economic self-interests. For that reason, such groups could never be trusted to run the state. "Lovers of honor," people such as those in the military, likewise could also not be trusted to govern the country equitably. The aim of the soldier, thought Plato, was to gain

[82] Wiarda, *The Soul of Latin America*, 20–21.

fame and admiration through military exploit. Plato believed that military leaders were too narcissistic for the public good. And politicians, if that was their life's aim, were by nature crafty, adept at manipulating people through rhetorical persuasion. Essentially, believed Plato, the democrat is incapable of healthy self-rule because people are prone to be swayed by their desires and personal interests. However, Plato didn't just criticize the democratic system; the Athenian sage offered an alternative.

In *The Republic*, Plato posits a solution: What were needed were "lovers of wisdom"—in short, a class of people who possessed a superior intellect, which Plato equated with love of philosophy. Come to think of it, Plato may have been the first to conceive of a think tank, people dedicated to nothing more than solving the prickly problems of making a society work for all. But Plato also understood it would not be in their general makeup for lovers of wisdom to govern; their main passions focused on the mind and thinking through ideas. Nevertheless, having been born and bred to think impassively, they should be compelled by force, if necessary, to run the state. Thus, Plato boldly asserts, "Until philosophers are kings or the kings and princes of this world have the spirit and power of philosophy . . . cities will never have rest from their evils."[83] Plato espoused the need for an elite class of people, nurtured in the art and science of governing the masses, people he called philosopher kings. Moreover, since philosophy always leads to real knowledge, as Plato maintained, wise leaders should not be overly concerned with the grumblings of the ignorant or ill-informed masses.

Plato also wrote on the nature of society. One of his most profound seminal ideas was his view of an underlying corporate system that was practically immune to change. In Platonic thought, people were born into distinct groups, which together made up the social fabric. One was born into nobility, the priesthood, some guild, peasantry, even slavery. He might have considered otherwise but, for the most part, Plato never held that a craftsman, for example, could, or should, aspire to become

---

[83] Plato, *The Republic,* 5.473d, 484a–502c.

a part of another group. In the broad scheme of life, the ultimate good was to realize one's function within their group and perform his or her duty to the best of one's ability. In Plato's ideal world, individuals only really mattered insofar as they worked to maintain the viability of the group they belonged to, thus insuring the stability of the social order.

Plato's pupil, Aristotle, held to this same organic dissimilarity among the classes. There was, for him, a natural hierarchy that institutionalized domination and submission. The wife naturally submits to her husband, the child to the parent, the slave or servant to the master, etc. With such a view, Aristotle could write of "equality for those who are equal," however, "not for all."[84]

For Aristotle, social conventions were sacrosanct for they exhibited a "power" and a kind of immutable "quality" that elevated them above any concept of individuality. He reasons:

> Further, the state is by nature clearly prior to the family and to the individual since the whole is of necessity prior to the part; for example, if the whole body be destroyed, there will be no foot or hand except in an equivocal sense, as we might speak of a stone hand; for when destroyed the hand will be no better than that. But things are defined by their working and power; and we ought not to say that they are the same when they no longer have their proper quality, but only that they have the same name.[85]

Aristotle believed people were born into ranks, with deescalating levels of inferiority. The lowest human rank was that of a slave. However, under his ideal social construct those born or sold into slavery would be under the care of civilized and righteous rulers who would train them

---

[84] Aristotle, *Politics,* Book 4.

[85] Ibid., 1.2

in "virtuous behavior."[86] Rightly does Wiarda note about Aristotelian politics, "Only rarely does Greek political thought recognize concepts of social change, dynamic modernization, or the possibilities of raising oneself in the social hierarchy. One is born into a certain station in life and one remains in that station throughout the generations."[87] In fact, though both acknowledge the necessity of democracy, neither Plato nor Aristotle offer any real path for people at the lower rungs of the pecking order to aspire to a better life for them or their children after them.

That such stagnant prospects should prevail in ancient Greek and Hellenic thought is not inconceivable to fathom once we understand how the social fabric of ancient Macedonia held together. One thing was sure, "In the Greek political structure," notes Wiarda, "individuals derived their identities as citizens from membership in a *deme* . . . each of which was comprised of clans from distinct economic and geographical regions of Attica."[88] Macedonia was, at that time, a league of city-states bound together out of a need for defense and survival. People didn't so much see themselves as Macedonians, but rather as citizens of cities—places like Thebes, Sparta, Corinth, Athens, Thessaly, Pella, and so forth. Since the ultimate question of concern was the viability of the city, logically, the concerns of individuals would hardly register. For someone from the lower echelons of society to seek or assert a personal right or privilege not inherent to their clan's station would be extremely grievous.

The Greco-Roman Contribution

The distance between Athens and Mexico City, or Pella and Lima, or Sparta and Buenos Aires is thousands of miles. It would take centuries for the musings of fourth-century BC philosophers to influence Latin

[86] Ibid., Book 5. See also Lewis Hanke, *Aristotle and the American Indians* (Bloomington: Indiana University Press, 1970).
[87] Wiarda, *The Soul of Latin America,* 21.
[88] Ibid., 23.

America, but that they shaped her way of thinking about life and its possibilities is beyond question. As history reveals, Platonic and Aristotelian ideas on the nature of government and society did not stay within the boundaries of Macedonian city-states. In time, Rome annexed Macedon and Achaia, along with all the Aegean islands. And with territorial expansion came exposure to Greek and Hellenistic political ideas.

When Rome conquered the Greek peninsula in 146 BC a reciprocal "conquest," and one more enduring, happened as well. Rightly did the Latin poet Horace observe, "Captive Greece took captive her savage conqueror and brought her arts into rustic Latinium."[89] Though the Romans were always careful to clothe their political conversation in native dress, there is no doubt Greek political theory fit their growing needs. After all, society worked best when governed by an enlightened body of rulers (the Senate) morally obligated to act benevolently toward its subjects, but with an important caveat. In keeping with stratified society, rulers needed to listen to corporate interests that held the Roman ship of state afloat; individual grievances would have been out of the question. Thus, Wiarda repeats, "Rome believed—like its 'children' in Latin America—in hierarchy and rank . . . locked in place."[90]

The record speaks unequivocally. Even as Christendom grew and gained political power, it did not put forth a vision of the equality of all people. The church's first instinct was to baptize the existing Roman system, encompassing a segment of Europe under the aegis of what would come to be known as the Holy Roman Empire.[91] With respect to the Iberian Peninsula, this social legacy solidified. The Iberia of the medieval ages embodied the concept that people were born into separate and unequal bodies or corporations. While individuals might have

---

[89] Horace, Book II, Epistle I, 156–157.

[90] Wiarda, *The Soul of Latin America*, 32.

[91] This title dates to Charlemagne in the eighth century AD. However, it fell into disuse after the death of the Franc and was revived by Otto I becoming the first emperor of the Holy Roman Empire. It lasted from AD 962 to 1806, when it was finally dissolved by Francis II in the wake of the Napoleonic wars.

rights within their group, such rights could not be extended beyond proscribed limits.

By the year of our Lord 1492, the Roman Empire had long fallen, but Spain, which some considered to be Rome's greatest prodigy, had emerged as a sovereign and powerful country all her own.[92] It was that year that Columbus, with the backing of the Spanish Catholic monarchs, Ferdinand of Aragón and Isabella of Castile, sailed to the islands of the Western Hemisphere. By that time, the political ideas discussed above had been honed to perfection, and in just a few years Spain exported them to her newest acquisition. But, if the truth be fully told, we cannot leave the impression that this kind of social structuring was solely the product of pagan Greek and Roman thinkers. In fact, the church had also made her considerable contribution.

The Theological and Ethical Moorings of Spanish Society

The political concepts described in the previous pages were founded almost exclusively on the deductive pillars of nature and reason, philosophy and ethics. As Christianity grew in prominence, however, these same concepts needed to be grounded on revealed truth—Holy Scripture, if you will—recasting them in the clothing of biblical principles.

Enter Saint Augustine of the fifth century AD, who wrote that, although inferior, civil society could still be used by God to advance his kingdom. By Augustine's day, Christianity had become the state religion of the Roman Empire, so it was only natural for him to believe that the organization, hierarchy, and discipline of the state should be grounded on the Christian gospel. For Augustine, the concept of unity so prominent in the writings of the New Testament (e.g., John 17:11–22; 1 Cor. 12:13; Eph. 4:4–6; Phil. 2:2), could only truly reach its highest earthly expression through the marriage of church and state on the basis of Christian love. It should not come as a surprise therefore that early

[92] There is a saying about Spain: "más papista que el Papa" (more popish than the Pope).

church fathers would develop a theological justification for the nuptial. Professor Wiarda has identified fifteen religious ideas espoused "derivative of earlier Greek and Roman sources."[93] Of these, four concepts go directly to our topic:

- Life lived under a divine immutable law
- No real distinction between law, politics, or religion
- Life as essentially organic and corporatist
- A focus on community rather than individualism

For the church, these ideas were seen as having a biblical base, providing the Christian authority that had been lacking. To be sure, Augustine's concerns to build an earthly "City of God" went a long way toward blessing the marriage of the church with the state. But it was Thomas Aquinas who, more than any other, developed the most complete theo-political worldview.

Doctor Angelicus Thomas, a Dominican theologian of the thirteenth century, accepted Augustine's hierarchical social model and anchored it securely to Christian doctrine. He believed that the believer's heavenly hope should drive Christianity to perfect the human condition, after the divine pattern. In his *Summa Theologica,* Aquinas wedded philosophy with theology to explain all of life in terms of a God-centered universe where society, politics, religion, and education worked as a seamless whole.

Of course, we know that in due time the Protestant Reformation would challenge many, if not all, Thomistic assumptions, but these challenges rarely rang out in Spain.[94] His synthesis of philosophy and

---

[93] Wiarda, *The Soul of Latin America,* 40–42.

[94] There was a short-lived reformation movement in Spain during the early sixteenth century. It was centered around the Monastery of Santiponce, near Seville, ironically where the office of the Spanish Inquisition had its headquarters. The history of this fleeting movement can be read in Dale V. Vought, *Like a Flickering Flame: A History of Protestant Missions in Spain* (Sevilla: Publidisa Publishers, 2001).

theology provided the ideal God-ordained life, and the Reformation made these southern European countries want to reinforce such ideas with all the more vigor.

As Wiarda details, Saint Thomas turned to the Bible to advance an organic and functional organization of society, and he found his inspiration in the writings of the least of the apostles.[95] For Thomas, Romans 13:1–2 provided the foundation for the biblical authority of the Roman Catholic Christian state. Why? It called for every person to

> . . . be in subjection to the governing authorities. For there is no authority except from God, and those which exist are established by God. Therefore, he who resists authority has opposed the ordinance of God; and they who have opposed will receive condemnation upon themselves.

As Thomas saw it, to resist such authority was to resist God at the risk of hell. Moreover, in Romans 12:4, which reads, "For just as we have many members in one body and all the members do not have the same function," Thomas found more than ample support for holding that the divine plan for society was stratified along functional lines. God certainly loved the individual, but people's worth to society was based on their ability to perform their preordained service. For Thomas, Paul's first epistle to the Corinthians provided a blueprint for a corporatist societal hierarchy. As Thomas interpreted 1 Corinthians 12:11–14, Paul lays it out:

> But one and the same Spirit works all these things, distributing to each one individually just as He wills.
>
> For even as the body is one and *yet* has many members, and all the members of the body, though they are many, are one body, so also is Christ. For by one Spirit we were all baptized

[95] Wiarda, *The Soul of Latin America,* 45.

> into one body, whether Jews or Greeks, whether slaves or free, and we were all made to drink of one Spirit.
>
> For the body is not one member, but many.

Yes, Thomas knew this was Paul's vision of the church. However, since he also accepted Constantine's fourth-century integration of the government with the church, Paul's instruction extended beyond the distribution of spiritual gifts to individual believers to the distribution of stations, functions, and responsibilities to sustain the existing social structure. This, of course, has strong obvious implications. People had no standing to question the station in life into which they had been born. Holy Scripture offered no avenue for an individual to seek a higher station that God had not willed for them.

Saint Thomas believed allegiance to the social order was essential, and it worked in both directions. For one, Thomas never considered that denial of individual rights and freedoms was tyrannical. God's plan had a safety net, for if the lower rungs of society owed obedience to those with rank and authority, those whom God had placed in ascending positions of privilege owed to their subjects a responsibility to rule wisely and with compassion. Alas, when the Spaniards and Portuguese colonized the Western Hemisphere, they considered no other form of governance than that conceived by Macedonian philosophers, adopted and implemented by the Roman Empire and made sacrosanct by the Holy Roman Catholic Church.

As history shows, Spain discovered the New World at about the same time that northern Europe would recover a conception of the Christian faith: by grace through faith in Christ. The Protestant Reformation was challenging many of the tenets of Medieval Christendom. Moreover, the Age of Enlightenment would soon dawn, putting into question old assumptions about the absolute right of kings and the circumscribed rights of their subjects. Moving forward, Spain could not simply continue to apply its system of government imperiously, but this did not mean they would reject it outright. The Hispanic colonial population was overwhelmingly native and *Mestizo*, and their voices could not be denied. Change was in the air and Spain would have to bend, at least to a point.

Enter Jesuit Francisco Suárez, a Spanish philosopher and theologian who provided a way forward.[96] Though he was fully committed to the church and imperial rule, Suarez was a pragmatist who saw the world changing. While he continued to support what he considered to be the "higher ends of the state" at the expense of private interests, his revised theory of organic society was revolutionary. For Suarez, power still emanated from God to the crown, but only in so far as the king or queen governed justly. In stating this, Suárez is the first Spaniard to place a check on absolute monarchy, legitimizing resistance in the face of imperial cruelty. Here, Suárez echoed the Magna Carta, proposing a contract between recognized corporate entities and the monarchy. Under Suárez's reformulation, people in their corporate spheres gave consent to be ruled by a monarchy, so long as they ruled wisely and benevolently. However, while Suárez sounds republican, he never advocated for individual rights. The only voice, or voices the crown were obligated to acknowledge, were those of corporate interests within the realm.

Most scholars who have studied Suárez and others concede that through history, Spanish monarchial power usually found a way to exert its control in the *colonia*. While the compromise envisioned by Suárez was practiced in Spain, colonial corporations were not allowed the same kind of representation before the royal court. So, it may be in large measure due to frustration with not implementing Suárezian changes in the colony that Latin America struck out for independence. But this is not to say that it was inspired by the principles that had driven the American Revolution. This much is true: While the Spanish and Portuguese monarchies were banished, imperial ambitions were not. Mexico made its liberator an emperor, and then went further. For most Latin American countries, their leaders—*caudillos*, as they came to be known—tended to rule as ostensible monarchs. In doing so, these

[96] Francisco Suárez, *De Legibus,* Book 8.

new countries moved valiantly forward, but with old, ancient cultural ideas still in place, adopting the Suárezian understanding of governance, which the Iberians had denied them.

To be sure, after the wars for liberation Latin American leaders could not act with impunity, not for long. Bowing to Suárez, Latino political figures became deft in negotiating with powerful industries, foreign governments and internal syndicates that had coalesced. With this change, the stage was set for patronage and cronyism to reach unprecedented heights. In all this, a basic tension emerged between the values of Latin American corporate society against those of innate individualism. For many, this created a tug-of-war that continues in the heart of many a Latino. Most have a love for their *tierra querida* (beloved country) that is praiseworthy. But they also have personal hopes for their families—aspirations which neither their colonial creators nor their post-colonial representatives dared acknowledge, much less helped them realize.

This contra-wise reality is baffling but understandable; for Latinos, like all peoples, did not have the advantage of hindsight to see what the end results of their struggles for liberation would produce. How could they know not only what they had never known, but what their minds were hard-pressed even to understand? Though Hispanics fought for independence from colonial control, they were not thinking of putting in place a new governing model. Their philosophical views of society remained intact and so, the ideas of the American Revolution did not ring true in their context. The belief that people have rights as individuals, the principle that justice and law should apply equally to all citizens, ensuring the right for people to worship freely without governmental coercion—these concepts made a late showing, coming after the various revolutions had already been fought. Few, if any, had spilled blood for such ideals. To the contrary, such things were strange-sounding, indeed revolutionary, to their struggles for independence.[97] Alas, the political ideas that prevailed over colonial society for more than three hundred years endured

[97] Wiarda, *The Soul of Latin America,* 136–137.

through the shaping of their national identities. And even if equality and democracy was preached from bully pulpits, a deeper innate voice spoke, reminding Latinos that God had created their world with firm, inviolate lines of social distinction. Despite countless overtures to representative democracy, such ideas are not really championed in the region.[98]

Positivism in Latin America

I can't say for sure what the producers of the 2006 comedy *Nacho Libre* were thinking of, but whatever they had in mind they seem to have touched on a significant philosophical development in Latin America, and it has to do with the introduction of logical positivism into the region. Integral to the movie is a certain character, a thin as a rail wrestler who goes by the name of *Esqueleto,* literally "Skeleton." I only bring him up because unlike the character Jack Black plays, *Nacho*, a monk who moonlights as a masked wrestler, *Esqueleto* sets himself apart as "a man of science." I ask, does this movie poke fun at Latin American positivism? *Esqueleto* is hilarious because he claims to be governed by reason and logic, yet he makes his livelihood in arenas rampant with brute emotion, hardly places that promote dispassionate, objective scientific inquiry. Moreover, his tag-team partner is *Nacho*, a Roman Catholic monk! Indeed, the more I think about it, and regardless of whether the producers of *Nacho Libre* were conscious of it or not, the old adage is true, at least in this case, art truly does imitate life.

If ever there was a socio-scientific philosophy that promised to provide a way forward from the impasse of old worn feudal thinking, surely logical positivism was it.[99] Introduced into the Latin countries

---

[98] For a study of Latin America's continued interest in non-democratic principles, see Douglas W. Payne, *Storm Watch: Democracy in the Western Hemisphere into the Next Century* (Washington, DC: Center for Strategic and International Studies, Policy Paper on the Americas, 1998).
[99] For an overview of Latin American positivism, see Jorge G. E. Garcia, "Importance of the History of Ideas in Latin America: Zea's Positivism in Mexico," *Journal of the History of Ideas,* Vol. 36, No. 1 (Jan.–March 1975).

in the mid-1800s, this philosophy of social evolution laid great stress on the need to move past outmoded superstitions, and Latin America was filled with them. Auguste Comte (1798–1857), its most popular advocate, believed that societies needed to evolve past what he believed to be primitive theological worldviews.[100] At some point, taught Comte, societies need to be freed from their religious chains to begin conceiving of a social order based on laws and principles deduced from the natural order of things—through dispassionate scientific observation, and not as governing principles given by revelation from above.

Comte, considered to be the father of the social sciences, called for a necessary metaphysical phase of social development. This was an interim state where humanity begins to use reason to detect abstract principles of rights that are natural and logical, not theological, religious, or based on superstitions. This French philosopher believed that the metaphysical stage prepared society to enter into the scientific phase of social development. By embracing a world where science dominates, any values it could not scientifically measure would no longer hold society captive. Instead, societies would be guided by objective science, providing the proper mechanisms to address long-standing social evils. Comte once said, "From science comes prediction; from prediction comes action."[101] For many at the time, positivism was that scientific philosophy of human social development, which would suggest the action necessary to eradicate Latin America's political malaise.

---

[100] Comte (full name: Isidore Auguste Marie François Xavier Comte) is considered to be the founder of sociology and of the philosophy of positivism. See his *A General View of Positivism*, available at Project Gutenberg, http://www.gutenberg.org/ebooks/53799 (accessed November 18, 2017).

[101] Sociologist Anthony Giddens has rightfully noted, "[T]he irony of this series of phases is that though Comte attempted to prove that human development has to go through these three stages, it seems that the positivist stage is far from becoming a realization. This is due to two truths. The positivist phase requires having a complete understanding of the universe and world around us and requires that society should never know if it is in this positivist phase." Giddens argues that since humanity constantly uses science to discover and research new things, humanity never progresses beyond the second metaphysical phase. See Anthony Giddens ed., *Positivism and Sociology* (London: Heinemann Educational Publishers, 1974), 9.

Positivism made a big splash throughout Latin America. It came on with the intent purpose of wiping away the Latino feudal society that had been in place for centuries. Latin American political liberals believed positivism was just what the region needed.[102] Somehow, the whole region needed to be unshackled from their common plight, their colonial past, and all the religious trappings that came with it. There were enthusiastic hopes that this philosophy, which interpreted the past in such a way that it denied its relevance for moving forward, would be the savior of Latin America. The past had been a necessary stage, but it needed to be left behind; the region needed to move on to more progressive stages of development.

Concerning Latin American positivism, Leopoldo Zea makes the insightful observation that Spanish-speaking countries saw it as extending their revolutions. Whatever they had failed fully and totally to discard when they banished Spain and Portugal, positivism would help them eliminate intellectually. Thus, observes Zea:

> Hispanic Americans always reacted violently; they always tried to eradicate once and for all any influence which they considered foreign. They attempted to destroy all traces of their so-called colonial heritage, as if such a thing were at all possible. . . . By following positivism, the Mexicans thought that they could put an end to the almost perpetual anarchy which kept them in turmoil. In Argentina, positivism was considered a good instrument for eliminating the absolutist and tyrannical mentalities which had scourged them. The Chileans considered positivism as an effective means of converting the ideals into reality. In Uruguay, positivism was regarded as a moral doctrine that could put an end to the long era of military uprisings and corruption. Peru and Bolivia found in

[102] Among Latin American flags, Brazil stands out, displaying a constellation of stars and the positivist slogan "Order and Progress" written on a yellow band around the globe.

> positivism a doctrine which would strengthen them after the great national catastrophe which they had suffered in their war against Chile. The Cubans looked upon it as a doctrine that would justify their desire for independence from Spain. Positivism was in every case a radical remedy which Hispanic America attempted to use to break away from a past that was overwhelming it.[103]

Again, fundamental to the promise of these positivistic systems was the belief that people could only move forward as they left behind the feudal life, replete with its religion and customs which had defined the region over centuries.

The jury is still out on whether logical positivism helped Latin America move forward. Some maintain that this social science is still present in the region, and there is a case to be made—you can see its vestigial remains emblazoned on the Brazilian flag! One thing is true: Early on, positivism attempted to drag Latin America from her feudal history into the modern era. Whether it was Domingo Faustino Sarmiento, Juan Bautista Alberdi in Argentina, Gabino Bareda and Jose Luis Mora in Mexico, Enrique Jose Varona in Cuba, Jose Victoriano Lastarria in Chile, or Alejandro Deustua in Peru—and whether they drew their inspiration from Henri de Saint-Simon, August Comte, or the social Darwinism of Herbert Spenser or John Stuart Mill—Hispanic positivists saw this social science as providing the conceptual mechanism necessary to complete the intellectual emancipation of the Latin American mind.[104]

Specifically, these liberal thinkers believed that education was the key to move their countries forward, and that positivism would lead the way. Since education had been controlled by the Roman Catholic Church, stripping her of that powerful influence was job one. In

---

[103] Zea, *The Latin American Mind,* 28–29.
[104] Ibid., 256.

Mexico, President Benito Juarez (1806–1872) had already done much to curtail church power by nationalizing lands owned by the church. But it was President Porfirio Diaz (1876–1911) who gave Mexico its full positivistic dose.[105] Diaz convened a cabinet of social engineers headed by Justo Sierra and Gabino Barreda, known as the *científicos* (scientists), who secularized the public-school system. Much the same happened throughout other Latin American countries.

Positivism was applied ardently, but the experiment was less than successful. It wasn't long before it became apparent that progress could not be achieved in lands so attached to their past and their mystical traditions. Only at the expense of selling their very soul could Hispanics buy into the belief that clinical, dispassionate scientific inquiry held the key to their future.

We should not conclude that positivism evaporated within fifty years. Even today, the need to help people move past primitivism, especially in rural areas, is an important national goal. It may no longer be thought of as positivism, but the ideals of secularism appeal to many who are convinced that Latin America's fixation with their past legacies keep her from advancing.

The Romantic Reaction

To be sure, positivism gained a foothold in Latin America, but its ideals were met by formidable resistance, and this wasn't because Latin America was backward. They knew their countries would need to modernize in the fields of education, land management, agriculture, medical services, city and urban planning, industrialization, and so many other areas. But the notion that progress in these areas could only happen at the expense of abandoning their core societal and religious convictions did not necessarily follow—not for most Latinos.

---

[105] John Charles Chasteen, *Born in Blood & Fire: A Concise History of Latin America* (New York: W. W. Norton & Company, 2006), 195–196, 220–221.

And so, it happened, early at the beginning of the twentieth century—and on the heels of the Mexican Revolution (1910–1920)—that a revival of nationalism and a romantic attitude toward their history, particularly pre-Columbian history, began to take hold. Positivism, had it prevailed, would have brought aboriginal peoples kicking and fighting into modernity. But romanticism valued the *Indio* as such. Hispanics didn't need to modernize the native peoples; they needed to value them as symbols of their national identities.

Then came José Enrique Camilo Rodó (1871–1917), a Uruguayan writer, who penned *Ariel*, and by so doing gave voice to this romantic spirit that was flowering throughout the Spanish-speaking hemisphere.[106] In this work, Rodó calls on Latin America to reject positivistic and utilitarian philosophies, and to revert to Greco-Roman ideals. Sound familiar?[107] Rodó feared the debilitating effect of the Industrial Revolution upon Latin American society. With its emphasis on science, positivists would scarcely value virtues that had stamped the Latino mode of being. For Rodó, the kind of modernization that the prophets of positivism promoted could only happen at the expense of Latin America losing her soul.

In Rodó's *Ariel*, Próspero the teacher and Ariel are Shakespearean characters, which Rodó typecasts as metaphors who symbolize beauty, spirit, and that which is good. Caliban, on the other hand, represents the heartless forces of materialistic utilitarianism. Caliban, writes Rodó, is too myopic to take into account the whole, causing the mutilation of the person. In his mind specialization, a hallmark of the scientific method, caused societies to become culturally immature.

True to his fondness for the Greco-Roman way of life, Rodó also criticized US democracy. He believed the masses were foolhardy and incapable of making good decisions; democracy could only lead to

---

[106] Jose Enrique Rodó, *Ariel* (Middlesex: Echo Library, 2008); Chasteen, *Born in Blood & Fire,* 207–208.

[107] Kalman H. Silvert, *The Conflict Society* (New York: Harper & Collins, 1966), 140. Silvert notes the inability of Latin American societies to pull away from the Greek ideal.

social suicide in the Latin countries. Like Plato, Rodó believed that the governance should be done by the elite, and those most capable among them.

One of the interesting aspects of Rodó's book was his constant critique of *nordomanía*, the obsession many influential people had for all things "North." Indeed, many Hispanic leaders in Rodó's day saw the United States as a model to emulate, but Rodó would have none of it. By contrast, he echoes the importance of regional identity and how it should be rooted deeply in the ethos of each country. Rodó puts forth the idea that even though influences from other countries could be beneficial, the potential for cultural harm was too great. Rodó urges the youth of Spanish America to help form and maintain their regional and cultural identity.

The Uruguayan proved to be very influential for a movement that began to embrace the past as the cultural repository of everything that Latin America was. The message was clear: Rather than rushing headlong into modern times, Hispanics needed to make sure that the culture they had inherited and shaped during their colonial period remained alive.

Then came José Vasconcelos, an influential minister of education in Mexico from 1921–1924, who penned the small treatise *La Raza Cósmica* ("The Cosmic Race").[108] Vasconcelos can be seen as a thinker of his time who also challenged the promise of positivism for a more romantic future. He saw the *Mestizo* (along with other mixed blood peoples of the world) as the saviors of the human race. Mexico, he believed, needed to embrace fully the indigenous culture, rather than long for whatever North America offered.

Both Rodó and Vasconcelos challenged positivistic programs in vogue. It is no overstatement that Rodó, Vasconcelos, and others reignited a passion for everything that had defined Latin American history.[109]

---

[108] José Vasconcelos, *La Raza Cósmica* (México, D.F.: Espasa-Calpe, Mexicana, S. A., 1992).

[109] Gary Prevost, H. E. Vanden, eds., *Latin America, an Introduction* (Oxford: Oxford University Press, 2011), 177–179.

Conclusion

In surveying the philosophical challenges like positivism, which tried to strip Latin America from her ancient roots, one lesson is clearly learned: One would be better off believing the earth is flat than to wait for the day when Hispanics might dispossess themselves of those mystical and spiritual things that make them Latino. After all, when the brutal realities of modern life threaten, the Hispanic way, ancient as it is, roars in defiance.[110]

The Latino philosophical community has surrendered to this reality, for the time being.[111] We know this to be true, for when Latin American philosophy is so attuned to the ethical and existential problems that face the Hispanic world does it not, in fact, show the weakness of its hand? While some Latino thinkers have proposed that a genuine Latin American philosophical tradition can emerge, the major focus has always been, and continues to be, a pursuit for defining the essence of the Latino predicament.[112] As Risieri Frondizi acknowledges about his life's work as a philosopher, it is intimately linked "with the problems of the sociocultural milieu."[113] Simply put, Hispanic philosophy cannot afford to pursue questions of speculative interest—not when the tumultuous history and conduct of the Latin American needs to be understood and explained. And so, whether by way of religion, mysticism, or philosophy, the focus is on the perennial historical challenges of the Latino.

---

[110] Chasteen, *Born in Blood & Fire,* 15–24. Chasteen acknowledges the vast diversity that exists throughout Latin America, yet maintains that the twenty countries "have struggled with similar problems in similar ways," giving the political history of the Latin American countries "a unified ebb and flow."

[111] Jorge G. E. Garcia, ed. *Latin American Philosophy in the Twentieth Century: Man, Values, and the Search for Philosophical Identity* (Buffalo, NY: Prometheus Books, 1986), 17.

[112] Ibid., 21. For a review of attempts at undertaking original Latin American philosophy, see Ricardo Vélez Rodriguez, "La Filosofía en Latinoamérica y los Problemas de la Originalidad y del Método," Universidad Federal de Juiz de Fora, http://www.ecsbdefesa.com.br/defesa/fts/FLPOM.pdf; accessed May 15, 2018.

[113] Ibid., 22.

But what of the Hispangelical? Does he have an answer to the "Hispanic Condition," to quote Stavans? Well, we believe he does! When we see a confluence of interest from people of religion, as well as from those committed to philosophical humanistic solutions, I can't help but think that Hispangelicals have come unto their own at a propitious moment in time.

Christians of Paul's era also lived in a world filled with philosophers, sages, mystics, mendicant teachers, prophets, rabbis, and priests. There was no end to the ideas that flowed throughout the world. Belief systems ranged from devotion to the ancient Greek pantheon, to innumerable local and provincial deities, to the Roman state religion, to the moral philosophies of Stoicism and Epicureanism, to eastern Mithraism and Zoroastrianism. And of course, Jewish monotheism also attracted many. Every one of these philosophical, religious, or moral schools had some persuasive message to sell, and it was within this world wind of ideas that the gospel made its unique appeal.

In addressing the church at Colossae, which was being inundated by a syncretistic fusion of Jewish legalism, Greek philosophy and Eastern mysticism, Paul assured the church there was a "treasure" of wisdom and knowledge to be discovered (Col. 2:2–3), but it was not found in "persuasive argument" (v. 4), nor in "empty deception, according to the tradition of men" (v. 8). Human intellect and reason, persuasive as they might seem, were ultimately bankrupt. With "Christ" in grammatical apposition to "God's mystery" in verse 2,[114] Paul shows that "Christ Himself" was the mystery, the treasure. The masculine relative pronoun "in whom," which follows in verse 3, solidifes Paul's conviction that the wisdom and knowledge people sought could only be found through knowing Christ through that believer's redemption. Not merely doctrine, or the teachings of the Galilean, but Jesus himself was the source for those who lived "in Him."

---

[114] Cleon L. Rogers and C. L. Rogers III, *The New Linguistic and Exegetical Key to the Greek New Testament* (Grand Rapids, MI: Zondervan Publishing House, 1998), 463.

All believers spend a lifetime growing in spiritual wisdom and knowledge as they mature and their personal relationship to their Savior and Lord deepens, and the Hispangelical is no different in this respect. However, the way Hispangelicals express their life "in Christ" may be directly challenged by the conditions their life, their culture, their circumstancess have laid before them. The issue is not insignificant and we will have more to say about it in chapter seven, "Then Came the Hispangelical's Challenge."

CHAPTER THREE

Then Came Culture

While a culture may be defined by the customs and accepted practices of its people, it is critical to understand that it is the thinking of its people that creates a culture in the first place. Knowledge of this difference is so significant as to be the key to life or death for civilizations. Indeed, it has been for thousands of years.

Andy Andrews
The Noticer Returns[115]

Recently, a former student forwarded a YouTube video to me that has received over seven million views as of April 2017. She was sure it would catch my attention, and indeed it has, for it says in images what ten thousand words can never communicate. The video is titled "Alma y Colores de Mexico," a visually stunning production that extenuates Mexico's culture.[116] What is so striking about this video is that apart from a fleeting clip of sailboats, the rest of the five-minute presentation could have been videotaped centuries earlier (if videotaping

---

[115] Andy Andrews, *The Noticer Returns* (Nashville: W Publishing Group, 2013), 162.
[116] Los Cojolites, "Alma y Colores de Mexico," January 7, 2012, YouTube video, 5:20, posted October 6, 2014. https://www.youtube.com/watch?v=aavRzHta1YM (accessed June 3, 2017).

had existed). There is almost nothing in the video that showcases Mexico's current twenty-first-century culture, or does it? Does it, in fact, say proudly, "This is truly who we are"?

Go to Mexico and you will see a concerted effort to develop and to modernize. There is construction, road building, and industrial development everywhere you look.[117] And yet, despite remarkable advances, there is always the tug of what Guillermo Bonfil Batalla has labeled a *México profundo*,[118] somewhat akin to what I would call a Latino cultural "Pied Piper."[119] But actually, what is true of Mexico is true to one degree or another of the various regions that make up the Latin American countries.[120] This cultural allure is so irrepressible that it has a way of clinging to the heart of even the most assimilated, even resistant, US-born Hispanic.[121]

Recently, my wife reminded me of a comment made by a cousin years ago. Upon crossing the border for the first time in his life, Tacho was left speechless at the sudden change. "How could things be so different," he thought, "when all that separates the two countries is a third-rate river?" To be honest, throughout my formative years as we regularly traveled from San Antonio, Texas to Monterrey Nuevo Leon, I also marveled at the stark divide. Of course, it started with the change in language spoken, but it extended to virtually everything my senses took in. It took years for

---

[117] Gary Prevost and Harry E. Vanden, "An Introduction to Twenty-First Century America," in *Latin America: An Introduction* (Oxford: Oxford University Press, 2011), 1–18.

[118] See Guillermo Bonfil Batalla, *Mexico Profundo: Reclaiming a Civilization* (Austin: University of Texas Press, 1996). The word *profundo* can mean "deep" or "profound." Here Batalla uses it to speak of a mystical Mexican parallel culture, which exists beneath the veneer of contemporary secular Mexican civilization.

[119] Manuel Vargas, "On the Value of Philosophy: The Latin American Case," *Comparative Philosophy,* Vol. 1, No. 1 (2010), 36. Some say "pied" piper, referring to a person who offers others strong yet delusive enticements.

[120] The Western Hemisphere is generally divided into seven distinguishable regions: North America, Mesoamerica, and Intermediate, Caribbean, Amazonian, Central Andes, and the Southern Andes regions.

[121] Susan E. Keefe and Amado M. Padilla, *Chicano Ethnicity* (Notre Dame, IN: University of Notre Dame Press, 1987), 8. Keefe and Padilla show that while cultural awareness can decline, feelings of ethnic identity intensify.

ıne to realize that the differences were due to cultural factors. From the Latino side of things, it was the logical end result of a Baroque world that the Roman Catholic Church had set into motion centuries before. This is so patently true; whoever said that the Baroque Era ended around the 1800s was not entirely correct. Certainly some aspects of baroque influences, particularly as related to the fine arts, architecture, and so forth, gave way to more modern, progressive developments. However, when it comes to culture—a way of life—and particularly in Latin America and among Latinos, the baroque heart has not missed a beat.

Baroque Beginnings

While we can agree that there have been broad cultural movements that emerged by happenstance with no discernible forethought, we cannot ascribe it to baroque influences, not in Latin America. Its development can be traced to soon after the Reformation took hold. Within three decades, in fact, from the diffusion of Luther's Ninety-Five Theses northern Germany, Holland, the Scandinavian countries, England, and Scotland had all severed ties to Rome and embraced Protestantism. For her part, the Catholic Church did not let the Reformation continue unchecked, allowing other countries to follow suit. Catholics mounted a defensive action that would have implications for theology and culture in Europe and across the Atlantic.

Led by the Society of Jesus, a church council was convened in Trento (Trent), Italy from 1545–1563. Although billed as ecumenical, Protestants never had a hearing, and we can see why. The Jesuits moved to strengthen Catholic doctrines and ecclesiastical authority. Though the council issued a number of important decrees, one aspect concerns us: the place of art and iconography in the life of the church.[122] While disil-

---

[122] Helen Gardner, Fred S. Kleiner, and Christin J. Mamiya, eds. *Gardner's Art through the Ages: Book D: Renaissance and Baroque*, fifteenth edition (Belmont, CA: Wadsworth Publishing, 2015).

lusioned with the state of art—like, for example, Michelangelo's works, which put artistic effect over religious objectives—artists and sculptors created art that went over the average worshipper's ability to appreciate. At Trent, the Jesuits saw it necessary to encourage the creation of art that was more devotionally oriented. With that in mind, the council convened for its twenty-fifth and final session in December of 1563. The council addressed the issue of the invocation, veneration, and relics, or Saints, and other sacred images. In it the council states:

> The holy Synod enjoins on all bishops, and others who sustain the office and charge of teaching . . . instruct the faithful diligently concerning the intercession and invocation of saints; the honour (paid) to relics; and the legitimate use of images: teaching them, that the saints, who reign together with Christ, offer up their own prayers to God for men. . . .
>
> Moreover, that the images of Christ, of the Virgin Mother of God, and of the other saints, are to be had and retained particularly in temples, and that due honour and veneration are to be given them . . . because the honour which is shown them is referred to the prototypes which those images represent; in such wise that by the images which we kiss, and before which we uncover the head, and prostrate ourselves, we adore Christ; and we venerate the saints, whose similitude they bear . . .
>
> And the bishops shall carefully teach this,-that, by means of the histories of the mysteries of our Redemption, portrayed by paintings or other representations, the people is instructed, and confirmed in remembering, and continually revolving in mind the articles of faith; as also that great profit is derived from all sacred images . . . .[123]

---

[123] J. Waterworth, ed. and trans., *The Canons and Decrees of the Sacred and Ecumenical Council of Trent* (London: Dolman Publishers, 1848). Text found at https://history.hanover.edu/texts/trent.html (accessed October 6, 2017).

In reading the council's decrees, there is an unambiguous hope that visual features within the church should be used to "communicate religious themes in direct and emotional involvement."[124] And it went further, for the Jesuits also incorporated theatrical methods into their liturgy.[125] In doing so, we should not cynically condemn Jesuits as manipulative. Inspired by their founder, Ignatius of Loyola himself, they understood the educational power of professional theater, so Jesuits drew from the craft of actors to create dramatic liturgy that would inspire devotion. As Michael Zampelli has observed, they saw dramaturgy as "thoroughly incarnational," believing theater had the power to ignite the imagination, achieving spiritual transcendence by means of the physical, "through the word-made-flesh."[126]

Of course, that the Council at Trent should concern itself with artistic matters is itself a testament to the effect that Protestantism was having throughout Europe. As history shows, most Reformers were antagonistic to the proliferation of images, icons, and relics that filled Catholic churches. And despite official pronouncements, like we see expressed at Trent, the need to warn against idolatry is telling. We should not forget that Protestant Reformers were not writing or preaching as uninformed outsiders. Having been Roman Catholic and wanting to reform the church rather than leave it, they knew that people went beyond veneration to outright worship of those visuals in the churches. Protestants railed against what they considered to be a gross endorsement of idolatry, and their response was iconoclastic—painting over, shattering, or removing anything that could turn the people's attention away from the preaching of the Scriptures.

---

[124] Ibid., 516.

[125] Marcia B. Hall, Tracy E. Cooper, eds. *The Sensuous in the Counter Reformation Church* (Cambridge: Cambridge University Press, 2013), 10.

[126] John W. O'Malley, Gauvin A. Bailey, Steven J. Harris and T. Frank Kennedy, eds., *The Jesuits II: Cultures, Sciences, and the Arts, 1540–1773* (Toronto: University of Toronto Press, 2006), 563; Hall, *The Sensuous in the Counter Reformation,* 11. Hall notes there were popes and Jesuits who opposed theatrics.

The Council at Trent strongly disagreed. They held that God should be worshiped with great flair and grandiosity, and that art could certainly be an aid in that endeavor. So, Jesuits drew from both the plastic and performing arts in the hope of instructing people, as they put it, in the "mysteries of our Redemption . . . confirmed in the habit of remembering, and continually revolving in mind the articles of faith."[127]

The council that convened at Trent could not have imagined it at the time, but their dictates had far-reaching implications, bleeding over into architecture, church construction, music, and more, so much more. This strengthening of all that had sensual appeal turned out to be a stroke of genius for keeping the illiterate within the Catholic fold, but how did it accomplish this? The dictate became a catalyst, weaving its way into the very fabric of culture itself. And so it was that the impetus for what would evolve into the baroque and rococo world was sparked.[128] And those same impulses were brought to the Latin American colony, where no protestant threat existed.

In the colony, the Spanish crown effectively quarantined millions of Hispanics from ever having to deal with the teachings of Protestant beliefs. This was accomplished largely through the tight regulation of foreign enterprises and the establishment of Inquisitorial offices opened first in Mexico City and Lima; a third office opened later in Cartagena.[129] The resulting seclusion to which the Spanish colony was subjected allowed a baroque veneer to permeate the culture, unaffected by Protestant teachings and secular ideas shaping countries elsewhere.[130]

---

[127] Waterworth, *The Council of Trent*, 234.

[128] Thomas F. O'Meara, "Baroque Catholicism," *The HarperCollins Encyclopedia of Catholicism* (San Francisco: HarperCollins, 1989), 140–141.

[129] In the Americas, King Philip II set up two tribunals (titled *Tribunal del Santo Oficio de la Inquisición*) in 1569, one in Mexico City and the other in Lima, Peru. The tribunal at Cartagena was not established until 1610.

[130] This isolation went beyond keeping Protestant teachings away. There were important developments in all the sciences, laying the groundwork for advancement in agricultural development, industrialization, and medicine. These things were known in colonial Latin America, but the will to put them to good use rarely developed.

In Latin America, the baroque mood reached beyond the dictates initially articulated by the Tridentine council. Life itself became essentially baroque, the worldview weaving its way into the very fabric of colonial life. If art, music, and architecture were tools used to indoctrinate the faithful masses, people expanded its influence by taking that very sentiment into their *barrios, ranchos, haciendas,* and *favelas*. Latin American religion and culture, fused into one indivisible whole. So far as people were concerned, they might just as well have been living on a desert island the size of two continents.[131] As Steve Wakefield has so astutely noted, the baroque was like a Medusa "taken to the Americas to 'petrify' the indigenous peoples and subject their culture to the dominant ideology."[132] Latin America looked deeply into the baroque Medusa, and it cemented the colony in time and space.[133] But it had verbal help.

Words Matter

As the vagaries of history would have it, the Spanish language also contributed to seal this outcome.[134] Peter Burger and Thomas Luckmann remind us that language "is the most important sign system of human society . . . grounded in everyday life and . . . pointing back to it."[135] The Latin colonizers brought with them a language that was salted with Catholic themes one could hardly avoid. Much of the spoken Spanish was framed so as to begin, end, or interject somewhere in between the language of the mother church. If something caught the Hispanic by surprise, "*Jesús, María, y José*" were invoked to express the emotion. Those needing comfort, solace, or protection had only to call out to

---

[131] See Véliz, *The New World of the Gothic Fox,* 33–34.

[132] Steve Wakefield, *Carpentier's Baroque Fiction: Returning Medusa's Gaze* (Woodbridge, Suffolk: Tamesis, 2004), 330–333.

[133] The term "baroque" may also evolve from the concept of an irregularly shaped pearl.

[134] See Véliz, *The New World of the Gothic Fox,* 35–36.

[135] Peter L. Berger and Thomas Luckmann, *The Social Construction of Reality: A Treatise in the Sociology of Knowledge* (New York: Doubleday, 1966), 52–53.

their "*Virgen Purísima,*" "*Diosito Santo,*" or "*Madre de Dios*" as their refuge. And when someone left home for work or any other reason, you were sure to hear a loving "*Que Dios te guarde.*"

Of course, all languages are capable of speaking of the divine. Yet, it is probably true to say that English speakers tend to speak a more secularized language, unless they intend to use "church talk." However, in his *Teología,* Luis G. Pedraja muses over the nature of language and asks about the word "God": "Could it be that the very meaning of God might be colored and affected by who we are, by our culture, our biases, and our assumptions?"[136] Latinos tend to use religious language as a matter of fact, finding the old religious idioms and imagery emotive and perfect to express their most modern thoughts and emotions.[137]

I was reminded of the importance of God-language recently when we celebrated the birthday of a family member. Initially, someone asked the guests to join in singing the English "Happy Birthday." But then, some five minutes later, another guest, perhaps feeling somewhat underwhelmed by the English song, asked those attending to sing the Spanish "*Feliz, Feliz Cumpleaños.*" No doubt, my working on this chapter heightened my sense of awareness. Immediately, it struck me how different both songs are. While the English song is secular, and frankly, redundant, the Spanish song tells a story, invoking God, asking him to grant the person a long, healthy, and joyous life.[138] The more I think of it, the more I am convinced the man roused everyone to sing the Spanish birthday song to make sure that God was welcomed into the celebration.

---

[136] Luis G. Pedraja, *Teología: An Introduction to Hispanic Theology* (Nashville: Abingdon Press, 2003), 89.

[137] Seymour Resnick, *1001 Most Useful Spanish Words* (Mineola, NY: Dover Publications, 1996). Resnick lists "God" as useful for speaking Spanish.

[138] "Las Mañanitas" is traditionally sung to young girls on their birthday, and contains religious language noting King David, Saint Peter, Saint John, the baptismal font, and reference to the person's matron or patron saint.

It is possible, and I know from personal observation, that the language of the church is so embedded into the Hispanic mindset that one can hardly express an idea without inserting something of a religious tone within the normal course of conversation. "Dios" language, for example, abounds: *válgame Dios, solo Dios sabe, Dios mío, que Dios te bendiga,* and *Diosito Santo* are just a few phrases people use, even if they are discussing what items to buy at the store. Although you can certainly bid farewell to someone by saying *ciao* (or *chao*), *hasta luego*, or *hasta la vista,* the most popular way, *adios,* commends people to God in their journey.[139] The same can be said about calling on the names of Jesus, Mary, and Joseph.

But it did not start and stop with religious language. Spaniards also brought with them the language of serfdom and patronage, reinforcing deeply held social beliefs that were also common to pre-Columbian civilizations.[140] Spanish and Portuguese, steeped with religious concepts and ideology of hierarchy, class distinction, and patronage, keeps the Latino grounded in that very same history—for, as Burger and Luckman remind us, language always points back to itself. Who could have guessed that the Spanish Crown and the Roman Catholic Church would happen upon a land mass complete with whole civilizations which proved to be largely amenable to their overarching baroque worldview?

In his excellent work, *The Latin Americans: Understanding Their Legacy,* Randall Hansis makes it clear that Spain never had to conquer the New World through fierce protracted wars. Yes, there were skirmishes and battles, and some indigenous tribes did fight to the bitter end. But, by large measure, the native peoples of the New World simply handed themselves over to the "fair-skinned gods," who imposed upon them the

139 *Chau* is regional and limited to a few South American countries. *Adiós* literally means "to God" and is used to commend the person to God as they part company. Other languages that use this expression include French, Portuguese, Italian, and Catalan.

140 Wiarda, *The Soul of Latin America*, 105–106.

baroque way of life.[141] It is stunning but true that within fifty years after Columbus arrived on the shores of *Guanahani,* the New World—along with its millions of natives—had surrendered itself, at least outwardly, to this monolithic ideology that Spain and Portugal introduced.[142]

Hispanics and Hispanic-Americans are a "Baroque" People

While it is true that all Latin American countries have distinct cultural characteristics, there is one thing that is common among them: baroque influences.[143] These don't end at the US-Mexico border either, for wherever Hispanics are likely to live or travel, they will carry with them, to one degree or another, something of that ornate worldview. But, just what is the baroque lifestyle?

When I click the synonym finder for "baroque," my word-processing program gives an almost endless list of adjectives: ornate, ornamental, decorative, elaborate, exaggerated, rococo, extravagant, flamboyant, overdone, and over-the-top. From this list, we get the sense that baroque was a cultural movement that tended to err on the side of extravagance. Given the submersion of Latin American cultures to baroque influences, it should not surprise us that evidences of its continuing influence abound.

La Fiesta

There can be little doubt but that partying among Latinos is thoroughly baroque. While most people live a secular lifestyle, many celebrate birthdays, *quinceañeras*, and the like by going first to the local parish to light a candle to thank a patron saint or the Virgin, followed by a

[141] Randall Hansis, *The Latin Americans: Understanding Their Legacy* (New York: McGraw Hill Publishers, 1997).
[142] Wiarda, *The Soul of Latin America,* 86.
[143] Pablo Alberto Deiros, *Historia del Cristianismo en América Latina* (Buenos Aires: Fraternidad Teológica Latinoamericana, 1992), 396–397.

lively fiesta. If they can afford it, the neighborhood is invited, filling the evening's activities with music, dancing, and all-around partying. While the festivities may begin with due reverence paid at the church, the actual fiesta is a time to let loose. The music played, as we shall shortly see, is usually of baroque cloth, all of which encourages drama, passion, and over-the-top displays of emotion and flair.

Don't misunderstand—a fiesta can be a very sacred event; nevertheless, it reveals its baroque influence. Throughout Latin America, *matachines*, indigenous ritual sword dancers, venerate either Mary in any of her local modalities, a local saint, or perhaps *El Niño Dios*, The God Child. These native dancers mix pre-Columbian beliefs with Roman Catholic traditions specifically dedicated to venerate the statue or relic being paraded through the village. Some partygoers will prepare themselves mentally and spiritually throughout the year to undergo bodily scourging, as demonstrations of affection to the holy icon. As one can see, whether it is corporal flagellation, the tearing of one's knees for having walked on them in pilgrimage, or any other act of physical trauma, it all heightens emotion. When the religious procession ends, the fiesta begins, leading to a time of drinking, dancing, and partying that can go for days.

La Música

What fiesta can there be without music? We should remember that a key tenet of the Baroque Era was the belief that music could be a potent tool to arouse the deepest religious sympathies of the people. Did the Jesuits of Trent seize upon this genius idea from the pages of Scripture? Young David, we will recall, was summoned to bring relief to the tortured soul of Saul by the playing of his harp, as 1 Samuel 16:23 tells us:

> So it came about whenever the evil spirit from God came to Saul, David would take the harp and play it with his hand;

> and Saul would be refreshed and be well, and the evil spirit would depart from him.[144]

Whether the Tridentine Council was guided by Holy Scripture is a topic for another day. What is beyond doubt is that after Trent, the Roman Catholic Church became a major patron of music, intentionally funding the movement. The number of recognized Baroque composers born between 1550 and 1700 figures in the hundreds.[145] Over the course of the following years, especially from 1600 to 1750, many gained great acclaim throughout Europe for their creations, most of which were written and played to the glory of God. But what of music in the colony?

Latin America, for her part, never produced an Antonio Vivaldi or a Johann Sebastian Bach, much less a George Fredrick Handel, to name the most well-known Baroque composers. But, this is not to say that the baroque attitude to music did not find a receptive ear. It most assuredly affected the way music would evolve in the Latin American colony and afterward.

Today, it would be wrong to say that Latin Americans don't enjoy modern music. Indeed, much music is thoroughly secular and influenced by the same trends that influence music in the West. Yes, Latino Elvis Presley and Michael Jackson impersonators do exist. And I can attest to having heard a Spanish rendition of Frank Sinatra's "My Way" at a family wedding in Monterrey, Mexico. Yet, despite the popularity

---

[144] In this context, there is an interesting story offered by Artus Thomas, a French scholar describing the effect that the musical performance of one *Sieur Claudin Le June* had on a person who happened to hear him sing: "I have oft times heard it said . . . that he had sung an air (which he had composed in parts) . . . and that when this air was rehearsed at a private concert it caused a gentleman there to put hand to arms and begin swearing out loud, so that it seemed impossible to prevent him from attacking someone: whereupon Claudin began singing another air . . . which rendered the gentleman as calm as before. This has been confirmed to me since by several who were there. Such is the power and force of melody, rhythm and harmony over the mind."

[145] For a list of Baroque composers, see http://www.ask.com/wiki/List_of_Baroque_composers?o=3986&qsrc=999 (accessed June 12, 2017).

of modern and contemporary music, there is an enduring love for music that goes back to ancient baroque traditions.[146]

The earliest Hispanic musical developments date back to the colonial era when the Spanish introduced the *son*, a style of music tied particularly to stringed instruments. In Mexico, the *son Jaliscience*, for example, is known to be the predecessor to *mariachi* music, which achieves a mixture of cultural influences that span centuries.[147] It was also the baroque *son* that gave rise to extravagant costumes such as the *charro* outfit, the *sombrero* with the extravagant brim, and the "*Ajuaa!*" emotional outbursts associated with those musical styles.

Pulitzer Prize winner Oscar Hijuelo's *The Mambo Kings Play Songs of Love* (1990) is considered to have been a catalyst for the "debut" of Latinos onto the American stage.[148] But notice what brought them to the limelight. Though Hispanics have long been involved in business, medicine, academia, entertainment, sports, and politics, it is their exaggerated music and lyrics that caught world attention. The sensual music of Hector Lavoe, Gloria Estefan, Tito Rodriguez, Celia Cruz, Ricky Martin, and others is unabashedly baroque, expressing passion in the rhythms and bodily gyrations of Latin and Caribbean *salsa*.

But if the melodies are baroque, the lyrics send raw emotion through the stratosphere. You cannot hear the lyrics of songs by earlier luminaries such as Trio Los Panchos, Los Dandys, or Trio Matamoros, or contemporaries such as Los Tri-O, or *boleros* sung and played by José Feliciano, or even the modern Spanglish renditions of Los Lonely Boys, or the sensual lyrics of Fato or Julio Iglesias to see that Latin music

---

[146] See David R. M. Irving, "Latin American Baroque," *Early Music,* May 2011 39(2): 295–298; see also chapter 12, "Spain, Portugal and Latin America," in *A History of Baroque Music*, George J. Buelow, ed. (Bloomington: Indiana University Press, 2004).

[147] There is also the *Son Jarocho, Huasteco,* and *Chiapaneco*; see Hermes Rafael, *Origen e Historia del Mariachi*, segunda edicion (Republica de Colombia: Editorial Katun, S.A., 1983). So popular is the mariachi is that its influence is felt throughout Latin America, the US, Europe, Israel, and as far away as Japan.

[148] This in itself is revealing, for Hispanic music had been sung throughout North America for centuries.

has not ventured far from its baroque roots. Note the song "*Ódiame*," wherein a jilted lover asks the woman who is leaving him to muster the vilest emotion possible against him, and why? Self-interest, as the man confesses:

> *Ódiame por piedad yo te lo pido; ódiame sin medida ni clemencia, odio quiero más que indiferencia, porque el rencor hiere menos que el olvido.*
> *(Hate me, by God, I'm asking you; hate me without measure or clemency; I desire hatred more than indifference, for rancor injures less than forgetfulness.)*[149]

Similarly, "La Copa Rota" centers on a man tormented for having discovered the treachery of his lover. Drowning his sorrows in a bar and overcome with sadness, he breaks the glass with his teeth as he drinks and asks the bartender to refill the broken glass. Why?

> *Mozo . . . sírvame la copa rota, sírvame que me destroza esta fiebre de obsesión Mozo . . . sírvame la copa rota, quiero sangrar gota a gota el veneno de su amor.*
> *(Barkeep, fill the broken glass, give it to me that it might tear this feverish obsession*
> *Barkeep, fill the broken glass, for I want to bleed out drop by drop the venom of her love.)* [150]

As you might sense, the emotional involvement is extreme, inviting the hearer to live the intensity of the moment. Such lyrics are common in Latino music.

---

[149] "Ódiame," composed in 1959 by Peruvian, Rafael Otero Lopez (1921–1997); lyrics inspired by a sonnet written by Federico Barreto, "El último ruego" (The Last Plea). Lyrics at https://www.lyrics.com/lyric/34006432/La+Santa+ Cecilia/Ódiame (accessed May 6, 2019).

[150] "La Copa Rota," composed and written in 1966 by Puerto Rican Benito de Jesus (1912–2010). Lyrics at https://genius.com/Jose-feliciano-la-copa-rota-lyrics (accessed May 6, 2019).

Additionally, most songs are played with the guitar, the sound of which immediately conjures great sentimentality. This stringed instrument, which made its way across the Atlantic, found a people who one could say were awaiting its arrival. This was certainly true in the case of Agustín Barrios, one of the best guitar composers Paraguay has ever produced. His more than three hundred compositions reveal his masterful mix of baroque folklore, religion, and romanticisms. Barrios, who died in 1944, was particularly fond of Johann Sebastian Bach; his 1921 composition "La Catedral" (The Cathedral), considered his crowning achievement, is clearly influenced by Bach. John Williams, composer extraordinaire, once said of Barrios, "As a guitarist/composer, Barrios is the best of the lot, regardless of era. His music is better formed, it's more poetic, it's more everything! And it's more of all those things in a timeless way."[151]

Yes, Latino guitarists create sounds that immediately bring up all the range of emotions: from great pride in one's homeland like the Argentine tango, to sadness for a loss ("La Camisa Negra"), to joy for having the simple pleasure of going out on the town ("Me Voy al Pueblo"). As Kelly Trottier, a contemporary music critic observes, "Latin music covers it all with a passion that is somehow different from other cultures."[152] I dare not make comments about other cultures, but Latino music touches the raw nerves of hard-lived life. The dictate of the church to engage emotion through music could not be limited to the church. If Latinos found ways to express their love for church with passion, it was natural to extend such investment to the realities of life, and they did it musically; they still do.

In the interest of full disclosure, I confess my affection for baroque Latin music. Some time back a colleague told me of his disdain of mariachi music, and I pitied him. After all, what is more romantic yet

---

[151] "Agustín Barrios Mangoré," Philadelphia Chamber Music Society, https://www.pcmsconcerts.org/composer/agustin-barrios-mangore (accessed April 27, 2019).

[152] See http://www.mademan.com/mm/10-best-latin-songs.html (accessed November 14, 2016).

tragic than "La Malagueña," as interpreted by no greater champion of that style than Miguel Aceves Mejia, *¡Ajuuuuuaaahh!*

El Arte

In Europe, it was the visual arts that were most immediately influenced by the cultural shift that in time came to be known as the Baroque Era. In Latin America, this same exuberance swept through the colonies, leaving a definite and enduring imprint in place.

We can see this legacy by taking a close look at the paintings of prominent Latin American artists. Though realism was and still is a style of artistic expression, Spanish art hardly ever seeks to recreate a true-to-life depiction. Among Hispanic artists, landscape naturalism, for example, is practically nonexistent.[153] Whether it is Salvador Dali, Pablo Picasso, El Greco, Diego Velasquez, Francisco Goya, Freda Kahlo, or Diego Rivera, these and many others tend to focus on creating visual impressions that stimulate the senses, creating a definite mood. Spanish and Hispanic Baroque artists were not known for adherence to realism, but rather for painting intensely emotive subject matter.

One good example is that of Pablo Picasso's 1937 "Guernica." The subject matter of this painting is the bombing of a Basque village by the Nazi air force. In terms of actual style, it is certainly not classical baroque, but probably a blend. What is for certain is that it depicts the atrocity creatively, intensifying the drama of the event. Likewise, Diego Rivera's "Man Controller of the Universe," his "Exploitation of Mexico by Spanish Conquistadores," or any of his other works defy realism. Rivera wants to create an impression, and that is the point.

Of course, it can be shown that most art seeks to move the observer emotionally. This was true before the Baroque Era, and is true of modern art as well. But one thing is for certain, the impressionistic styles that came into their own in the nineteenth century came on the heels

---

[153] Véliz, *The New World of the Gothic Fox,* 82–83.

of baroque influences, which opened the door for art to move creatively away from the realism and formal perspective that had taken hold during the Renaissance. We should not think that the impressionism of Edgar Degas, cubism of Pablo Picasso, or surrealism of Freda Kahlo and Salvador Dali might not have developed if the Baroque Era had not arrested its classical forerunner. Who's to say what paths cultural development might have taken? Historically, we know that the Jesuits of Trent ordered something upon the church, but which unbeknownst to them would spill out into art studios. This was a movement that encouraged artists to experiment beyond the limits of the observable and into the transcendental. If the ultimate aim was to glorify God, and Trent made that aim specific, Latino artists accepted the challenge.

Thus, while Protestants were busy effacing religious art, Catholic artists were creating it all the more. In doing so, they were going beyond the image itself, attempting to capture the emotion and the feeling it evoked. Others, not so committed to the church, would take their lead and advance the world of art. In that lineage, Latin American art is an offspring of the Baroque Era.

One other observation must be noted, more pedestrian but also relevant to this issue: This baroque attraction for color and flamboyance happens at many levels. In the 2001 movie, *Fools Rush In*, the plot focuses on an Anglo man who marries a Mexican girl. No sooner does the family of the *novia* hear of her marriage than they take it upon themselves to deck out the groom's home appropriately—for a Hispanic couple, that is. Her brothers paint and redecorate the suburban Las Vegas home in a variety of vibrant colors. And of course, the couple also receives a family heirloom: a huge crucifix for good fortune, for no Hispanic home is complete without one.

Yes, the whole scene is blatantly stereotypical, but I am not offended; very few Hispanics are. Go to two or three Mexican food restaurants and you will likely see the same splash of color and religious iconography on the walls. The extravagance of it all screams baroque: vibrant primary colors, gaudy pictures, the Virgin of Guadalupe, the "Sacred

Heart," the crucifix, along with pictures and statuettes of any number of other virgins and saints prominently displayed. Family-owned eateries proudly display their heartfelt devotion, and superstition, believing such religious artifacts ward off evil and misfortune.

Later-Generation Hispanics

One last issue needs to be taken up. While some believe that first- and second-generation Hispanics still hold emotional and cultural ties to Hispanic ways, later-generation American-born Hispanics, it is believed, are not so connected. The truth, however, is not so clear-cut. I will readily admit that many Hispanic young people and couples live seamlessly in our English-speaking world. That cannot be denied. Still, it must be asserted that not all young Hispanics in the US live in lockstep conformity to the so-called "American way."

Consider the emerging presence in North America of young Latinos who reject being classified as Millennials, or Generation X or Z; they choose to call themselves *Generación Ñ*.[154] Or listen to Sebastian De la Cruz, a young mariachi crooner who was so powerful in singing the national anthem at game three of the 2013 NBA Finals in San Antonio that he was invited to repeat it for game four. Young people such as these speak English, but not exclusively. They also speak Spanish, and often both at the same time. Most are American-born, but there are also "dreamers," a political designation given to foreign-born children brought illegally to the United States. These young Latinos are fully acclimated to the American way of life, but that doesn't keep them from embracing old-world baroque influences without apologies.

[154] *Generación Ñ* embrace both the American and the Latino fully. Their philosophy states, "It's loving *Star Wars* and yet growing up with your *abuela*'s *novelas*. Intimate knowledge of the musical catalog of both U2 and Celia Cruz. It's a space where your Latin heritage influences your choices but doesn't define you." For more on *Generación Ñ,* go to http://generation-ntv.com (accessed April 19, 2016).

In a day when some are saying that third- and later-generation North American Latinos are abandoning their roots, there are countless numbers of young Latinos that defy the prevailing belief. Many embrace their heritage, giving great value to the lifestyle and traditions that their *padres y abuelitos* (parents and grandparents) bequeathed to them. For many, living the dream goes beyond the way it has been understood traditionally in the United States. Theirs is an "*Américas* Dream," a dream that isn't circumscribed by the Anglo-American vision, but one which is more attuned to celebrating pre-Columbian traditions mixing them with colonial values.

Conclusion

Just this week I was reminded again of this exaggerated approach to life, which can be linked back to baroque influences. It happened as I visited my elderly mother at a rehabilitation center. When I arrived, she was watching TV, so I sat down with her to watch a segment of *El Gordo y La Flaca* (The Fat Man and the Skinny Lady), a popular Spanish-language program which airs on Univision. The segment running focused on Mexican soap opera star Eduardo Yáñez, who, at a red-carpet event, slapped a reporter whose questioning was clearly getting under the actor's skin. I have no doubt the incident was newsworthy but, in viewing it, you might have thought Yáñez was delivering blows like a prizefighter. Throughout the segment, the slap was shown in regular time, in fast motion, slow motion, in color, panned out, up close and tight, in black and white, and with electro-static *ZAPS!!* that coincided with the moment Yáñez made contact with the reporter's face! The slap was repeated at least thirty times! Need I say more?

Hispanic evangelicals must come to grips with the fact that they live within a culture seriously committed to melodrama and exaggeration as normal life expressions. In saying this, it doesn't mean that Latinos do not appreciate reason, logic, and common sense. It is simply that, in the Latino mind, emotional investment is not seen as something that undermines or trivializes the legitimacy of an issue. Quite the opposite: Extravagance, even if it does tend to gush beyond the limits of decorum, is much admired. For most Latinos, passion reinforces conviction, emotion boosts resolve; and the more meaningful something is perceived to be, the more it demands one's emotional investment.

For their part, Hispangelicals are new creatures in Christ, who have left many aspects of their former life behind (2 Cor. 5:17), but this does not include discarding the expression of heartfelt emotions. Moving forward, we will need to find a way to express feelings thoughtfully to highlight truths that matter, like joy over the birth of a child, sadness at the death of a friend, or thrill when our team comes from behind to win the game. Though they can be exaggerated, all emotions are legitimate at one time or another. With that in mind, Hispangelicals will lose an important aspect of their witness to their community if they buy into the "I feel it but don't show it" mentality.

When Hispangelicals place their emotions and general temperament under the leadership of the Holy Spirit, they recover their maximum effectiveness to bear witness to the redeemed life in Christ. This is of great importance, for as J. Oswald Sanders notes, it is the influence and presence of the Spirit that provides the "power to change the atmosphere around you." It is the Spirit-filled life "that makes Christ real to others."[155] The Hispangelical must never react in knee-jerk fashion, as opposed to the exaggerated displays that abound in the Latino world. It is enough to let the opportunity be a proto-evangelistic moment, thanking God, "who always leads us in his triumph in Christ, and manifests through us the sweet aroma of the knowledge of him in every place" (2 Cor. 2:14).

[155] J. Oswald Sanders, *Spiritual Leadership* (Chicago: Moody Press, 1994), 31.

CHAPTER FOUR

Then Came Syncretism

[T]here are many religiously grounded refutations and condemnations of syncretism. I would like to promote the idea that jealousy is a key term. I also want to claim that jealousy as grounds for judging syncretism, syncretistic comportment, or syncretistic ideas entails a relational aspect, giving a place to sentiment and emotions.

Patrik Fridlund
Theological and Philosophical Responses to Syncretism[156]

My older brother is named Jose Guadalupe. Joe, as he is also known, is named in honor of one of my father's uncles, but his middle name reveals that he was also dedicated to the matron Virgin of Mexico. This is nothing unusual; if there is one José Guadalupe, there are probably ten million José Guadalupes throughout Latin America; my father in-law has the same name. The naming of children, often the firstborn, in honor of the Virgin Mary or some other saint is

[156] Patrik Fridlund and Mika Vähäkangas, eds., *Philosophical and Theological Responses to Syncretism* (Leiden, Boston: Brill Academic Publishers, 2017), 13.

common throughout Latin America. Indeed, there probably isn't a family anywhere in Spanish-speaking countries that doesn't have at least one member of their extended family with a religious name including the possible use of Jesús, its feminine form Jesúsa, or even Jesusita, adding a note of endearment to the name of Christ.

But it goes further, for Latin America found a way to take teachings, places, and artifacts of the Christian faith and use them as proper names. Of course, we do this in English-speaking countries. We may know someone named Immanuel, or Mercy, or Christian, even Evangeline, but Hispanic peoples take it further. And truthfully, its practice is so ingrained it sounds normal to fluent Spanish speakers. Thus, parents will name their newborn Consuelo (Consolation); Natividad (Nativity), Trinidad (Trinity), Salvador (Savior), Confesor (Confessor), Belén (Bethlehem), Santos (Saints), Encarnación (Incarnation), Fidel (Faithful), Martirio (Martyrdom), Milagros (Miracles), Pascual (Paschal), Rosario (Rosary), Cruz (Cross), Transfiguración (Transfiguration), even Socorro (Salvation, or as a cry for help, "Save me!)"

I imagine it is possible to write about some countries so invested in modernism that religion is peripheral, limited to a subset of the population. But, with some exceptions, Hispanics could never be understood without taking into consideration their religious character. Despite all the advances of the modern age—and indeed, even in the face of a concerted effort—that secularized Latin American governments have wielded to marginalize, if not banish, religion's considerable influence, this is not one of those things that most Latinos have ever thought to discard.

Hispanics and Religious Pluralism

As modern studies reveal, Latin America continues to be religious, but no longer singularly Roman Catholic. It was inevitable that on the heels of her political emancipation, non-Catholic religions would move in to stake their claims, and now it is in full swing.[157] Today, Hispanics embrace the full gamut of religions, as current studies reveal.[158] These show that though Roman Catholicism is still the dominant religion, the Church's prominence in the region continues to erode. Protestantism, as we have noted, is making steady gains.[159] But it goes further, for Hispanics have also embraced sectarian religions like Adventism, Christian Science, and heterodox religions like Mormonism and the Jehovah's Witnesses. Most recently, Hispanics have also embraced world religions with some enthusiasm. Finally, though small by comparison, Judaism has long been a part of Latin America's religious landscape.[160]

But statistics also show another sober trend. A significant percentage has become agnostic, even atheistic, indifferent to matters of faith. Recent studies suggest that those who choose not to affiliate with any religion can go from as low as one percent of the population to as high as seventeen percent.[161] The sex and pedophile scandals in the Catholic Church, along with blatant evangelical huckstering, have caused many to turn away. But apart from those things that can rightly be pinned to organized churches, the secularization of the West, which challenges the validity of most religious claims, continues to place religion in doubt. The positivistic philosophy of the late nineteenth century, fiercely anticlerical, certainly laid the groundwork, encouraging people to abandon religion as a relic of the past. Many have done so, never to return. But despite the many factors that have contributed to shape and alter

---

[157] While a comprehensive treatment of religion in Latin America and among Hispanics is beyond the scope of this study, notes 2, 3, and 4 provide the reader so inclined with resources to pursue a deeper understanding of the religion/s of Hispanics.

[158] See Geoffrey W. Conrad, *Religion and Empire* (Cambridge: Cambridge University Press, 1984); Justo Gonzalez, O.E. Gonzalez, *Christianity in Latin America* (Cambridge: Cambridge University Press, 2007); Gary Prevost and H. E. Vanden, *Latin America: An Introduction* (Oxford: Oxford University Press, 2010); and John Lynch, *New Worlds: A Religious History of Latin America* (New Haven, CT: Yale University Press, 2012).

[159] David Martin, *Tongues of Fire: The Explosion of Protestantism in Latin America* (Oxford: Blackwell Publishers, 1990).

[160] Jacob Beller, *Jews in Latin America* (New York: Jonathan David Co., 1969).

[161] Prevost and Vanden, *Latin America: An Introduction,* 142.

religious beliefs and affiliations, most Latinos continue to be deeply religious.

Latin American Syncretism

As noted, it would be wrong to think that all Hispanics are Roman Catholic. Still, this is not to say that Roman Catholicism's influence has disappeared altogether. As John Charles Chasteen, historian for the University of North Carolina at Chapel Hill, has observed, "Most of the world's Roman Catholics are Latin Americans,"[162] all of which means Hispanics continue to live under its significant influence. In fact, even if someone could show that their family has not been Roman Catholic for generations, their exposure to the region's highly syncretistic religious culture is not something which should be summarily dismissed.

Defining Religious Syncretism

But what do we mean by "syncretism" anyway? When most people hear the word they either don't know what it is, or they tend to think of it as a religious phenomenon. However, its origins are more political in nature. The Mediterranean island of Crete provides the backdrop for its earliest mention. It was the philosopher/biographer Plutarch (AD 46–120) who observed the ability of citizens of Crete to reconcile their differences, especially when facing a common danger, and he chose to comment on it. Though the fusing of separate entities had existed over the centuries, it is Plutarch who coined the term *syncretismus*, from the Greek, which literally means "the coming together of Cretans" or, more succinctly, "Cretan confederation."[163] As Plutarch saw it, syncretism was not something that happened as a natural development among Cretan islanders; it was sparked when people felt a common threat. At such

---

[162] John Charles Chasteen, *Born in Blood & Fire: A Concise History of Latin America* (New York: W.W. Norton & Company, 2006), 16.

[163] Plutarch, *Moralia*, 2.490b.

moments, people who might not otherwise have anything in common, or indeed may have even been enemies, found it advantageous to come together in a desperate hope of survival.

There are many examples of nonreligious syncretism when facing some menace, and we don't have to travel back too far in time to see it. During the Second World War, the Allies banded with the Soviets, no political soulmates, to defeat the Nazis. In modern times, syncretism is alive and well. In countries like England, or Israel, with numerous political parties, rivals will often confederate to gain majority control, particularly if they hold some policy interest in common. In fact, the North Atlantic Treaty Organization, aka NATO, is quintessentially syncretistic. This alliance between the US, Canada, and other western European powers was created in 1949 as a way to ensure mutual security against possible Soviet aggression.

Still, while syncretism may have started out as a political coping strategy, in time people would see it as a religious process.[164] Today, the term is rarely applied to politics. Rather, it is seen as the commingling, or fusing, of religious ideas and rituals, precisely as happened in Latin America.

The Emergence of Latin American Religious Syncretism

There were many dangers sensed by the natives of Central and South America upon the arrival of the white gods, and one that was felt deeply was the challenge that Roman Catholicism posed to their religious beliefs. Across the colonial claims of Spain and Portugal, indigenous tribes, whole nations, with histories and complex civilizations to rival European civilizations, were being forced to abandon the religions they had practiced for millennia. But how did the native peoples cope with

[164] Erasmus of Rotterdam coined the modern usage of the Latin word in his *Adagia*, published in 1517–1518 to designate the coherence of dissenters in spite of their differences in theological opinions; "Syncretism," New Advent, http://www.newadvent.org/cathen/14383c.htm (accessed October 27, 2018).

it? One researcher notes that pre-Columbian societies already had "a tradition of accepting the gods of conquering civilizations," and so it may be that these native civilizations were preconditioned to take up syncretistic practices when it seemed necessary.[165] If that is so, those same strategies used throughout their pre-Columbian rivalries served them well. Far from abandoning their religions, the Mesoamericans created associations between their own deities and practices and the invading Roman Catholic religion. But what is ironic is that this was inadvertently facilitated by the church herself.

The Roman Catholic Church believed she stood at the pinnacle of society ordered by God, so it is inconceivable that she would enter into a syncretistic alliance willingly. The problem, however, was that Mesoamericans also saw their world as composed of hierarchically ordered societies that reflected a divine pattern.[166] The very concept of the Catholic Church and her role in the world mirrored the grand Mesoamerican cosmic vision. Given that, there is no doubt there would have been a fierce struggle to the death—that is, if both religious pugilists had had similar economic and militaristic strengths. Of course, Roman Catholicism, when it set foot on the Western Hemisphere, overwhelmed the natives in relatively short order, and maybe they thought they had thus decimated their religions as well. Alas, the *conquistadores* should have taken the time to decipher and read, rather than burn, the religious texts of their conquered subjects. In doing so they might have realized they were providing them with a "Trojan horse" of sorts, enabling the conquered to infiltrate their own catholic religion! For their part, given their mirror-image religious structures, the natives embraced the Catholic religion, which imposed a social structuring and ordering that was congenial to their own view of society. Thus, they syncretized and

---

165 Bowling Green State University, "Popular Religion and Festivals," http://blogs.bgsu.edu/span4890/files/2012/02/Popular_relgions-Pop-culture-in-Latin-America-2.pdf, 286 (accessed September 25, 2017).

166 David Carrasco, "Religion as Worldmaking, Worldcentering, Worldrenewing," in *Religions of Mesoamerica* (New York: Harper & Row Publishers, 1990), 19–23.

why not? The fact that Catholics built cathedrals and basilicas atop places where pagan temples had stood before only encouraged it all the more.[167] When all was said and done, they could still worship in many of their sacred pagan sites. To be accurate, yes, the natives were conceding to the Roman Catholic Church's dominance; but really, it never kept millions from maintaining their animistic and pagan beliefs alive, albeit in an altered form.

The Origins of Latin American Catholic Syncretism

As I began my ministerial training, and being of Hispanic ancestry, it was predictable that the topic of syncretism would stoke my interest. One thing that caught my attention whenever it was discussed, however, was that syncretism was always associated with the interaction between Roman Catholicism, Latin American pre-Columbian culture, and West African slaves in the Caribbean and Brazil. I can't say if my fellow students ever had this thought, but I wondered why it was never applied to other contexts in the Western Hemisphere. For example, there was never, to my recollection, any lecture on Protestant or evangelical syncretism. And even though Roman Catholicism also existed in the United States, native North Americans never seem to have had the need to confederate their religious beliefs. Why was this so, given that American churches interacted with native tribes and West African slaves as well? I wondered, why was syncretism so prominent in Spanish-speaking America but not in English-speaking America?

When the Spanish and Portuguese conquistadors arrived on the shores of the Western Hemisphere, they brought with them their Catholic religion. This, in and of itself, is not unusual by any means. If those who crossed the Atlantic on the *Mayflower* had their faith convictions, why should the Spaniards, who had made the trek more than a century

---

[167] According to the Oxford Dictionary, the first reference to syncretism in English appears in 1618.

before, not also have theirs? When we look closer into this development, however, we quickly note that despite surface similarities, there was one undeniable difference: Unlike the Pilgrims, who were fleeing the religious persecution of their native England, the Spaniards were zealous Catholic advocates of their native Iberia. This suggests the reason why syncretism flourished in the Spanish and Portuguese colony, while it never materialized further north in the English colonies.

We will not belabor the point. The main motivation that drove the Pilgrims to cross the Atlantic was their desire for religious liberty, to be free to worship in accordance with the dictates of their faith and conscience. And it is arguable that though it took 168 years (1621–1789), that same desire for religious liberty prevailed when the newly coined American country added amendments to its Constitution insuring such freedoms. In contrast, Catholic colonizers didn't cross the Atlantic hoping to break free from the heavy hand of their "mother Church." To the contrary, they hoped to fulfill a Roman Catholic aspiration long delayed.

It is a known fact that once the Moors were expelled in 1492, Ferdinand, Isabella, and Manuel I of Portugal picked up where the Visigoth kings had been stymied eight hundred years before. The desire to create a Roman Catholic state may have been interrupted when Tariq ibn-Ziyad crossed the Mediterranean in AD 711, but that dream was never abandoned. In fact, the discovery and colonization of the New World meant that a Roman Catholic realm, greater than the Visigoths had ever before imagined, could now be realized, and its ramifications are telling.

In North America, Indian tribes were certainly evangelized, but this happened through the efforts of concerned individuals and denominations. It is a sad fact that sometimes Indians were induced, and perhaps even bribed, into conversion, but these were the misguided efforts of some missionaries that led to such dubious tactics. In point of fact, neither during colonial times, nor later as a nation, were there ever policies in North America that sought to force Christianity upon the Native

American.[168] Protestantism never waged a religious campaign against the beliefs of the Chesapeake, the Algonquians, or the Mohawk. The US never sought to pacify the fierce Sioux nations or the Apache by forcing them to become Christians. This was true in the seventeenth century, and it was true as westward expansion continued in the eighteenth and nineteenth centuries. As we shall soon argue, the Mezoamericans and West Africans found a syncretistic opening in Catholicism, but the North American native tribes never found, nor needed, such an opening with Protestant end evangelical denominations. To the best of our knowledge, the indigenous nations that were eventually subdued and banished to reservations were allowed to keep their ancestral religions. This continues today.

By contrast, Spanish and Portuguese colonizers were intent on realizing their dream of a vast Roman Catholic realm; thus, the reason for religious intolerance surfaces. It should come as no surprise that far from ensuring the religious freedom for the civilizations they encountered, Spain and Portugal forced Catholic conversion upon the natives, baptizing them wholesale, bringing them under the fold of their mother church.[169] Many historians have pointed to the work of Catholic orders that labored benevolently to give the Indians a Catholic education, to show them how to farm and raise cattle, providing hygiene, and so on. But seriously, the Indians or Africans who came later never had the freedom to say, "Thanks, but no thanks; we have our own religion and culture." And it was this chauvinistic policy, which the Catholic Church took as she moved to burn pagan sacred texts and to raze cultic places of worship to the ground, which forced the issue. Ironically, in seeking

---

[168] See James Axtell, *The Invasion Within: The Contest of Cultures in Colonial North America* (New York: Oxford University Press, 1985), 91–178; Bolton and Marshall, *The Colonization of North America*, 87–91; Henry Warner Bowden, *American Indians and Christian Missions* (Chicago: University of Chicago Press, 1981), 124–128.

[169] Pedro Menéndez de Avilés (1519–1574), founder of St. Augustine, Florida suppressed native Floridians, forcing submission to the Catholic faith. See Randolph J. Widmer, "The Rise, Fall, and Transformation of Native American Cultures in the Southeastern United States," *Reviews in Anthropology* 39, no. 2 (2010), 108–126.

to impose Roman Catholicism, the church inadvertently provided them with the religious garments necessary to successfully dress their ancestral religions.

The Birth of a Syncretistic Alternative

As David Carrasco has noted, Mesoamericans devised "strategies to survive and maintain human integrity in relation to their lands and selves."[170] And what they did proved permanent. Today, the strata of religion with which the syncretistic process worked in Latin America cannot be peeled off like the layers of an onion, for the Catholic teaching and the ancestral beliefs of the natives fused for all time. The earliest generations who consciously subjected their religion to Catholicism may have been able to keep *Quetzalcoatl*, the serpent god of the *Nahuatl* (Aztecs), distinct from the biblical God of all creation, but the Catholic conquerors never left, or relented. It was inevitable that later generations would lose sight of such distinctions.

As one generation passed and a new one came, the elements of the native religion blurred. Thus, the syncretistic process gave birth to a third religion—one not Roman Catholic by standards of orthodoxy, nor true to the religions of pre-Columbian peoples either. This third alternative was an amalgam wherein gods of food, rain, and other natural processes, ancestral traditions and Catholicism, biblically incompatible, comingled, as we shall illustrate.

Along Came Mary, Then the Next Mary, Then the Next, and the Next . . .

Nothing says Latin American syncretism quite like the phenomenon of Marian apparitions, which abound throughout the Spanish-speaking hemisphere.[171] While there are more than 230 pilgrimage sites and

[170] David Carrasco, *Religions of Mesoamerica,* 128.
[171] Ruben Vargas Ugarate, *Historia del culto de María en Iberoamérica: y de sus imágenes y santuarios más celebrados* (Madrid: Editorial Huarpes, 1947).

thousands of shrines, here we give a partial list of those Marian apparitions most significant in the various Latin American countries:

- 1510, Lady of la Antigua, Panama
- 1531, Virgin of Guadalupe, Mexico (1643, San Juan de los Lagos, 1653, Zapopan)
- 1500s, Lady of Miracles, Paraguay
- 1555, Virgin of the Rosary, Colombia
- 1562, Virgin of the Immaculate Conception, Nicaragua
- 1594, Lady of Quinche, Ecuador
- 1612, Lady of Charity, el Cobre, Cuba
- 1616, Lady of Alta Gracia, Dominican Republic
- 1630, Virgin of Lujan, Argentina
- 1635, Lady of Los Angeles, USA
- 1717, Lady of Apreciada, Brazil
- 1747, Lady of Suyapa, Honduras
- 1787, Lady of Peace, El Salvador
- 1800s, Lady of Mt. Carmel, Chile
- 1821, Lady of the Rosary, Guatemala
- 1825, Lady of 33, Uruguay
- 1850s, Lady of Providence, Puerto Rico
- 1921, Lady of Mercy, Peru
- 1942, Lady of Coromote, Venezuela
- 1949, Virgin of Copa Cabana, Bolivia

As we consider these "apparitions," certain things bear notice. First, it is important to realize that many of these alleged manifestations of the Virgin Mary on colonial soil are not original to Latin America. For example, this is true of La Virgen de Guadalupe of Mexico, of Our Lady of Mercy of Peru, and of Our Lady of Antigua of Panama, all of which have a European antecedent. Our Lady of Coromote of Venezuela is said to have left a Baroque painting of herself, largely of Portuguese style.[172] As any objective researcher would be hard-pressed to ignore, such things put into question the validity of these manifestations, for they invariably tie back to the most devoted Catholic countries.[173] A sceptic might ask, "Was Mary that partisan? Did the Queen of Heaven not reach out to Protestant America?"

Without a doubt, the proliferation of Marian apparitions was a religious strategy meant to solidify the church's hold on people. For example, it was a Catholic pilgrim who in 1630 commissioned a terracotta statue of the Immaculate Conception with the intent purpose of honoring the Virgin Mary, but also encouraging people to remain faithful to the Church. This statue became Our Lady of Lujan, venerated in Argentina. When we note that the bulk of such appearances happened just as the Baroque Era was dawning across the Latin American colony, this only fueled their exaggerated increase. Thus, it was zealous Catholics who turned to a well-known script, using images and statues of the Virgin Mary, the Mother of God, and the Queen of heaven to tug at the heartstrings and lure people away from lingering pagan practices—but did the strategy succeed? In fact, none of these Marian manifestations remained orthodox Roman Catholic. The Catholic Church has tacitly acknowledged as much by not officially sanctioning some apparitions. But even here, the Church has tried to have it both ways, for all these

---

[172] For more on this phenomenon, see Veronica Mena, "20 Marian Devotions by Country in Latin America," July 10, 2015, The Catholic Company, https://www.catholiccompany.com/getfed/20-marian-devotions-latin-america (accessed November 12, 2017).

[173] The first recorded apparition of Mary on American soil is said to have happened when Mary appeared to Adele Brise, a Belgian immigrant, on three occasions in October of 1859. The confirmation of this apparition did not happen until 2010. See Benjamin Mann, "Wisconsin Chapel Approved as First US Marian Apparition Site," Catholic News Agency, December 9, 2010, https://www.catholicnewsagency.com/news/wisconsin-chapel-approved-as-first-us-marian-apparition-site (accessed September 22, 2017). Post-Vatican II, there have been more than thirty reported visions of Mary in the United States. See Bryan J. Walsh, "Marian Apparitions in the Americas," EWTN.com, http://www.ewtn.com/library/mary/marian.htm (accessed September 22, 2017).

apparitions have a shrine, church, cathedral, or basilica devoted to their veneration.

Official dictates aside, when we consider the festivals and pilgrimages associated with the cult of so many of these regional matrons of the faith, we soon discover significant elements that tie back to ancient pre-Columbian religions.[174] The Roman Catholic Church was aware of such developments, but was never successful in correcting the deviation—and maybe, there was no sustained interest in doing so. I say this in light of the fact that there is no case of Marianism throughout Latin America that is faithful, or limited to a biblical portrait of Mary. For their part, *feligrés*, devoted followers of that cult, contextualized their "lady" or "virgin" with elements that fit their pagan world vision. One can't help but see an accommodation take root. If the natives took up a syncretistic process to keep faith with their own beliefs, the colonial church could nevertheless count on people returning to their shrines in pilgrimage and devotion.[175]

The Virgin of Guadalupe

To illustrate the point, we will focus on perhaps the most popular Marian apparition, *La Virgen de Guadalupe*. Though Mexican, its roots reach back across the Atlantic. Centuries before *La Guadalupana* would make her debut in the New World, the *Real Monasterio de Nuestra Señora de Guadalupe* in Extremadura, Spain dated to the late thirteenth century. This *Señora* already had a three-hundred-year Spanish history. Nevertheless, though an import, Guadalupe's cult in New Spain would be vastly different than its European predecessor. While the Guadalupe of Extremadura is a triangular figurine made of ivory and clothed with

[174] Indeed, most Marian festivals in Latin America have pre-Columbian religious elements. See Bowling Green State University, "Popular Religion and Festivals," 287.

[175] Most pilgrimages in Latin America are of Roman Catholic origins by far and date to the sixteenth century. For an analysis of this phenomenon see M. Ross Crumrine and Alan Morinis, eds., *Pilgrimage in Latin America* (Westport CT: Greenwood Press, 1991).

rich embroidery, the colonial Guadalupe is a human brown-skinned woman who identifies with the indigenous and Mestizo people. Significantly, Juan Diego's cloak, upon which the image of the Virgin was first revealed, was made of cactus fiber, rejecting any conceivable association with her regally adorned Iberian figurine. With a stroke of genius, Juan Diego's Mary is presented in something that touches the very heart and soul of the Mexican people.

Spaniards generally considered cactus to be nothing more than food for hogs and cattle. However, while *Méjico* and *pulque* go together like hand in glove, you couldn't have the latter without the *maguey* cactus.[176] More tellingly, the center panel of the Mexican flag depicts an eagle perched on a *castilla* cactus as it devours a snake. And on a tastier note, the prickly pear fruit is eaten throughout the region, like North Americans eat pears or apples. Yet, there is one more way this succulent of the wilderness defines what it is to be Mexican.

Here, I am reminded of an experience my father had while employed as a chef at the North Moor Country Club in Chicago during the 1950s. One day, a member of the club caught him and said, "Rudy, I have traveled all over the world, but I don't think I have ever eaten a Mexican omelet. Is there such a thing?" My father assured him there was, and offered to prepare one for him on the following Sunday brunch. During the week, my father went to a local *tienda*, a small store that catered to Hispanics, and picked up the necessary ingredients. When Sunday arrived, the gentleman showed up for brunch and chef Rudy delivered on his promise. The man ate the omelet, remarking, "This isn't anything like the Spanish omelet," and my father agreed. Chef Rudy explained the reason he had never eaten a "Mexican omelet" was because Mexicans didn't normally prepare eggs in that style. However, what made that omelet truly Mexican were three key ingredients: chorizo, cilantro, and, you guessed it, *nopalitos*—cactus! Indeed, despite any misgivings about

[176] Additionally, both mezcal and tequila are also native fermented drinks distilled from the *maguey* cactus, and Mexican in origin.

eating it, Amerindians, Mestizos, *criollos,* in short, Mexicans, have been eating cactus since time began.

And so, is the iconic image of Guadalupe, emblazoned on Juan Diego's cactus-fiber cloak, coincidental? Hardly, for cactus has meant the difference between starvation and survival, and more. Cactus provides not just the *pulque* but the *mezcal* and *tequila*, drinks that that help them party hard or wash their sorrows away. And for the poorest of the poor, cactus provided the fiber necessary to weave their humble clothing. For the pre-Columbians and their *mestizo* offspring, cactus is a staple of Mexican life, of its very existence. Truly, Guadalupe's portrait on cactus cloth fuses essential indigenous values onto a Catholic frame.[177]

Are there other syncretistic features associated with the cult of *Nuestra Señora de Guadalupe*? F. Gonzalez-Crussi, professor of pathology at Northwestern University Medical School, wrote "The Anatomy of a Virgin," providing a detailed analysis of the emergence of this cult—and showing how in spite of its ties to a Catholic predecessor, *Tonantzin*, the pagan nature goddess, which Spaniards had counted out, was not quite dead, and did not take kindly to the humiliation. "Chthonic force that she was," says Gonzalez-Crussi, "she drew strength from being buried in the earth, and from her burial place began a silent, obstinate resistance."[178] David Carrasco agrees, for "while strongly Catholic in meaning," the fact that the Virgin appears on a hill dedicated to the Aztec goddess Tonantzin, Guadalupe "also expresses an Indian sense of sacred space and worship of the goddess and her cults."[179]

Is it not more than coincidental? *Tonantzin* is a native Aztec Nahuatl term meaning "our mother," and we should not forget that *Nuestra Señora de Guadalupe* quickly became the matron of Mexico, deposing her Aztec rival. But it goes further—for while Tonantzin claimed the

---

[177] The prickly cactus is also an important aspect of the Mexican flag.

[178] F. Gonzalez-Crussi, "The Anatomy of a Virgin," in *Goddess of the Americas: Writings on the Virgin of Guadalupe,* Ana Castillo, ed. (New York: Riverhead Books, 1996), 6.

[179] Carrasco, *Religions of Mesoamerica,* 137.

love of her Aztec children, Guadalupe is now *La Madre de las Américas*, Mother of the Americas, a patent article of faith for her devotees.[180]

Today, Guadalupe of Mexico is whoever her followers need her to be. Unlike the biblical Mary who pointed people to God's acts in history and to her Son (Luke 1:46–56; John 2:1–5), Guadalupe draws attention to herself. She is the focus of a procession that has gone on for hundreds of years, dating back to ancient pilgrimages undertaken to plead the rain gods of Tenochtitlan. For those who venerate her, Guadalupe is a mother, an intercessor, a fearless destroyer of serpents, and a fighter against all forms of injustice. Oh, and she is also a feminist sex goddess. As Carrasco notes, "In Guadalupe we see a curious and even furious syncretistic mixture. She is Indian and Spaniard. She is an Earth Mother and a Holy Mother."[181]

When all is said, the Virgin of Guadalupe may well have provided the hemispheric template for the many other Marian permutations that would follow. Not that there were no earlier Marian apparitions, but Guadalupe, as we have noted, came into prominence early in the sixteenth century, not long before the Baroque Era would be launched in earnest upon the world. Having had her beginning at such a strategic time in history, this "Mexican Mary" rode the waves of Baroque enthusiasm like none before her, inspiring devout Catholics throughout the Latin colonies to do the same. In light of this, it is arguable that Guadalupe is not only the Mother of the Americas, but the mother of most, if not all, the Virgin Marys of the Americas.

It should not surprise us to see that throughout the centuries, many more apparitions of Mary are recorded. As we survey this occurrence, we are struck by the fact that there is no Latin American country that does not have a Mary of its own and often, more than one. Given such facts, it is telling to note that each Marian cult adheres to an established

---

[180] Virgilio Elizondo, A. F. Deck, and T. Matovina, eds., *The Treasure of Guadalupe* (New York: Rowman & Littlefield, 2006), 85.

[181] Carrasco, *Religions of Mesoamerica*, 138. See also Castillo, *Goddess of the Americas*.

Catholic script, yet also pays homage to the distinct and regional cultures of the people that support its cult.

Santeria

If Latin American syncretism began in the sixteenth century, it was not limited to the interaction between the Mesoamericans and Europeans. A century later, when the Spanish and Portuguese began importing West Africans into Brazil and the Caribbean, these enslaved people also brought their animistic religions with them, and yet another brutal reality must have soon hit them: If their conquered predecessors who had lived in these new lands for millennia were forced to alter their religious practices, what hope could they, who had been forcibly ripped from their lands and families, have for maintaining their ancestral beliefs?[182]

Interestingly, the way slaves were managed in the two Americas was different, all of which fueled syncretistic measures in Latin America. One researcher notes the way slaves were bought and sold in the Western Hemisphere, and it is worth reading. He goes on to note about slaves:

> When they were brought to the Spanish and Portuguese colonies in the New World, slaves were transported in groups that generally remained more or less intact after arrival, a policy that permitted them to retain elements of the African cultures they left behind. In contrast, the British colonies separated slaves who might have language or customs in common, thus systematically erasing cultural roots in order to better acculturate and control them.[183]

---

[182] See Julio A. Sánchez Cardenas, *La religión de los Orichas: Creencias y ceremonias de un culto afro-caribeño,* (Hato Rey, PR: Esmaco Printers Corp., 1978, 1997).
[183] See Bowling Green State University, "Popular Religions and Festivals."

As one can note, the result of the Spanish and Portuguese policies with respect to the handling of slaves was different and, one could argue, more benevolent. Unlike Anglo America, where slaves were sold off piecemeal—making it impossible for tribal connections and religious and cultural practices to survive in the Latin colony—African cultural and religious practices were able to continue. However, it is ironic to think that in North America where no one religion ruled, the religions of the slaves withered, but in the Latin colony where the Catholic Church sought intentionally to monopolize all religion, slaves—who at least were allowed to keep the vestiges of family, culture, and religion—managed to keep the vital elements of their religions alive.

Still, while slaves in Latin America maintained their animistic beliefs, they were not free to practice their religions openly, so it was inevitable that they would turn to syncretism. The Africans intertwined their deities with the saints and virgins of the Roman Catholic Church, and with God Himself. In Cuban *Santeria*, for example, its seven major deities were conflated with a Christian counterpart. The god *Olofi* was identified with God, *Obatala* with Our Lady of Mercy, *Yemaya* with Our Lady of *Regla, Chango* with Santa Barbara, *Eleggua* with St. Anthony, *Ochun* with Our Lady of Charity, and *Babalualle*, with St. Lazarus.[184] And it went further, for Santeria incorporated many Catholic rites and traditions—things like baptism, the serving of a mass, the lighting of candles and incense, calling their priests *padrinos*, and the practice of maintaining home altars. How could this happen?

At first glance, one struggles to identify a theological basis for the choosing of the particular Catholic figures in the masking of pagan African gods. Apart from identifying *Olofi* with God, the rest don't offer rhyme or reason for their choice. Three are identified with different Marian apparitions, one with the biblical Luke, and two with Catholic

[184] The seven major divinities of Santeria are noted; however, there are many lesser deities to be cajoled and appeased through ritual action that is a mixture of Catholic ceremony and African religion. Also, being oral, Santeria lacks a sacred and authoritative source. Santeria is fluid and can vary from region to region.

saints of latter church history. Upon initial inspection, one might conclude that any number of other saints and virgins could have served just as well. However, even in this, the Roman Catholic religion may well have provided the religious framework necessary to move the syncretistic process along.

One distinctive of Roman Catholicism, which Protestant Reformers rejected, was the appeal to saints as intercessors for the faithful.[185] This practice, which may have started as early as the fourth century, was and is a great source of comfort for devout Catholics. In Roman Catholicism, many saints of the church are believed to have specific spheres of influence. Thus, for example, Saint Christopher is the traveler's saint; Saint Joseph is the underground real-estate agent; and Saint Monica, the patron saint of mothers, who helps recover wayward husbands and sons. In Central America, El Cristo Negro (the Black Christ) helps people prosper in their business enterprises; in Mexico, this same Christ is the antidote for poisoning. Globally for Roman Catholics, Saint Jude is the saint to turn to in the most desperate circumstances.

In my own extended family, San Martin de Porres, a Dominican and the first canonized African American saint, is greatly revered, and it is easy to see why. Unlike many other saints, who seem to function within a circumscribed area, Porres is seen as more democratic. Thus, San Martín is there for people of mixed race, for hairstylists, for innkeepers, for people who play the lottery, for public health workers, and the list continues. We could say that Porres, is the "duct-tape" saint, helpful in a myriad of ways, but he is by no means alone.

---

[185] The Roman Catholic Church posits the communion of the saints in three states: The Church Militant refers to those alive on Earth; the Church Penitent consists of those undergoing purification, and the Church Triumphant refers to those in heaven. Along with other church traditions, the Roman Catholic Church encourages the practice of seeking the intercession of saints in heaven. The earliest known practice of this dates to Saint Nicetas of Remesiana (ca. 335–414). See Encyclopedia Britannica, "Communion of the Saints." See also *Catechism of the Catholic Church*, Part One, Chapter Three, Paragraph 5.II (Libreria Editrice Vaticana, 1994), 954–957.

Indeed, the Roman Catholic Church acknowledges more than five hundred saints, each with a specific sphere of influence ranging from help for the poor and the blind to curing cysts, epilepsy, cancer, and other diseases. Some saints have guild, unionized, or associational concerns, being there for architects, boy scouts, soldiers, butchers, bakers, and candlestick makers.[186] As one website notes, "Catholics trust their favorite saints, they have confidence in them, they regard them as faithful friends who stand ready to use their influence on our behalf."[187]

The veneration of saints is linked to the communion of saints, a Catholic dogma which assumes an ongoing spiritual and reciprocal relationship between departed saints and faithful Catholics who still live on this earth. On the one hand, the saints are there to intercede for their devotees who appeal to them in their hour of need. The prayers of the saints also add to the treasury of merit for the benefit of deceased and departed souls in purgatory who need the constant intersession of their church and family and saints in heaven. On the other hand, devoted followers reciprocate by keeping the cult of a particular saint alive, venerating the saint by attending pilgrimages and by maintaining a home altar.

Amazingly, this aspect of the Catholic religion was not that far removed from the tribal religions of West Africans. After all, if faithful Catholics turned to saints for help in everyday circumstances, African slaves were no different. Africans sought the favor and help of their dearly departed, whom they believed cohabitated with angels or gods in the unseen world. It is thus likely that the naming of African gods and ancestral deities was made possible by linking them to saints who served the same purposes in the Roman Catholic religion.

---

[186] For a list of saints and spheres of influence, see http://www.catholicsupply.com/christmas/saint_meaning.html (accessed September 18, 2017).

[187] See "What Every Catholic Needs to Know about Saints: Our Friends in High Places," *OSV Newsweekly*, https://www.osv.com/OSVNewsweekly/Story/TabId/2672/ArtMID/13567/ArticleID/10325/What-every-Catholic-needs-to-know-about-saints--Our-friends-in-high-places.aspx (accessed September 27, 2017).

While theologians might draw distinctions between Catholic dogma and West African animism, it is doubtful whether African slaves bothered to consider such details. They were under pressure to practice their religion, yet also forced to submit to their Catholic overlords. And so, it didn't take long for African slaves to see how both pressures could be alleviated. African slaves adapted and found a way to continue. As we ponder this, it may very well have been this ironic correspondence that gave Santeria, along with its many derivatives, its staying power.[188] Today, Santeria has devoted followers across the globe.

Generally, it should go without saying that the study of Latin American syncretism could continue without end. If we focused specifically on the Marian cult and Santeria, we did so because of the overwhelming popularity of these cults, one emerging from pre-Columbian roots, the other developing from African slave traditions. Together they show that religious syncretism has long ago stopped being a coping strategy. We know this because even though Hispanics no longer live under the same conditions, the syncretistic product is now normative for multiple millions of Latino adherents. Because this is beyond dispute, living with, experiencing, and being challenged by syncretistic ideas is something all Hispangelicals will likely face.

Conclusion

In working through the elements of this chapter, I couldn't help but think: If the Roman Catholic Church had sought really to eradicate all the pagan religions they encountered, they might have come to a realization as old as time itself—the devout will die rather than surrender their sacred beliefs. Under this scenario, countless tribes and civilizations would have been wiped off the face of Latino soil, with only the

---

[188] Fernando Ortiz, *Los Negros Brujos (Apuntes para un Estudio de Etnologia Criminal)* (Madrid: Lib. de *Fernando* Fé, 1906). Ortiz was a student of Afro-Cuban culture, who saw Yoruba mythology as comparable to that of ancient Greece.

remnants surviving. On the other hand, had the Catholic Church tolerated the practice of other religions, allowing unfettered religious liberty, it is doubtful whether syncretism would have ever taken shape. Those ancient religions might have continued intact to our day. But as we know, neither of these two paths were followed.

In his indictment of Protestantism, J. K. Van Baalen famously asserted that the cults were "the unpaid bills of the church."[189] When Protestants and evangelicals consider this statement, as we sometimes do, we focus on our shortcomings that perhaps allowed for the proliferation of cults in nineteenth- and early-twentieth-century North America. But the more we think of it, no one denomination can be blamed for this, for no one religious group ever held a monopoly in the American colony, much less in the United States. Besides, once freedom of religion was legally enshrined into our Bill of Rights, it should not surprise us to see aberrant groups flourishing. No, despite Van Baalen's charge, the rise of cults is not the fault of the church failing to pay her bills, but the inevitable development of living in a country where freedom of religion prevails.

In Latin America, things were different. From Argentina to Mexico, and throughout much of the Caribbean, Roman Catholicism was the sole religious overlord for centuries. It is no overstatement to say that the Church sought to control the spirituality of her massive colony. Yet, her hegemonic strength proved to be her weakness. In her belief that she could force loyalty to the Catholic cross, her arrogance blinded her to the simple and effective counter-strategy of lip service and appearances.[190]

---

[189] Jan Karel Van Baalen, *The Chaos of the Cults* (Grand Rapids, MI: Wm. B. Eerdmans, 1942).

[190] Upon visiting Puerto Rico in 2002, I was shown a picture of Pope John Paul II wearing the vestments of a *Babaloa,* a Santeria priest while holding an open-air mass in Havana, Cuba, during his visit in 1998. Papal embrace of syncretistic religions is well documented. See John Kenneth Weiskittel, "Voodoo You Trust? John Paul II's Betrayal in Benin," Novus Ordo Watch, http://novusordowatch.org/voodoo-you-trust-weiskittel (accessed May 22, 2017).

If there ever was a church that failed miserably to "pay her bills," the Roman Catholic Church in Latin America qualifies.[191]

Today, we can be thankful that countless Hispanics are turning to faith in Christ's atoning salvation, but Hispangelicals should learn from church history. During the first decades of the early church, many Jews came to faith in Christ and what is today referred to as "Judaizing" soon appeared. In fact, since it was the intent purpose of some Jews to mask the gospel so as to make it amenable to orthodox Jews (Gal. 6:12–13), we could say this Judaizing tendency is the earliest case of Christian syncretism. Disturbingly, so powerful was this phenomenon that it drove even pillars of the faith to hypocrisy (Gal. 2:11–14) and precipitated the need for the church to convene and deliberate (Acts 15). For our part, Hispangelicals should not be so naïve as to think that upon conversion, the syncretistic mishmash which has defined Latino popular religion for centuries simply disappears.

While most North American evangelicals rarely consider that syncretism could impact them in significant ways,[192] the Hispanic evangelical must know otherwise. Even if they are personally dispelling such notions, they should know that they live with family members and/or within a community that continues to harbor, and celebrate such beliefs, superstitions, and traditions. As such, the thoughtful Hispangelical will anticipate the syncretistic challenges he or she is likely to encounter. There will be more to say about this challenge in chapter seven, "Then Came the Hispangelical's Challenge."

---

[191] Leoncillo Veguilla Cene, *Cinco Formas de Sincretismo Religioso en Cuba* (Masters thesis for Seminario Teologico Bautista "R.A. Ocania," Habana, Cuba, 1997). Cene gives five reasons: 1) the failure of the Catholic Church to evangelize and disciple those who she baptized, 2) the brutal treatment of the slaves by Catholic slave traders and owners, 3) the belief by many colonials that blacks were subhuman, not possessing souls, 4) the sanctioning by the church of practices viewed as cultural, but in reality religious, and 5) the gradual acceptance and embrace of the religions of the blacks by *mestizos* and whites.

[192] This is not entirely true. See Ed Stetzer, "Avoiding the Pitfalls of Syncretism," *Christianity Today,* July 15, 2014, http://www.christianitytoday.com/edstetzer/2014/june/avoiding-pitfall-of-syncretism.html (accessed November 12, 2017).

CHAPTER FIVE

Then Came the Ahistorical Hispangelical

If you don't want a man unhappy politically, don't give him two sides to a question to worry him; give him one. Better yet, give him none. . . . Peace, Montag.

Ray Bradbury
Fahrenheit 451[193]

Introduction

I think most people would click their heels and agree with Dorothy that "there is no place like home." Author Lyman Frank Baum may have tapped into this sentiment when he published *The Wonderful Wizard of Oz* in 1900, but, as you may have read, the patriarch Jacob experienced homesickness long before (Gen. 31–33). Truth be told, this feeling of longing for home has been felt across time immemorial, and who can deny it? Though there may be more beautiful homes, none compares to our own. After having been gone for years, or simply after

[193] Ray Bradbury, *Fahrenheit 451* (New York: Ballantine Publishing Group, 1953), 61.

a hard day's work, home is the cure for all that ails. It's easy to get lost among the anonymous mass of humanity, but at home you are known.

When Pentecostalism reached into the Latin world, something unexpected happened: Many Latinos felt at home with it. Have you ever wondered why Hispanics are so drawn to Pentecostalism? In attempting to understand and explain its appeal among Latinos, a number of answers have been offered. Some, for example, have suggested Hispanics gravitated toward Pentecostalism because of the emotional character of its services. Since Hispanics are also prone to be driven by emotion, it was only natural that they would find "spirit-filled" services appealing to their temperament. Thus, some will point to the lively music of the Pentecostal services and suggest that the drama of it all is what draws them in. There may be truth in this, for Latinos do tend to be a lively people. Daisy Rodriquez, for example, is one former Roman Catholic who confessed she left her church because she felt greater freedom to express her love of God within the Pentecostal faith. "In the Pentecostal Church," said Daisy in an interview, "I feel more freedom to perform what the Lord wants me to do."[194] So, there may be reason to believe that a church that encourages active personal participation in the worship service can be a powerful draw. Others find the discrepancy of economic and education factors compelling. Since Latinos tend to be poorer and less educated, they naturally shy away from affluent churches or from congregations made up of college-educated professionals, where they may feel that they don't fit in. And so, the Pentecostal church is appealing to Hispanics because it tends to draw people like themselves who come from a lower social class, or perhaps from less economic means.

There may be other reasons students of this trend will give to account for Hispanic interest in Pentecostalism, and I would not deny that such observations have validity. But the fact is, many have found

---

[194] Jeff Kunerth, "Hispanics Flock to Pentecostal Churches," *Orlando Sentinel*, January 2, 2010, http://www.orlandosentinel.com/features/os-hispanic-pentecostals_3-20100101-story.html (accessed August 15, 2017).

the Pentecostal church appealing, and it isn't only the poorer or less educated Hispanics either. While cultural and economic factors certainly play a role, I am not convinced that such reasons explain this shift, not fully. And so I ask again, "Why have so many Hispanics embraced Pentecostalism? Why has Pentecostalism reached more Hispanics in just a few decades than all the other Protestant and evangelical denominations combined were able to reach in the last two centuries?"[195]

Often, "why" questions can be uncomfortable, and even irritating, especially when they are repeatedly asked. But we should not be too quick to banish those who have honed the "why" question into a refined tool, for they may be doing us a service. Since the question before us goes to the heart of what it is that makes us human, could continuing to ask why help us understand the Latino's turn to Pentecostalism? If we ask why Hispanics have been drawn to the Pentecostal movement, some of the answers, like the ones noted, may well provide some explanation, but they don't answer the question fully. But if we keep asking why, two further answers surface.

Then Came the Ahistorical Hispangelical

In continuing to ask why, someone might eventually say, "Well, Latinos seem to feel more at home in the Pentecostal church," and in saying so, they would touch on a deeper reality that, surprisingly, rings true. Unlike other Protestant denominations, Pentecostalism, as we will note, resonates with an ancient mode of being, which is at home in the Latino context. The passage of half a millennium has not dissipated its strength. To the contrary, if history is its womb, the continuation of factors ground in history keep it alive. No one could have foreseen this, but Hispanics and Pentecostalism are essentially "a-historical." If we should ask what this means, I know of no better way to

[195] The modern Protestant missionary outreach to Latin America began piecemeal after the wars for liberation in the 1820s.

explain it than by appealing to personal experience and to recorded history. As I hope to show, while history accounts for the conditions that made ahistoricity possible, personal experience couches it in a way we can all understand.

The Challenge of Ahistorical Christianity

For myself, I came to faith in Christ as a young adult, and my sense of the Christian faith was self-centered, to put it mildly. The way I understood it, salvation focused on me and me alone. I took comfort in the knowledge of God's unconditional love for me, sending his Son to die for me, and securing a heavenly mansion for me. Yes, I knew God had saved others, but it was their responsibility to look after their relationship with God; I was absorbed in my own.

This self-absorption was evident even when I shared my faith with others. My witnessing never went beyond encouraging people to consider the gospel based on what God could do for them. I cannot remember ever perceiving the bigger picture—that is, of God's grand plan of redemption encompassing the whole of his created order, or how we as his redeemed factored into that plan. There is no telling how long I might have continued with this self-centered view of the Christian message. My pastor's preaching tended to emphasize God's love for the individual. Church members were encouraged to give testimonies that were often emotionally charged, thanking God for what he had done for them on a personal level. The worship choruses found ways to place me smack in the center of God's unmerited favor.

I know I run the risk of being misunderstood, so I should state for the record that anyone's encounter with God's saving grace is by definition personal and individual. To my knowledge, no one is ever saved apart from a personal encounter with God's grace. That said, if there was one thing I learned, it was that my relationship with God was so overwhelming and secure. Whatever else Scripture talked about came in a distant second; it didn't matter.

It was about a year after my conversion that I sensed God calling me to vocational Christian ministry. As that call became clear, I acted on it immediately. Within a month, I was pastoring a small church in Hobbs, New Mexico, but it wasn't too long after that I realized I needed some serious ministerial training. I returned to Texas and enrolled at Criswell Bible College in Dallas, expecting to learn the nuts and bolts of ministry: how to marry, bury, baptize people, and how to preach a sermon as well. You see, I believed I had it all down, I just needed to learn the mechanics of it. Man, was I in for an eye-opening surprise!

It wasn't long before I was introduced to the historical nature of the gospel; the professor used Paul's introduction in Romans to drill the point home. The apostle, I was shown, began his letter by affirming that his gospel had been "promised beforehand through His prophets in the holy Scriptures, concerning His [God's] Son, who was born of a descendant of David according to the flesh" (Rom. 1:2–3). I remember it struck me as a revelation to learn that Paul's gospel was rooted in the prophecies of the Old Testament.

The implications of that early lesson soon began pouring in. Christ had done infinitely more than just drop from heaven to die for me on the cross. There were ancient promises to Israel, which were being kept through his Passion. Moreover, his redemption reached to the furthest corners of space, reconciling back to himself something lost at the very dawn of human history (Rom. 8:19–23; Col. 1:20). The thing that I began to learn and appreciate (as basic as it may seem to most) was that the gospel came as an answer to a chain of historical occurrences and expectations. It was grossly naïve for me to think of Christ's atonement only regarding my own need.

As I continued to study, I learned that this appreciation of history went beyond biblical limits. Through the study of history, theology, and philosophy of religion, I came to see that the Christian faith was, in a way, continuing the story. As my understanding grew, I learned that the very articulation of a theology could not happen without the work of serious Christians, and that this process took centuries. The writings of ante- and post-Nicene church fathers revealed the struggles that came with interpreting the Bible at a time when the question of the canon of the New Testament was not settled. Even more, heretical teachings were sometimes the catalyst that prompted early church fathers to come to a more acute understanding of the faith. It took the work of early church councils in the fourth century to work through so many matters of Christian doctrine. Through it all, church history and historical theology taught me how those who had gone before had laid the groundwork for the doctrine that I had embraced.

Throughout the Bible, God's people are admonished to remember the mighty acts of God through history (e.g., Exod. 15; Luke 1:46–56; Acts 7) and that, more often than not, God did his redemptive work through people who served him faithfully (Heb. 11). Scripture reminds us to remember those who came before us, "and considering the result of their conduct, imitate their faith" (Heb. 13:7). It was my earliest ministerial formation that, more than anything else, opened my eyes to the fact that God continued to work through believers enmeshed in history. It thrilled me to know that I was part of a "spectacle" presented for the benefit of men and angels (1 Cor. 4:9; Heb. 10:33). This drama was being rolled out through the lives of his people, through revivals and missionary movements, and yes, even through theological developments.

I don't remember when it first dawned on me, but once I learned this lesson, I never forgot it. To the degree that my redemption was exclusively or even primarily about me, my faith was essentially ahistorical—that is to say, narrow-minded—because I devalued or ignored what did not seem to concern me. In my ignorance, I had failed to realize that it *all* concerned me. I have been reminded of this marvelous truth many times again and especially when I relish the fact that I have been spiritually joined "to Mount Zion and to the city of the living God, the heavenly Jerusalem, and to the myriads of angels, and to the general assembly and church of the firstborn who are enrolled in heaven" (Heb. 12:22–23).

Historical Evangelicalism

And what are we to make of the evangelical movement? Did it spring from nowhere? Mark Knoll, now retired Professor of Christian Thought at Wheaton College and cofounder of the Institute for the Study of American Evangelicals, shows that evangelicalism can be linked to Protestantism by way of the Anglican Church, Puritan Calvinists, and European Pietists.[196] The obvious point to make is that evangelicalism was the product of the Reformation, and as such, it was historically anchored.

To pose a question: Evangelicalism began what Knoll labels a "protest movement," reacting to the lifeless spirituality that prevailed over Protestant churches—so, didn't that divisive move sever its historical ties? No, the evangelical movement never advocated a total break from Protestantism. Perceptively, the Puritan fathers of the movement knew that the church's spiritual health was tied to her theological moorings—both went together. Thus, for example, this did not lead to disaffected evangelicals producing a new theology. Classic evangelicalism set forth a core set of beliefs, for the most part in tune with those of the Reformation yet advancing in the areas of evangelism, personal piety, and so on. We could say that evangelicalism branched out from Protestantism. Despite whatever misgivings mainline Protestantism might have had about evangelicals,[197] it did not see evangelicalism as a movement unconnected with its concerns. Protestants knew that the seeds of discontent, which would produce this movement in time,

---

[196] Mark A. Knoll, *The Rise of Evangelicalism: The Age of Edwards, Whitefield, and the Wesleys: A History of Evangelicalism* (Downers Grove, IL: InterVarsity Press, 2004). See also Clyde L. Manschreck, ed., "The Rise of Evangelical Pietism," in *A History of Christianity*, Vol. 2 (Grand Rapids. MI: Baker Book House, 1964), 263–314.

[197] Leonard Verduin, *The Reformers and Their Stepchildren* (Sarasota, FL: The Christian Hymnary Publishers, 1964). Verduin documents the animosity of Reformation leaders toward the so-called radical reformers, the Anabaptists of the sixteenth-century Europe.

were sown in the fields of the Reformation and its later theological wars and skirmishes.[198]

Pentecostal Evangelicalism

But what about Pentecostalism? Were the dictates and emphases of this new movement in continuity to some degree with the shared concerns of Protestants and evangelicals? On this question, I would argue that Pentecostalism revealed quite early the net effects of an ahistorical approach to the Christian faith. For even though they did originally emerge from within the Holiness branch of the Wesleyan denomination, the theological and ecclesiological concerns of Protestants and evangelicals were never really embraced. This movement did not inspire its followers to fight for upholding doctrinal orthodoxy, to defend the inspiration and infallibility of the Bible, or to affirm Christ's bodily resurrection from the grave, etc. It's not that Pentecostals didn't believe in these things; they did. It's just that early on, Pentecostalism focused on a critical circumstance it was attempting to address, and it had little time to focus on theological concerns between Protestants and evangelicals.

At the same time, Latin America was undergoing turbulent social upheaval, and it brought critical problems to the surface. Would the Catholic Church, which had traditionally sided with more conservative governments, continue its affiliation against the best interests of the Latino masses? Not surprisingly, many citizens were being alienated from their political leaders and religious institutions. Sociologist David Martin has noted about such desperate times that, "What moves people on the move and turns their atomized being into a corporate movement is a repertoire of religious images corresponding to their

[198] Thus Wesleyans, for example, who expounded Arminianism, did so in the knowledge and repudiation of the hyper-Calvinism of their day. Their doctrine was rooted in the history of that theological debate that could be traced as far back as St. Augustine's attack of Pelagian Soteriology.

circumstances."[199] Darren Dochuk agrees and adds that it was precisely at this crucial moment in Latino history that Pentecostals were successful, creating the "reenchantment and mystification of economic systems."[200]

In answer to the disillusionment Hispanics were experiencing, Pentecostals made their life experiences the hermeneutic key for their faith. Rather than hitch on to orthodox Protestant and evangelical statements of faith, they never really hitched on to the long train of Protestant evangelical history. It was ahistorical because it offered an "otherworldly" spirituality that gave Latin Americans a "repertoire of religious images" that promised a release from their oppressive realities. Pentecostalism accomplishes this by mystifying the circumstance of the Latino, offering a religion that "allowed for the signs and wonders of the unseen realm."[201] For Hispanics, the theological concerns that energized evangelicalism were foreign in their context. Real-life conditions needed to be addressed; all else paled in importance.

This same concern holds true today.[202] Overwhelmingly, the Pentecostal movement has been about one thing: attacking with extreme prejudice the demonic forces of evil and despair. Pentecostals see themselves as God's champions in this arena. Perhaps they more than any other Christian group, they would argue that they have been gifted—or, indeed, have taken for themselves—the aptitude and audacity for spiritual battle, and God has responded. In answer to their simple but undaunted faith, God has given Pentecostals weapons to vanquish the devil and release people from bonds of generational curses and oppres-

---

[199] David Martin, *Pentecostalism: The World Their Parish* (Malden, MA: Blackwell, 2002), 168.
[200] Heath W. Carter and Laura Rominger Porter, eds., *Turning Points in the History of American Evangelicalism* (Grand Rapids: Wm. B. Eerdmans, 2017), 270.
[201] Carter and Porter, *Turning Points*, 268.
[202] Doctrinal matters are often relegated to people who are seen as spiritually lifeless. There is a broad belief that one can either be educated or Spirit-filled, but not usually both. However, things are changing. See Julian Lukin, "Professor Proves Pentecostalism and Scholarship Can Coexist," *Charisma*, http://www.charismamag.com/site-archives/570-news/featured-news/11969-a-professor-with-spirit (accessed September 20, 2017).

sion. In all this, one thing is true: Whether it is the prosperity gospel, a strong emphasis on miraculous signs and wonders, or on healings and the like, just about every Pentecostal message is aimed to some degree against the circumstances the Hispanic people have had to endure.

Then Came the Ahistorical Latino

As we began, we made a startling statement: namely, that Pentecostals resonate with Latin American culture. This happened as the result of key decisions undertaken by the Catholic Church centuries before. On its face, it sounds incredible to sustain. But then again, while there are innumerable differences that can be drawn to show that both Catholicism and Pentecostalism are light years apart, the fact of the charismatic movement, which is largely Catholic, suggests that there is significant overlap. Certainly, the doctrines and practices that can be seen in both groups reveal this similar interest to address the Hispanic condition.

That said, have we ever stopped to consider that the Roman Catholic Church might have prepared the region for the eventual rise and growth of Pentecostalism? Here we argue that the notion that Latin American Pentecostalism is ahistorical can be traced to the very nature of the Latino experience. In his groundbreaking work *Understanding the Latin American Mind*, Leopoldo Zea describes the inability of Latin American countries to enter the historical stream.[203] Even after their wars of liberation in the early nineteenth century, these emerging countries found it impossible to get past the feudalism that colonial Spain and the Catholic Church had set in place centuries before.

This well-known history is relevant to our subject, for Latin America continued a way of life that minimized whatever contribution other countries could have made to ease them into the modern world. With a 350-year lag in her development, it was inevitable that the historical disconnect between Latin America and progressive Europe and North

---

[203] Zea, *The Latin American Mind,* 44–45.

America would be painfully felt. To be sure, there were the trappings of modern democratic order here and there. Latin Americans were writing democratic-style constitutions like mad. However, very little of it made any real difference. Howard Wiarda warns us, "Latin America will often pay lip service to a way of life it has never understood and doesn't really desire."[204] Believe it: Latin American history offered the perfect womb for the Pentecostal Hispangelical's gestation.

When Pentecostals began to reach out to Spanish-speaking countries, it continued something of this same characteristic trademark, bypassing the doctrinal connections and challenges that shaped the European and American evangelical world. In a way this makes sense, for the theological wars would have sounded like gibberish to Latinos who were effectively segregated from the discussion for hundreds of years. They had no way of knowing how the evangelical message had begun as a form of dissent from Anglicanism, or as a form of support for dissenting groups in England, or Moravians and Pietists. Again, Pentecostal Hispangelicals tend to be ahistorical in that their faith focuses on immediate existential concerns, rather than trying to show any continuity with historic evangelical concerns.

Overwhelmingly, Hispanic Pentecostalism is true to its roots, addressing pressing needs felt quite literally in the flesh. As such, the Pentecostal Hispangelical rarely preaches the gospel without also casting it as liberation from poverty, illness and disease, the ravages of drug addiction, family violence, crime, and so on. You see, for Latinos, the salvation they seek had better address their immediate circumstance.

Ironically, liberation theology had a concern to alleviate the deplorable conditions that many impoverished peoples faced throughout Latin America. Their social consciousness initially won over many followers. However, it did not deliver on its promise. Those theologians who took their message to Latin America, always more sophisticated than the peasants they hoped to liberate, tied the movement to an

---

[204] Wiarda, *The Soul of Latin America*, 322–323.

imported European ideology. Marxism, they believed, was the answer, but this was largely rejected in Latin America.[205] Liberation theologians forgot that Hispanics wanted a pragmatic faith that promised to work in the context of their daily struggle. They had little time to hear quasi-Christian philosophical sermons on the historical grievances that caused their struggle.[206]

In a way, it seems incredible that the Roman Catholic Church, with its long history, should create the conditions that would welcome the Pentecostal Hispangelical, but that is what happened. Spurred on by the Counter-Reformation, the church sought to insulate their newly acquired lands from any influence that would threaten her grip on their Western subjects. By so doing, Catholicism held Latino minds and hearts in mental quarantine for centuries. It didn't help that the church perpetuated a religion that gloried in medieval obscurantism, deepening a faith that was disconnected from the historical developments of Protestantism and evangelicalism happening elsewhere in the world.

We can get a sense of this isolation by focusing on the sixteenth century, a time that saw the beginning of the Protestant Reformation, leading to a host of sweeping changes that were felt throughout Europe. In light of this religious earthquake that was rocking Europe, it is appropriate to ask if any tremors were being felt in the Latin colony, which was also being formed and shaped at the same time in history. You read and decide:

---

[205] Ibid., 212–245. Wiarda shows the shortcomings and rejection of Marxism in Latin America. However, in 2015, Pope Francis engaged with Peruvian Gustavo Gutierrez to rehabilitate liberation theology, showing that some failed theologies refuse to surrender to their inevitable demise. See Steven F. Hayward, "How Is 'Liberation Theology' Still a Thing?" *Forbes*, May 10, 2015, https://www.forbes.com/sites/stevenhayward/2015/05/10/how-is-liberation-theology-still-a-thing (accessed September 15, 2017).

[206] Emilio A. Núñez C., *Liberation Theology* (Chicago: Moody Press, 1985); see Part Two, "Historical Outline of Liberation Theology," 35–130. For a classic articulation of liberation theology, see Gustavo Gutierrez, *A Theology of Liberation* (Maryknoll, NY: Orbis Books, 1990), first published in 1971.

- 1517—Martin Luther's Ninety-five Theses were published and circulated across Europe, fueling the Protestant Reformation. However, in the Latin colony, the Catholic Church was putting in place a system that would vanquish all opposing religions. Thus, as early as Cortez (1520s) and Zumárraga (1530s), the church instituted tribunals to adjudicate such things as heresy, blasphemy, bigamy, Judaism, Protestantism, idolatry, sorcery, and superstition.
- 1522, 1526, 1569—The publication of the Bible into modern languages (German, English, Spanish) allowed people the freedom to read Scripture for themselves. In the Latin colony, the reading of the Bible was limited to the Vulgate, and available only to Catholic clergy. The congregant had no access to a Bible in Spanish or Portuguese.
- 1529—The Marburg Colloquy focused on the theology of the Lord's Supper, setting the stage for a Lutheran and a Reformed split. However, in the Latin colony, no split from Roman Catholicism would be tolerated. The church established offices for the Inquisition in Mexico City and Lima (1569), and Cartagena (1610), fighting against any challenges to the church's dogmatic supremacy in the region.
- 1555—The Peace of Augsburg brought about the end of religious war on European soil allowing nations to choose their religious commitments. Latin America was a colony of Portugal and Spain and, as such, had no similar freedoms, liberties, or prospects.
- 1559—John Calvin wrote *The Institutes of the Christian Religion*. Thus, Protestantism was evolving beyond reacting to conflicts with Roman Catholicism to produce a theology that was wholly the product of the Reformation. In the Latin colony, the church continued promoting the medieval scholasticism of Thomistic theology.

- 1545–63—The Council of Trent, decidedly anti-Protestant, eliminated any hope for reconciliation between the Catholic Church and the Protestant movement. Trent codified Roman Catholic theology for the next four centuries, offering no quarter for Protestantism to gain a foothold in Latin America.
- 1598—The Edict of Nantes was penned, considered to be the basis for a secular society that in time would lead to freedom of religion. However, after one hundred years of colonial rule, Latin America continued under Roman Catholicism with no expectation of religious tolerance, much less of religious freedom.

In studying this timeline, we note that Protestantism may have begun as one individual's protest, but over the course of the sixteenth century it expanded to include whole nations, articulating principles that would reach across the north Atlantic. During this same time, however, Latin America was hermetically sealed from any form of religious development that was not in line with the Roman Catholic Church. We could continue with the seventeenth, and eighteenth centuries, but it would be an exercise in redundancy.

History registers theological developments and revivals that were shaping the very character of Protestantism elsewhere in Europe and North America. History also notes that little of it made any appreciable impact in the Latino colonies. Perhaps, Catholicism believed Protestantism might implode as it fought through its internal struggles. What it could not foresee, however, was the rise of evangelicalism, a protest movement, within Protestant ranks. Once evangelicalism was established, the possibility for further religious variation grew. For their part, the Latin countries could not fathom such religious pliability, free of hierarchical control. But this much is true: Religious liberty, which evangelicals demanded for themselves, made Pentecostalism possible. Neither the Protestants nor Catholics nor even evangelicals could see that, in time, ahistorical Pentecostalism would appeal to Hispanics by the millions.

As history reveals, in Latin America, the Catholic Church engineered a people who were practically dependent on the priests, friars, bishops, and monks. The Catholic Church did not set out to disciple a population of faithful Catholics who could hold their own and advocate for their mother church. Why would they need to do such a thing? There was no such person to react against anywhere in Latin America. In the West, the four horsemen of deism, rationalism, skepticism, and higher criticism were pillaging the theological landscape, challenging such orthodox tenets as the historical validity of miracles, rewriting the nature of divine revelation, casting the resurrection as myth, and evangelicals were making a stand on all fronts. But the only thing sounding from Hispanic lands—crickets![207]

And so it was that the Roman Catholic Church sealed the ahistorical nature of the Hispanic religious experience. The church insulated her Latino children from ever having to test their faith apologetically in a world where competing versions of the Christian faith were being heralded. No sooner were Protestant footholds identified on Hispanic and Brazilian soil than the Holy Office of the Inquisition moved to crush their presence,[208] and this had a downside. When Latin America finally opened her doors to her western and northern neighbors, Hispanics were seen as infantile and naïve in their faith. Their religion was medieval, ignorant of the challenges Protestantism had leveled at the church over centuries.

In some respects, Hispanic Pentecostals are like a static blip on the radar screen of church history. Because the blip remains in place, it leaves no trajectory to track. They are ahistorical, locked into a very narrow sliver

---

[207] Though there were earlier Roman Catholic scholars who addressed critical issues raised by protestant liberal research (e.g., Merrie-Joseph Lagrange), the church only really engaged theologically post-Vatican II. See William Baird, *History of New Testament Research,* Vol. Three (Minneapolis: Fortress Press, 2013), 395–444. Baird identifies European and North American Catholic scholars, but no Latin Americans.

[208] Pablo Alberto Deiros, *Historia del Cristianismo en América Latina* (Buenos Aires: Fraternidad Teológica Latinoamericana, 1992), 585–616. Deiros gives a summary of the many failed attempts to introduce Protestantism into the Spanish colony.

of history. Yes, as Pentecostalism has grown they have become more theologically engaged and, as such, more intertwined with the complex evangelical family of faith. But that said, their progress has never come at the expense of easing up on the spiritual crusade that has defined them. As Luis Lugo, Director of the Washington-based Pew Forum notes, wherever Pentecostals may venture to influence their world, it will never be at the expense of leaving behind "their world of spirit."[209]

Then Came the Baroque Pentecostals

Certainly, Latinos were the product of a quarantined existence, and it resulted in creating a cultural bubble so durable it continues today. That bubble, as noted, was a baroque approach to life, providing our second reason. It is ironic, but true, that it is the natural appropriation of baroque culture that makes the Pentecostal church so appealing to many Hispanics.

We have earlier argued that the ahistorical nature of the Pentecostal movement appealed to Hispanics because of its resonance with realities close to home and hearth—a fact we cannot attribute to all evangelical missionary efforts in Latin America. The earliest Protestant churches were established to service the religious needs of their own who had been invited in by the emerging governments to help stimulate economic development. As such, these earliest churches ministered in the languages of the foreign community, rarely in Spanish. This limitation, coupled with the fact that Protestant missionary agencies had deemed the region to be "Christian," helped implant the idea that Latinos had their Catholic religion and those who came from Europe or the US had their "Lutheran" religion.

Things pretty much continued under this arrangement until the end of the American Civil War. After the defeat of the Confederacy, beginning in the late 1860s, churches—primarily from the southern

---

[209] See Kunerth, "Hispanics Flock to Evangelical Churches."

states—began thinking about missionary excursions into Latin American countries. Initially, colporteurs began seeding the region with Bibles written in the language of the people, returning to the States with stories of their openness to read God's Word. Having laid that groundwork, Baptists, Methodists, Presbyterians, and evangelicals of all theological persuasions headed south to plant churches. But there was a momentous difference: Unlike the earlier churches that began as islands of Protestantism for foreign workers, these latter efforts were truly missions-minded—and, it should be noted, they had a desire to establish indigenous leaders and pastors. Still, there were significant challenges that lay ahead.

It didn't take long for missionary boards to realize that, despite their best efforts, the work of building up national leaders would take much time and treasure—foreign treasure. And so, the work continued largely under the direction of foreign missionaries and administrators, many of whom lived out their entire ministry in the host country. Whether by design or otherwise, a benevolent paternalism nevertheless developed, with American and European missionaries overseeing the work of the local leaders. There is, of course, much more that could be said about all the good that foreign missionaries have done around the world. But we must also acknowledge that, in some ways, the foreign missionaries' oversight helped to cement the impression that Protestantism, or evangelicalism (Latin Americans hardly knew the difference), was essentially a religious import not native to the people.

However, unlike other denominations, Pentecostalism was never seen as something foreign to the prevailing culture. While it may be true that the Azusa Street Revival of the early twentieth century had a strong influence, Allen Anderson, professor of mission studies at the University of Birmingham, has shown that Pentecostalism also had spontaneous beginnings throughout Latin America.[210] In fact, even in work initiated by North American Pentecostals, it wasn't long before indigenous believers of both genders took the lead. This important fact made a profound difference in the perception of the people.

While the Pentecostal message can clash with Catholic dogma, the packaging was and is homespun, thus baroque. In my estimation, the Catholic counterpart to Pentecostalism, the charismatic movement, reveals the affinity that both religious traditions share, and it has to do with music, with drama, and with emotional investment.

The Pentecostal Worship Service

One of the strongest attractions is the baroque atmosphere that permeates the Pentecostal worship experience. But we must be clear, Pentecostalism did not embrace baroque influences in the same way a Protestant or evangelical missionary agency might consider acculturation. The latter might do so in the interest of being more missional or relevant to the people they seek to reach. Pentecostalism was different. From its beginnings, it was native Hispanics, immersed in a baroque world, who drove the movement forward. They didn't have to embrace the culture to connect with the people in the *barrios*; they came from the *barrios* and *favelas*. The Pentecostal and Catholic living next to each other are cultural twins. While Protestants have been charged with being subversive to the culture because of their foreignness, that charge was harder to pin on Pentecostals. Mortimer Arias, a Uruguayan Methodist bishop, understood this all too well and asserted, "Pentecostalism is the most indigenous and popular protestant modality that Latin America has ever produced."[211]

---

[210] Allen Anderson, "The Origins of Pentecostalism and Its Global Spread in the Early Twentieth Century," Graduate Institute for Theology and Religion, University of Birmingham, October 5, 2004 http://www.ocms.ac.uk/docs/Allan%20Anderson%20lecture20041005.pdf (accessed July 18, 2016).

[211] Mortimer Arias, "El Protestantismo," *Presncia* [La Paz, Bolivia] (August 6, 1975), 184.

Given this important distinction, it was inevitable that Pentecostals would express their faith in a way that connected with the people, and indeed it has. In Pentecostal churches people felt free to play *la guitara, el requinto, el tololoche, el acordeón, las maracas, y los tamborines.* Until the late '60s, most Spanish-speaking evangelical churches sang only out of their denominational hymnbook, but not *Pentecostales.* From the start, worship incorporated the sounds of the *tríos*, the *norteño* bands, and *mariachis* to produce congregational singing that sounded like it was coming out of the radio they played at home. It was Pentecostals that created the *corito de alabanza*, the popular worship chorus, and they used the sounds and instruments of Latin folk music.[212] The rest, as they say, is history.

Additionally, the Pentecostal service invites unscripted "Spirit-filled" participation, but why? First, it's not that non-Pentecostal churches don't invite people to join in; they do. But *when* they do, their services are governed by a sense of denominational decorum. People are encouraged to participate through congregational singing, antiphonal reading, and corporate prayer. Anything that deviates from the program is to be shunned. The Pentecostal Hispangelical also sees great value in congregational singing, Scripture reading, and prayer, but these do not exhaust the ways God invites his children to worship. What about "praying in the Spirit" (Eph. 6:18), singing "spiritual songs" (Col. 3:16), or the sharing of the inner witness of God's Spirit with the believer's spirit (Rom. 8:16)? Pentecostals see these as aspects of worship, which cannot be controlled, nor should they ever be.

When Pedro C. Moreno, an international coordinator and lawyer for the Rutherford Institute and a Pentecostal, speaks of the dynamics of a Pentecostal worship service, he notes, "There is no clear beginning of the service, and usually no clear end."[213] You see, more important

---

[212] See David Masci, "Why Has Pentecostalism Grown So Dramatically in Latin America?" Pew Research Center, November 14, 2014.

[213] Pedro C. Moreno, "Evangelical Churches," in *Religious Freedom and Evangelization in Latin America,* Paul E. Sigmund, ed. (Maryknoll, NY: Orbis Books, 1999), 65.

than holding to any order or schedule is allowing for the full venting of the worshipper's emotion through shouts of praise, whistling, clapping, dancing, crying, lifting hands, and speaking in tongues, all of which validate the moment.[214] The point is important: The baroque cultural connection that exists between the Pentecostal and the Latino, generally speaking, is powerful and continues to draw millions of Hispanics to their churches, both throughout Latin America and in the United States.

Pentecostal Preaching

Baroque influences also extend to preaching, which within the Pentecostal church tends to be more dramatic, heightened by bodily movement and grand gestures. Preachers often move quickly to high intonation, sustaining prolonged moments of screaming, with sparse voice modulation. One feature that is almost always present is the repetitive appeal for people to say "amen." What is confusing is that the "amen," which is a biblical affirmation, is often expressed over statements which do not warrant it. But if you think such vocal affirmations are governed by reason, you miss the point. Most people motivated to express vocal "amen" are not necessarily driven to affirm orthodoxy or sound doctrine. For many, vocal "amen" is tantamount to the whoops and hollers of a cheering crowd, encouraging the preacher to set aside any inhibitions and express emotional involvement fully, without reservation.

As to the sermon itself, it tends to fall short of the hermeneutical task. Many Pentecostal preachers, in fact, will claim to be "Spirit-led" in their preaching, thus not beholden to what they would consider to be spiritually dead and lifeless preaching. Predictably, it shows. For a myriad of reasons—economics, family priorities, personal lack of discipline, education broadly denigrated within Pentecostal circles—few Hispanic Pentecostal preachers seek out training in basic sermon preparation,

[214] Ibid., 64.

much less in developing the art and science of homiletics. Rather, their sermons are predictably allegorical, which allows for great subjective latitude in the way they interpret and apply the text. Often the text is used merely as a launching pad and little else. If the text is used, many focus on a word, a phrase, or an event, but rarely consider its context. This kind of preaching is highly subjective and selective, ignoring semantic structures and principles within the text. As noted, the baroque worldview encourages flamboyant, over-the-top expression, often encouraging optics over substance and Pentecostal preachers are masters at it. With allegory as the *modus operandi*, the preacher is free to say whatever they feel, for it is emotional intensity which guarantees that he or she is Spirit-filled, thus validating the message.

One other thing to note is the contrast with respect to the people's involvement in the preaching event. In many Protestant and evangelical denominations, the congregants will tend to listen to the sermon respectfully, but rarely interject themselves. However, Hispanic Pentecostal preaching is participatory. This means people are encouraged to rise from their seat during the sermon and get involved as the Spirit might lead them. All things considered, it is ironic, but the Hispanic Pentecostal preacher achieves what the Tridentine Fathers hoped for when they encouraged the Catholic Church to create an environment that would draw the people in.

Praying for the Sick

Pentecostalism connects with people's needs in a more direct manner as well. This is not to say that non-Pentecostals are indifferent; they care just as deeply. Yet, there is a palpable difference that can be easily observed, and praying for someone's healing offers a good example. Evangelicals and Protestants intercede for those who are ill and ask for healing, but usually within the boundaries of God's sovereign will. Pentecostals, however, are apt to interpret the illness as a demonic attack, even presence, and deal with it through aggressive spiritual warfare.

This difference between seeing an illness as a natural malady, as opposed to sickness brought about because of the presence of a malevolent spirit, signals a massive theological—and, I would add, cultural—divide. After all, most Latinos, as Latin writers themselves state, have lived "in a world where saints intervened, myth defined reality, time was cyclical, witches worked, and things flew around the room or disappeared in a whirlwind."[215] I am not accusing Pentecostals of being exploitive, but it is opportune that laying all the blame for illness at the feet of demonic forces dovetails perfectly with ancient beliefs about sinister spiritual forces. Thus, many will credit Pentecostals as more discerning, even daring, for their willingness to call out the spirit causing the sickness, and expelling it in the name of Jesus. This confrontation of spiritual forces fits with a worldview that accepts as fact unseen forces, ghosts, spirits, and where even nature itself can be a spoiler. While some evangelicals will refuse to believe that demonic activity is behind some human sickness, Pentecostals combat their destructive intent without apology.

The Second Blessing

Are there other points of contact that enhance Pentecostalism's appeal? Consider the resemblances between the rosary among Catholics and the signature Pentecostal doctrine of the second blessing, as exhibited by the gift of speaking in tongues.[216] I admit that at first glance, similarities may seem a stretch, but upon closer inspection interesting parallels do surface.

In our overview of the Baroque worldview, we made reference to the Catholic Church's desire to draw its members to the church through

---

[215] Sigmund, *Religious Freedom and Evangelization in Latin America*, 178.

[216] For a description of holiness, Pentecostal doctrine, see *Ted A. Campbell, Methodist Doctrine: The Essentials* (Nashville: Abingdon Press, 2011); and Stanley M. Burgess and Eduard M. Van der Maas, eds. *New International Dictionary of Pentecostal and Charismatic Movements,* rev. ed. (Grand Rapids, MI: Zondervan, 2002).

visual and emotional involvement. One of the most successful ways it accomplished this was by revamping the rosary in the wake of Trent.[217] With its new face, the faithful were encouraged to devote themselves to its recitation wholeheartedly. And there is no denying that through its practice, the rosary, with its repetitive prayer to Mary the "Queen of Heaven," became a touchstone which continues to invite Catholics to the fifteen, later twenty, mysteries of the religion.

Of course, Protestantism has never had anything like a rosary to offer. The Reformation principle *sola Scriptura* underscored the Bible's sufficiency. Even though some churches wrote creeds or confessions of faith to affirm key doctrines, these never usurped the Bible. But what about Pentecostals and the second blessing, as vouchsafed by speaking in tongues?

While there are doctrinal differences that separate the rosary from the doctrine of the second blessing, it is interesting to see how they are both promoted. Roman Catholicism is invested in the rosary, assuring by pontifical decree that those who recite it faithfully will:

- receive a gradual, perfect knowledge of Jesus Christ.
- be purified; their sins will be washed away.
- have victory over all their enemies.
- live more virtuous lives.
- be set on fire with the love of the Lord.
- be enriched with graces and merits from Almighty God.
- be supplied with what is needed to pay all debts to God and to their fellow men.[218]

---

[217] Though the praying of the rosary dates perhaps to the thirteenth century, Pope Pius V (1504–1572) gave the rosary its basic structure, consisting of fifteen mysteries and grouping them into three sets: the Joyful Mysteries, the Sorrowful Mysteries, and the Glorious Mysteries. In 2002, Pope John Paul II added an additional five and called them the Luminous Mysteries, bringing the total number of mysteries to twenty.

[218] The list is adapted from "Benefits of the Rosary," at http://www.theholyrosary.org/rosarybenefits (accessed October 15, 2017).

As for the so-called second blessing, its prophets and apostles have extended similar benefits to those who take hold of this gift. Kenneth Copeland affirms that the gift of speaking in tongues allows the person, among other things, to speak directly to God, to stay in tune with the Holy Spirit, and serves as a powerful weapon against the enemy.[219] Kenneth Hagin affirms that speaking in tongues "stimulates faith and helps us learn how to trust God more fully."[220]

In his book, *The Power of Praying in Tongues: Unleashing the Supernatural Dimension in You,* Glenn Arekion identifies one hundred benefits to *glossolalia.*[221] As we survey Arekion's list, note how the benefits of the rosary align with the benefits of the second blessing as exhibited in speaking in tongues:

- Reciting the rosary will obtain all kinds of graces from Almighty God. Speaking in tongues: #1, is the believer's entrance into the supernatural; #4, is the believer's direct access to the throne room; #5, is speaking divine mysteries—divine coded secrets; #11, strengthens the inner man with might; #31, hones your sharpness and accuracy in the anointing; #38, is deep calling unto deep; #39, accesses revelation knowledge; #40, taps into the mind of God.
- Reciting the rosary provides a gradual, perfect knowledge of Jesus Christ. Speaking in tongues: #19, gives you unstoppable progress that your enemies cannot deny; #60, enables a closer walk with God; #61, is speaking the hidden wisdom of God; #99, makes you God-friendly rather than seeker-friendly, equips you for the

[219] See Kenneth Copeland Ministries, "5 Benefits of Praying in Tongues," http://www.kcm.org/real-help/prayer/apply/5-benefits-praying-tongues (accessed October 15, 2017).

[220] Kenneth E. Hagin, "Seven Reasons Why Every Believer Should Speak in Tongues," Kenneth Hagin Ministries, http://www.rhema.org/index.php?option=com_content&view=article&id=1053:seven-reasons-why-every-believer-should-speak-in-tongues&Itemid=145 (accessed October 15, 2017).

[221] Glenn Arekion, *The Power of Praying in Tongues: Unleashing the Supernatural Dimension in You* (Pescara, Italy: Destiny Image Europe, 2010).

wonders of God; #100, is a well, springing up into the God kind of life; #54, is a brainstorming session with God.

- Reciting the rosary purifies the faithful, washing away their sin. Speaking in tongues: #23, is help with your ultimate weakness; #58, removes you from the limitations of the flesh to God's abundant supply of the Spirit; #91, mortifies the cravings of the flesh.
- Reciting the rosary gives victory over all enemies. Speaking in tongues: #42, is part of the armor of God, the lance that will shoot down the enemy; #43, is the pilum to cause great damage to the kingdom of darkness; #51, is blowing the ram's horn for battle; #52, is the rallying sound of victory.
- Reciting the rosary makes it easier to practice virtue. Speaking in tongues: #26, renders you to be God-inside minded; #79, helps in living effectively in the last days; #80, is the ignition key to walking in the power of God; #81, is being endued with power from on high; #82, is rivers of living waters flowing out of you.
- Reciting the rosary will set the faithful Catholic on fire with love of the Lord. Speaking in tongues: #69, lights the fire of God in your life.

In considering these parallels, we can identify three broad areas of agreement. First, like the rosary, which promises to introduce the person into the mysteries of the faith, the gift of speaking in tongues connects Pentecostals ostensibly with the mysterious and supernatural world of the Holy Spirit. Second, like the rosary, which can be recited both at church and at home, the gift of tongues is not limited to a congregational setting. People are encouraged to express it at home through their personal prayer language; thus, tongues are ambulatory, for they go wherever the person goes. Third, and most importantly, like the praying of the rosary, which is said to lavish grace and merit upon those who practice it faithfully, the second blessing also promises blessings and spiritual empowerments for those who practice the gift. Though there are exceptions, for Pentecostals, speaking in tongues is a sign of sanctification, of greater spirituality. Thus, the person is said to move beyond the baptism of salvation to the second and third baptisms of holiness. Of course, in pointing out such things, I am not suggesting that the doctrine of the second blessing was developed to compete with Roman Catholicism, or to make up for the loss of the rosary among ex-Roman Catholics. Yet, it is uncanny to see how blessings associated with this so-called gift align with the rosary in so many ways.

It should be stated that evangelicals have always believed that God wishes to bless believers with the forgiveness of sins, increased spiritual power to overcome evil and temptation, spiritual discernment, and deepening intimacy with their Redeemer and Lord. For the vast majority of evangelicals, these blessings are freely available through the personal spiritual disciplines of prayer, obedience, the study and meditation upon the written Word, and corporate disciplines of the church. For Pentecostals, the second blessing, however, offers a religious experience that goes beyond. If the Roman Catholic Church has instilled into its flock the legitimacy of sacramental enhancements to devotion, the second blessing does the same for Pentecostals.

Conclusion

As of late, it is sometimes said that evangelicals are failing to take commitment to their Reformation moorings seriously.[222] Many, perhaps a significant majority, are more apt today to think of their faith mainly regarding a religious experience (e.g., as having been saved or born again), rather than as a conscious embrace of key and historical doctrinal distinctives (e.g., the doctrine of justification by faith and apart from works). Some critics go so far as to argue that the term "evangelical" has become so shapeless it can mean whatever one wants it to mean. For

[222] John H. Gerstner, "The Theological Boundaries of Evangelical Faith," in *The Evangelicals: What They Believe, Who They Are, Where They Are Changing,* eds. David F. Wells and John D. Woodbridge (Nashville: Abingdon, 1975), 21–37.

myself, I wonder whether this trend is fueled in part by a growing Hispanic presence. Could Hispangelicals, who continue to be influenced by Pentecostal tendencies, be less interested in the historical and doctrinal convictions of the movement—thus nudging evangelicalism more in the direction of a movement or orientation defined by emotion and experiences?

Whatever the case, Hispanic evangelicals need to work hard to overcome the oft-repeated and sometimes earned appraisal that they don't have anything substantive to add to the evangelical conversation. Sometimes this kind of critique is deserved, especially when our theology is born of the chronic conditions that have assailed Latinos. Don't misunderstand; it's just that when our theological offerings continue to sound like predictable grievances, it loses its broadest hearing. When Hispanics voice a theology that parrots the theology that was put forth by liberation theologians of the late twentieth century, it sounds like they are trying to revive a dead horse, lacking authenticity and depth of insight to speak to their day.

In saying this, I am not suggesting that Hispangelicals should abandon the call for justice, which is so often the call of the larger community. Sometimes what we cry out for, however, is found in the pursuit of other things. If Hispanic evangelicals can muster the courage to look beyond their immediate circumstance, to articulate Christian principles that speak to people beyond themselves, they may find the illusive butterfly of justice lighting on them.

If the Latino mantra holds true and God opts for the poor, does God decide on a people simply to look compassionately upon them? Or does opting for them include using them such as he finds them? Jesus surely ministered to the lame, the sick, the blind, and the brokenhearted, but he also reached out to the rich, to those supposedly in the know, and to the empowered. Is Jesus our model, and if he is, does the Hispangelical have a gospel for the world? Has liminality ever kept God's herald from saying, "Thus sayeth the Lord" to people oppressed by affluence, controlled by conspicuous consumption, or in the clutches of wealth? To be sure, Hispangelicals need to be keen interpreters of the Hispanic condition to their own, but they have been redeemed to do more. The Hispangelical can speak with authority and insight to people at large. But to do so, they will need to abandon their comfortable ahistorical bed.

That said, many Hispangelicals do understand that with growth in numbers comes increased accountability. In this vein, many Pentecostal churches are discovering that offering social services need not come at the expense of forsaking their spiritual roots.[223] Many are integrating the spiritual world with the very concrete material world around them, and it is adding to their appeal. And growth is also to be seen in formal theological and ministerial training. Though still lagging when compared to other ethnic groups within the evangelical fold, Hispanic Pentecostal ministers who attend Bible colleges and seminaries are steadily increasing.[224]

Lamentably, the Hispangelical world is filled with casualties—people who succumb to the consequences of prior bad decisions or ongoing chronic realities. In most cases, it is usually a combination of both. In light of this, the evangelical church would do well to note those who show potential for serious reflection and leadership, and encourage them in any way possible. Providing them with the tools that help them put their circumstance in a Christocentric light keeps the Hispanic reality from becoming ground for ill-founded hopes and futile aspirations, things that Latinos are notorious for harboring.

---

[223] See transcript, "Moved by the Spirit: Pentecostal Power and Politics After 100 Years," Pew Research Center: Religion & Public Life, April 24, 2006, https://www.pewforum.org/2006/04/24/moved-by-the-spirit-pentecostal-power-and-politics-after-100-years2 (accessed May 2, 2019). See also Kunerth, "Hispanics Flock to Pentecostal Churches."

[224] For an in-depth analysis of Hispanics and theological education, see Edwin I Hernandez, "Latino/a Research: An Educational and Ministerial Profile of Latino/a Seminarians," June 2007. This research can be assessed at https://latinostudies.nd.edu/assets/95307/original/lr_nd_v4n4finalweb.pdf (accessed August 14, 2017). See also, https://swbts.edu/news/releases/fields-ripe-harvest-hispanic-population-sanchez-says/ (accessed August 20, 2017).

CHAPTER SIX

Then Came the Hispanic Mind

The soul becomes dyed with the color of its thoughts.

Marcus Aurelius
Meditations[225]

In recent days, the call to recalibrate evangelicalism has intensified. Timothy Gloege, history professor at Calvin College, is one who suggests the relinquishing of long-held assumptions and the incorporation of new perspectives.[226] Gloege considers that evangelicalism should be recast as an "orientation," a paradigm, which he considers to be more flexible and amenable to the changes that are happening in the evangelical world. In all this, notes Gloege, "it's not enough just to jam new ideas into existing frameworks; we need everyone at the table building new frameworks together."[227]

As we think about it, Gloege's call for greater flexibility is not without precedent. Mark Knoll reminds us that evangelicalism has always been marked by impulses "in which groups, leaders,

[225] Marcus Aurelius, *Meditations*, Book V.16
[226] Chris Gehrz, "Recalibrating the 'Evangelical Paradigm,'" *Patheos,* July 13, 2017.
[227] Ibid.

institutions, goals, concerns, opponents and aspirations become more or less visible and more or less influential over time."[228] In light of evangelicalism's propensity to change, Gloege's call to create new frameworks may be warranted, but caution is always the better part of wisdom.

Evangelicalism may well be at a turning point—and if it is, the question we ought all to ask is, what ideas do we bring to this moment? Framed as such, the question is not meant to exclude, but rather to prompt anyone, or any group, who ventures to shape evangelicalism to engage in self-reflection.

For myself, I have no doubt that Hispangelicals have a contribution to make—I'm banking on it. Yet, because the shaping of Christianity has always been as much a human endeavor as it has been divinely providential, one important caution bears mentioning: All would-be contributors should remember that God holds us all accountable. As we push the evangelical envelope, we ought to do it with a bit of reverent fear and humility. In Matthew 12:36, we are warned to consider our words, for "every careless word that people speak, they shall give an accounting for it in the day of judgment." As we add our lines to evangelicalism's history book, we need to remember that God oversees the batting-around of our ideas, our newly constructed paradigms, and frameworks. After all, we are held responsible to the One who made the evangelical story possible. If we remain as mindful of our responsibilities as well as of the opportunity, we may well have reason to hope that evangelicalism's better days lie ahead.

An Overview of Biblical Accountability

Does God hold his creation accountable? From the moment of creation, all species are expected to thrive within their ordained environments.

[228] Mark A. Knoll, *The Scandal of the Evangelical Mind* (Grand Rapids, MI: Wm. B. Eerdmans, 1994), 8.

Their responsibility is to reproduce or, as Scripture says it, to "fill" the earth with its kind (Gen. 1:11, 20, 22–24). And what of the human race? Our first parents are bounded to live in a lush garden, to superintend it, to be fruitful and multiply, and to find their nourishment from within it (Gen. 1:26–30). The repeated "good" that Genesis sounds through the six days of creation (Gen. 1:4, 10, 12, 18, 21, 25, 31) suggests that had sin never entered into Eden, all creation would have lived up to expectations.

But of course, it isn't long until Genesis recounts the story of human sin, putting God's plan in doubt. A pertinent question to ask is, what happens to accountability when the circumstances under which creation was first set in place no longer exist? Is accountability in the context of a fallen world even possible? As the biblical story continues, we see that God still holds people accountable to him, but it become increasingly burdensome. In *Follow Me*, David Platt spells out the problem, which will render human accountability exceedingly difficult, if not impossible. Only six chapters into the book of Genesis, notes Platt, and "it becomes clear that the inclination of every person's heart is consistently evil, beginning from childhood."[229]

Given such a propensity to sin, a lesser god might have destroyed the world or simply abandoned it to its own devices. But the Bible never wavers on God, who continues to hold people answerable to him. As the biblical narrative rolls out the extent of humanity's spiritual and moral downfall, accountability never diminishes, even as evil intensifies. Generations later, Paul assesses the human condition with the backdrop of absolute holiness and declares "there is none righteous, not even one" (Rom. 3:10).

In the Bible, God certainly holds individuals accountable but he also goes further, for the ill-founded prejudices, beliefs, and actions of

---

[229] David Platt, *Follow Me* (Carol Stream, IL: Tyndale House Publishers, 2013), 29–30.

nations are also weighed in the balance.[230] God judged the whole of antediluvian society for its inclination toward evil (Gen. 6:5–8). God saw the problem with Babel's lust for glory and confused their language (Gen. 11:1–9). The ten plagues Egypt endured were certainly a judgment against their religion, and the drowning of its army at the Red Sea is cast as an archetype indictment against all nations that would trust in their military strength (Exod. 15:1–12; cf. Isa. 31:1).

This judgment of nations (e.g., Amalekites, Philistines) and city-states (e.g., Jericho, Ai) continues through Joshua's conquest, the time of the judges, and into the establishment of the monarchy. The book of Amos is notable for the way it begins, holding nations and city-states accountable for their militancy (Damascus, 1:3), deportation policies (Gaza, 1:6), breaking of alliances (Tyre, 1:9), hatred of a rival state (Edom, 1:11), unjust annexing of lands (Ammon, 1:13), desecration of rival human remains (Moab, 2:1), forsaking of God's law and statutes (Judah, 2:4), and the ill-treatment of the poor (Israel, 2:6). In surveying this list, we should not fail to note that God's judgment extends to national policies and international entanglements, but it also holds people accountable for their acts of social injustices and their religious failures. In almost every case, it is actions motivated by hateful beliefs and prejudices that provoke God to punish the offending states. Still, does human accountability ever hit closer to home?

[230] The Bible does not speak of "nations" in the modern secular sense of the term. In the Bible the nations are seen as people who have an inherent ethnic makeup. Moreover, in the Old Testament the nations are almost always named as the *goy,* or *goyim,* and not the *am,* the people of God. In the New Testament, the nations are identified as the *ethne,* routinely referring to the Gentile nations. The nations are thought of ethnically since they are almost always spoken of in contrast, and sometimes in consort with the only other ethnicity, Israel. See G. Johannes Botterweck, H. Ringren, eds., *Theological Dictionary of the Old Testament,* Vol. II, trans. John T. Willis (Grand Rapids, MI: William B. Eerdmans Publishers, 1975), Clements and Botterweck, 426–438; William A. Van Gemeren, ed., *New International Dictionary of Old Testament Theology & Exegesis,* Vol. 3 (Grand Rapids, MI: Zondervan, 1997), Robert H. O'Connell, 429–432; R. L. Harris, Gleason L. Archer, Jr., and Bruce K. Waltke, eds., *Theological Word Book of the Old Testament* (Chicago: Moody Press, 1980), 154.

Christ's Critique of His Generation

Throughout his ministry, Jesus had occasion to observe human attitudes and behaviors, and he doesn't shy away from evaluating them. Thus, Matthew 11:16–17 says:

> To what shall I compare this generation? It is like children sitting in the market who call out to the other children, and say, "We played the flute for you, and you did not dance; we sang a dirge, and you did not mourn."

As we consider the context of this passage, we note that this critique comes on the heels of Jesus' praise of John the Baptist (vv. 7–14). But the focus is also on the crowds that sought to catch a glimpse of this man. The three, "But what did you go out to see?" questions suggest that people were drawn by the wild and raw character of John's ministry, but were blind to his real purpose. Jesus held out hope that some might yet have discerning ears (v. 15), but he was not overly optimistic.

As he considered the throngs that made the effort to go out to the wilderness, Jesus judged them to be like children, but in a troubling way. They weren't like normal children—curious, eager for new experiences. As a matter of fact, on the surface of things some might have concluded that the crowds were showing all the signs of youthful curiosity. However, Jesus took a deeper look and concluded they were like jaded children, bored with it all. Jesus' assessment paints a tragic picture. People may have been titillated to go and "see" the wild man out in the wilderness but, once there, nothing moved them to "hear" his message. Our point is clear: Since Jesus makes an assessment which he applies to people in general, we know he was speaking of a broadly held attitude. But the question bears asking: Does Jesus ever hit closer to home?

Jesus' Critique of Samaritan Religion

Not long into Jesus' conversation with a woman he met as he traveled through Samaria, the woman perceives that she is speaking with a Judean prophet (John 4:19) and ventures to spar with him on the question of religion. Read her verbal challenge and Jesus' response in verses 20–22. "Our fathers," she lectures Jesus, "worshiped in this mountain and you people say that in Jerusalem is the place where men ought to worship." The woman is apologetic, seeking to validate the religious traditions of her community. She says in effect, "Hey, we worship here, you worship there; what's the problem?" For his part, Jesus could have steered clear from the rivalry of Samaritan versus Jewish religion, but he doesn't. He says to the Samaritan:

> Woman, believe Me, an hour is coming when neither in this mountain, nor in Jerusalem, shall you worship the Father. You worship that which you do not know; we worship that which we know, for salvation is from the Jews. (John 4:21–22)

Can we agree it takes some kind of chutzpah to say to someone, "You worship in ignorance"? Had Christ been concerned, he might have let her comments pass in the interest of better Jewish-Samaritan relations. But sidestepping the issue would have come at the expense of violating an important principle. Since both the Jews and Samaritans shared an overlap of Scripture, the relativism espoused by the woman revealed her gross misunderstanding of that very Scripture. She needed to be enlightened on the Bible's unified message: salvation was, and always had, emanated from the Jews.

With respect to evaluating religious beliefs, the case of the Samaritan woman brings us face-to-face with one of our most delicate challenges: God has not called us to trample over sincerely held religious beliefs, but, on the other hand, some things simply cannot be allowed to stand uncontested. For example, when some Jews unfairly accused believers of drunkenness on the day of Pentecost, Peter was compelled to set the record straight (Acts 2:13, 15). Later, in his first epistle, Peter encourages Christians to be apologists—firm defenders—for the gospel, yet to do it with gentleness and reverence (1 Pet. 3:15). Peter's defense at Pentecost teaches us that people are prone to misconstrue. Of course, timing and tone are always important considerations. But no matter when this happens, a believer should seek to correct misguided beliefs, especially when such beliefs distort the gospel message.

In our Samaritan example, Jesus saw a legitimate opening, since Jews and Samaritans drew from common Scripture. For our case, since most Latinos are "Christian" in the broadest sense, we share a common theological base. This overlap allows the thoughtful believer a point of commonality from which to assess the culture's consistency with biblical truth.

Though not easy by any means, upholding the integrity of God's message, coupled with a person's need to hear biblical truth, especially as it confronts faulty theology, is infinitely more important than us shying away from serious critique or anything that threatens our comfort zone. As we consider Jesus' words, we see that he told the Samaritan woman what she needed to hear, hurtful as it might have sounded. Since religion is almost always at the core of a person's hopes, the conversation was necessary if she was to understand the way of salvation.

Paul and the Case of the Cretans

In the foregoing cases, we have seen that Jesus held society and individuals accountable for their beliefs and prejudices, but he was not alone in this. In his epistle to Titus, the apostle Paul reminded his Gentile protégé that he had sent him to Crete to "set in order what remains and appoint elders in every city" (Titus 1:5). Paul was under no illusion that the job he had assigned Titus would be easy. By all appearances, Paul agrees with a local prophet who considered his fellow islanders to be "always liars, evil beasts, lazy gluttons" (vv. 12–13).

A question to consider is, why did Paul appeal to such a hurtful evaluation? Before charging Paul with gross insensitivity, it is probable that this was widely known in the Cretan community, akin to what behavioral psychologists consider to be cultural-bound syndromes.[231] Just about every society has them and Latinos are no exception, exhibiting things such as *susto, empacho, nervios, mal de ojo*, specific culturally bound pathologies the population would readily admit.

Still, the question remains, did these issues render Cretans morally bankrupt? Paul reminds the Philippians to always look for the better and noble qualities in people (Phil. 4:8); and to those in Thessalonica, he encourages them to hold fast to the good (1 Thess. 4:21). If we can agree that there are people in Las Vegas; Reno, Nevada; or Atlantic City, New Jersey who suffer from a gambling syndrome, and yet agree that most of those who live there are free of this vice, we can likewise believe that Cretans had many noble qualities, even if there was a propensity for laziness, gluttony, and lying among the citizenry.

For our part, we should not shy away from looking squarely at what Paul's approach might teach us. The apostle quoted from the very people he hoped to reach, which opens another avenue for assessment. This was not the only time he had appealed to local sources of moral authority. At Athens, Paul examined the Greeks' idolatry and turned specifically to their "unknown god" (Acts 17:16–34). In this, we discover that Paul was keen to consider their own voices and statements, letting them stand as planks from which to set forth the claims of the gospel.

The Redeemable Value of Cultures

In our foregoing comments, we have laid out a case which would seem to infer that all cultures are tragically flawed and deserving of the most severe criticism, but this is not entirely accurate. While God does hold

[231] Richard Cervantes, *A Guide for Conducting Cultural Assessment of Latino and Hispanic Clients* (Bayamon, Pr.: Universidad Central del Caribe, 2017), 15.

all nations and cultures accountable, he also bestows favor on those who seek to come under his rule. God showed favor to the Gibeonites (Josh. 10:1), Nineveh (Jonah 3:1–10), and Jerusalem (Josh. 15:63), among others. Jonah's prophecy is driven by God's desire that despite Nineveh's sin, she may yet be salvaged (Jonah 3:9–10). And with respect to Israel, though they are a rebellious and an obstinate people (Rom. 11:21; cf. Isa. 65:2), Paul dares to believe that in time "all Israel will be saved" (Rom. 11:26; cf. Isa. 59:20).

As the Bible repeatedly tells us, God always looks for something of redeemable value, but it must be on his terms. For example, righteousness is something that always exalts a nation (Prov. 14:34). In his Sermon on the Mount, Jesus notes a number of virtues like hunger for righteousness, peacemaking, humility (Matt. 5:1–10), as things that distinguish a shining city set on a hill (v. 14). When we apply God's Word to real-life cultures, some were so wicked that they were utterly destroyed. However, few are ever totally beyond reach. If nations and individuals are capable of gross immorality, they are also capable virtue, strength, and compassion. This is true of North American culture, and it is true of Latino culture as well.

Still, are any of us really fit to critique someone else's culture? In my estimation, we can't help but do so, for critiquing culture, national policies, social structures, and judicial rulings are things God's people have always been called to do. At first, God called prophets to hold nations accountable for such things. In our day, Christians are guided to seriously asses political and cultural conditions by the inner leading of the Holy Spirit, and God's written Word (1 Cor. 2:15, 6:2–4, 10:15). In my denomination, we believe in the need to assess cultural developments so strongly that we fund an agency dedicated, in part, to critiquing our national cultural values from a Judeo-Christian worldview.[232]

---

[232] The official Ethics and Religious Liberty Commission of the Southern Baptist Convention website is http://erlc.com (accessed October 25, 2017).

As we consider the sum of our observations, they suggest that all cultures ought to be scrutinized, but honestly. In such an endeavor, there is a place for broad evaluations, but also for delicate, even painful, critiques. When available, it is important to hear their own internal voices—for truth, understanding, and insight are not the exclusive possession of evangelical Christians. As we identify areas of concern, we gain much by recognizing the good and noble qualities of any culture as well, even if they should excel those of our own.

Assessing the Hispanic Mind

We begin by stating that despite a recent "most interesting man" advertising campaign, few people ever embody the Hispanic persona to a tee, so we should never paint in general with a broad brush. That said, I have met some who are Latinos *hasta el copete*,[233] and they can leave a lasting impression. One thing that immediately grabs you is their emotional transparency; whether they are happy, sad, determined, disgusted, whatever they are feeling, the emotion comes across honest and unvarnished. Many can toggle between the sacred and the profane effortlessly to speak on any subject, without finding it the least bit clashing. Moreover, their face, eyes, hands, their whole body is a fine-tuned instrument of communication. But what stands out most is their *sufrido,* painful love of country, and of their heritage—*y por tener la dicha*—for having had the good fortune to have been born *Mejicano*, *Cubano*, *Hondureño*, *Ecuatoriano*, or *Argentino*, to a people who hail from a land of "blood and fire."[234] More often, however, people convey their ethnic pride and heritage by degree, some more so than others; and in a rare few the Latino way is all but erased, if it was ever there at all. Knowing that Hispanics are a diverse people who come from different countries and cultures is important, for it reminds us that everyone carries the fingerprint of

[233] A colloquial expression, with the intended meaning "from head to toe."
[234] Taken from Chasteen, *Born in Blood and Fire.*

their own life experiences. A surname might be a good place to begin, but we dare not make judgments without knowing people for who they truly are.

The Lost Sheep of the Tribes of Latin America

In an earlier chapter, we took up three thoughtful Latino citizens to give us their sense of the Hispanic state of affairs. We deemed Leopoldo Zea, Claudio Véliz, and Ernesto Mayz Vallenilla reliable witnesses, for they have pondered the Hispanic experience seriously. While their observations vary, their thoughts do come together to verify a vital concern. Regardless of their vantage point, Zea, Véliz, and Mays Vallenilla testify to the persistence of a troubled Hispanic identity. And so, we ask, does God's Word speak to this condition?

The Bible addresses the state of fallen humanity in a variety of ways. Some of the concepts that are used to convey the depth of the predicament include those of alienation, sin, defilement, rebellion, madness, foolishness, hardness of heart, famine, enslavement, and sickness. Even physical defects like broken bones, blindness, stunted growth of members, mange, or even crushed testicles are also used metaphorically to speak of the way sin renders humanity unacceptable before God.[235]

One particular way in which Christ described Israel's troubled condition is that he saw them as "distressed and dispirited like sheep without a shepherd," and as "the lost sheep of the house of Israel" (Matt. 9:36, 10:6). This description is curious, for at the time that Jesus spoke these words the Jews were living in their ancestral land. Moreover, Jerusalem, their capital, was a thriving city that drew pilgrims from throughout the Roman Empire to her annual feasts and celebrations. The Jews enjoyed a magnificent temple, which some have identified as one of the wonders of the ancient world. Israel had a ruling class, a working priesthood, and a Sanhedrin that could adjudicate many domestic issues.

---

[235] Rudolph Gonzalez, *Acceptable* (Bloomington, IN: Crossbooks, 2012).

But it didn't stop at their Mediterranean shoreline. Beginning with Julius Caesar and continuing under Augustus, the Romans granted Jews the status of a *religio licita* (permitted religion), which benefited them throughout the Diaspora. With such unprecedented concessions, Jews living abroad used the Septuagint and the proliferation of synagogues throughout the empire to promote their monotheistic faith, bringing many Gentile God-fearers into its orb. These benefits helped dispersed Jews to maintain their cultural, social, and religious cohesion wherever they found themselves. So, the question is reasonable: Given all that Jews had going for them, in what credible way could they be seen as a distressed and dispirited people?

With the narrow parameters of our subject, a full-blown discussion of the problems and crises associated with Second Temple Judaism is beyond our purview here.[236] We can only offer the briefest of outlines:

- Geographically, Jews could hardly claim to possess the land in the full biblical sense. At the time, Israel was effectively balkanized.[237] The land was a patchwork of regions with non-Davidic ethnarchs and tetrarchs holding jurisdiction over various sectors of the land. Moreover, Rome labeled the province "Palestine," referring to the ancient Philistines.
- Religiously, Palestinian Jews were also divided with Pharisees, Sadducees, and the Essenes, each holding to different authoritative Scriptures. Moreover, Samaritans practiced a separate religion with its own priesthood. Since Israel was under Roman occupation, pagan religions would have been practiced wherever Roman soldiers were garrisoned, bringing religious defilement to the land.

---

[236] See B.D. Chilton, "Judaism and the New Testament"; C. Seeman, "Judea"; Craig A. Evans and S.E. Porter, eds., *Dictionary of New Testament Background;* (Downers Grove, IL: InterVarsity Press, 2000).

[237] Thomas Brisco, *Holman Bible Atlas* (Nashville: Broadman & Holman Publishers, 1998). See map, "The Divisions of Herod's Kingdom," and subsequent commentary, 208–212.

- Economically, Israel was under great stress. Roman taxation was always grievous, and Herod's extravagant constructions at home and abroad exacerbated the problem.[238] At the time of Jesus, poverty had swollen to unprecedented levels.
- Politically, Israel was decimated. The northern ten tribes had been wiped off the map in 722 BC. The Jews were ruled locally by the Herodians, puppets for the Roman Empire. Palestine was also under Pontius Pilate, a Roman prefect and governor of Judea.

Of course, Israel's problems did not start when the Roman general, *Gnaeus Pompeius Magnus,* arrived in 63 BC. The distressful conditions intimated by Christ had been the consequence of oppression experienced by Israel under multiple foreign powers, dating back centuries. And even when the Hasmonean dynasty gained Israel's autonomy, their Hellenistic appetites, along with external pressures from Parthians and Romans, made national sovereignty and political autonomy all but impossible to sustain. Yes, despite real-world advantages and covenantal privileges, the Jews were distressed, beaten down by their tragic history. As Christ assessed Israel, whatever benefits they had did not offset a fundamental problem:

> How often I wanted to gather your children together, the way a hen gathers her chicks under her wings, and you were unwilling. (Matt. 23:37)

Like sheep without a shepherd, like chicks, which resist being gathered under their mother hen, the Jewish people were living a "scattered" existence. This point is critical, for Moses had warned Israel how God would punish them if they should fail in their devotion to God:

---

[238] Stewart Perowne, *The Life and Times of Herod the Great* (Phoenix Mill: Sutton Publishing Ltd., 1956, 2003), 115–142.

> The LORD will scatter you among the peoples, and you will be left few in number among the nations where the LORD drives you.[239] (Deut. 4:27; cf. Neh. 1:8)

This concept of scattering is found mostly in the Old Testament. Though it is used in other ways, most of the time it refers to Israel being scattered by God for her disobedience. Thus, despite whatever advantages the Diaspora had brought to the Jews across the Roman Empire, from a biblical perspective their scattering among the nations was a sign of divine judgment.[240] For its part, Israel was not ready to be gathered up, and so her tragic existence, which any student of world history knows, was the sign of Israel's distress.

Does Israel's experience resonate in any way with the realities Latinos have had to endure? Here, I approach this question with abundant caution, for Israel holds a unique place in the pages of Scripture. Still, I can't help but find points of commonality, which should not be overlooked. Like Israel, Latin America was under the boot of foreign oppression for centuries. And even when she gained independence, her leaders, whether emperors, *caudillos*, dictators, or presidents, were predictably more accommodating to foreign interests than those of their people.[241] David Turner has shown that Israel's leadership was largely at fault, and that the people suffered as a consequence of it.[242] In similar fashion, Latin America has endured a relentless line of failed philosophies of governance and leaders that have resulted in the human predicament, which we see played out with sad regularity. At the turn of the twentieth century, between 1906 and 1934, we saw it in Haiti, the Dominican Republic, and Nicaragua. In the late 1950s and '60s, we saw it in Cuba.

---

[239] See also Lev. 26:33; Deut. 28:64; Ps. 44:11, 106:27; Jer. 9:16, 24:9; Ezek. 5:12, 12:15, 20:23; Zech. 1:21, 7:14; et al.

[240] However, the same God who had scattered them in judgment held out hope that his people might yet be gathered back unto him (Deut. 30:3; Neh. 1:9; Isa. 27:12; et al.).

[241] See Chapter 1, "Then Came History."

[242] David L. Turner, "Matthew 21:43 and the Future of Israel," *Bibliotheca Sacra* 159, no. 633 (Jan–Mar 2002), 46–61.

In the 1980s, we saw it in Panama, Argentina, and El Salvador. Mexico has experienced great turmoil for years. As I write this (2019), both Honduras and Venezuela are in the spotlight.

Once Israel divided after Solomon's death, there was never any real hope that the tribes would reunify, and it was much the same with Latin America. At their inception, both Mexico and Grand Columbia could claim grand aspirations, but their hopes were soon dashed. The lands were splintered into small and weak countries, making them ripe for the picking. Like the Babylonians who put in place a puppet ruler (2 Kgs. 24; 2 Chr. 36:10–13; Jer. 37:1); or later the Persians, who gave administrative jurisdiction to Samaritans (Ezra 4:2, 9–10); or the Romans, who installed the Herodians to rule Israel,[243] the French insulted Mexican sovereignty, imposing Emperor Maximillian even while Benito Juarez had been duly elected president. Latin American history is replete with German, French, British, and American intervention, imposing puppet regimes throughout Central America and the Caribbean.[244]

While the Jews managed to survive, they never really prospered under any foreign power. In similar fashion, whether it was the French, Germans, British, or Americans, whatever benefits Latin America received from their presence and investment also practically deepened dependency. And so it is no wonder that under such vexing conditions, vast numbers of their citizens would disperse, looking for a better life elsewhere. Like Israel, the Latin American Diaspora is essentially a tragic and desperate phenomenon caused as a result of failed internal policies and foreign entanglements that span centuries.

With that said, the Jews nevertheless held strong to their identity whether at home or abroad, and the Hispanic, to varying degrees, has done the same. Israel never forgot—even if they lamented it at times—that they were the chosen people of God; the apostle Paul acknowledges

---

[243] See Laurence H. Schiffman, *From Text to Tradition, a History of Judaism in Second Temple and Rabbinic Times* (Brooklyn, NY: Ktav Publishers, 1991).

[244] For a history of foreign interventions in Israel during the inter-testamental period, see Michael Brenner, *A Short History of the Jews* (Princeton, NJ: Princeton University Press, 2010).

this repeatedly about his kinsmen in his epistle to the Romans (2:17–20, 9:3–5, 11:28). Whatever their situation, the Egyptian bondage was in their collective memory, as was their deliverance, their sojourn in the wilderness, and their entry into the land of promise. In a way, just about everything that made them "Israel" was interpreted through the lens of history they had lived; it was formative for who they were.

And what about Latin Americans? As we have previously noted, Hispanics tend to be outspoken and proud of their heritage, even if their national leaders have done little to deserve their loyalty. In North America, Hispanics abhor being lumped together as "Mexicans." They want to make sure their nationality is known. Each of the twenty-plus nations has its own history, and few are apt to forget it. That said, there is one common experience, which the most desperate among them acknowledge.

For those who cross the US border illegally, music is a medium used to express a common lament. Many incorporate harrowing encounters at the *frontera* (the border), with the *rinches* (Texas Rangers), the *migra* (US Immigration Service), and *coyotes* (human traffickers), into *corridos* (folk songs) that tell of the risk they take in an effort to cross into the United States, but that is only the beginning. In fact, Psalm 137:1–6, which describes Israel's lament as she languishes under Babylonian captivity, might well echo the conflicted and emotional feelings many undocumented Hispanics sense:

Psalm 137	**Psalm 137, Latino Style**
By the rivers of Babylon,	*Al cruzar el Rio Grande,*
There we sat down and wept,	*Lloramos y lamentamos,*
When we remembered Zion.	*Recordando nuestra tierra querida.*
Upon the willows in the midst of it	*Rodeados de tanta abundancia*
We hung our harps.	*Colgamos nuestra guitaras*
For there our captors demanded of	*Los jefes gringos piden que cantemos*
us songs,	*Que cantemos con alegría,*
And our tormentors' mirth, saying,	*demandando*

"Sing us one of the songs of Zion."	*"Cántanos una canción de dónde eres."*
How can we sing the Lord's song	*Pero, como podemos cantar*
In a foreign land?	*¿Viviendo acá en el Norte?*
If I forget you, O Jerusalem,	*Si me olvido de mi tierra querida*
May my right hand forget her skill.	*Que mi mano derecha me falle*
May my tongue cling to the roof of my mouth	*Que nunca vuelva a cantar*
If I do not remember you,	*Si no me acuerdo de ti,*
If I do not exalt Jerusalem	*Si no ensalzo mi tierra querida*
Above my chief joy.	*Sobre todo mi gozo.*

Foreign-born Hispanics must be struck by the paradox of it all—to declare their love of country, yet to willingly leave it; to sing of their nation's beauty and values, yet to be living in a foreign place, and by their own choosing. That said, the fact that so many come to North America illegally should not be construed as blatant hypocrisy. Western Union's more than 32,000 offices throughout Latin America bears witness to the fact that many are here because of severe economic limitations, yet providing for their families back home. Despite the tens of millions of illegals who are in the United States at any moment in time, many do eventually return to their families and their beloved country.[245]

Of course, God's Word is a word for all people, so it should not surprise us if Psalm 137 rings true with people from any country who felt compelled to leave their native lands behind. In the United States, there is no doubt but that the English who first arrived—or later the Irish, Poles, Italians, Vietnamese, and all others—might identify with its sentiment. But there is one vital difference: With respect to these immigrant populations, mass immigration eventually slowed

[245] "Send Money to Latin America with Western Union," https://www.westernunion.com/au/en/send-money-to-latin-america.html (accessed November 3, 2017). The site lists over 32,000 agent locations throughout Latin America and the Caribbean.

to a trickle. For subsequent generations, the old country became something identified with their grandparents, or perhaps earlier generations; it was not their reality. However, with Latin America immigration, legal and illegal, always has been and will remain a constant, recharging the culture and those who live it with its enduring values and inconsistencies.

When all is said and done, Latino history underscores the sad reality that Hispanics never have had a real shepherd to guide them. Perhaps Simón Bolívar came close to being that leader for South America; he loved his *Gran Colombia* deeply. Yet Bolívar gave up in failure, confessing, "All who served the Revolution have plowed the sea." In expressing his frustration, Bolívar is not far from the Lord who also registered his own sadness over Israel's "lost sheep," a people unwilling or incapable of coming together under his caring wing (Luke 13:34). Bolívar died in Colombia of tuberculosis, but many historians believe it was the immensity of his country's dysfunction that really killed him. Like the Hebrews who desired the "cucumbers and the melons, the leeks and the onions and the garlic" (Num. 11:5) that kept them alive in Egypt, Hispanics are not likely to set aside those things that define them, but also enslave them.

Amazingly, some Hispanics are quite up front about this predicament. *Por Eso Estamos Como Estamos*, "This Is Why We Are the Way We Are," is a popular tune composed by *Los Intocables* (The Untouchables), a *Norteño* (Northern) band. The song gained almost immediate acclaim when released, but why? Listen to the song's refrain:

Por eso estamos como estamos,	This is why we are the way we are,
por eso nunca progresamos,	this is why we never progress (or get ahead),
si tal parece que gozamos	for we seem to enjoy (or relish),
poner las cosas al revés. [246]	putting (or arranging) things backwards.

[246] Los Intocables, "Por Eso Estamos Como Estamos," by Eduardo López, released 2009, track 12 *on Intocable—Classic*, Sony Music Latin, compact disc. Lyrics at URL: https://www.letras.com/los-apson/por-eso-estamos-como-estamos (accessed May 6, 2019).

But don't be fooled into thinking that musicians are the only ones who point out their problems. So true is this to the Latin American experience that eminent economist Carlos Elizondo Mayer-Serra adopted it as the title for his critique of the modern Mexican economy.[247] Note his economic assessment: "we never progress because we seem to enjoy putting things backwards." Meyer-Serra's title would have fallen flat if it had not resonated with pain and power—he was counting on it!

Critiquing Particular Cultural Traits

Oftentimes, our focus dictates how we evaluate something. Consider a beautiful rose. It is lovely, but can you get pricked if you're not careful when handling it? Is the Swiss Eiger not a majestic peak? Nevertheless, can seasoned mountain climbers lose their lives attempting to scale its "murder wall"? Few things are ever purely one thing or another, and this is especially true of cultures. If cultures have their deficiencies, they can also have their laudable traits.

Family

Take the issue of family. If Hispanics love their families one could easily ask, what culture doesn't? What may be important to underscore, however, is that this strong family tie is rooted to a great degree in the corporate mentality that has defined Latinos for generations.[248] If the Hispanic family is strong, it is probably because family members are taught to be interdependent, often making the values of the family indistinguishable

---

[247] Carlos Elizondo Mayer-Serra, *Por eso estamos como estamos. La economía política de un crecimiento mediocre* (México City: Debate Editorial, 2011). Mayer-Serra is a researcher and professor of politics at CIDE in México since 1991. He served as México's ambassador at OECD from 2004 until 2006. He studied international affairs at El Colegio de México. He has his Masters and PhD in political sciences from Oxford University, England.

[248] See Chapter 2, "Then Came Philosophy."

from their own. Many Hispanics grow up in very tight knit *pro-familia* households, where family always comes first.[249]

Still, though the Latino family is often depicted as strong, there are ominous signs that the modern Hispanic family is under stress. According to recent statistics, for example, 43 percent of Hispanic children born in the US are born to unwed mothers.[250] If this troubling fact doesn't challenge the rosy view that Latinos have strong family ties, then nothing will. It is only a matter of time before the absence of a strong father figure at home will lead to the inevitable problems that, in fact, are already present in many Hispanic communities.

More than anything else, the emergence of street gangs in the Latino *barrios* signals that all is not well in the home. Gangs thrive, as we know, to supplant the loss of a healthy family culture; and here is one instance, lamentably, where Hispanics excel. According to the National Gang Center, 46 percent of all gangs in the United States are Hispanic, beating the next group, African Americans, by 11 percent.[251] We can be thankful that the Justice Department is working hard to eliminate the vicious Salvadoran MS-13, but merely decimating one gang won't solve the problem. Whether the issue is drug abuse, dropout rates, violent crime, or rates of incarceration, the statistics reveal the grim reality that the healthy Hispanic family is under duress.

As a corollary to the issue, consider what illegal immigration creates on the other side of the border. Somewhere between eleven and twenty million Hispanic illegals in the US, mostly males, have left a huge vacuum in their native countries. As a result, many smaller villages have

---

[249] See Fabio Sabogal, et al., "Hispanic Familism and Acculturation: What Changes and What Doesn't?" *Hispanic Journal of Behavioral Sciences*, December 1, 1987, https://journals.sagepub.com/doi/abs/10.1177/07399863870094003 (accessed August 10, 2017).

[250] See Catherine Rampell, "Mapping Unwed Motherhood," *The New York Times*, May 2, 2013, http://economix.blogs.nytimes.com/2013/05/02/mapping-unwed-motherhood/?_r=0 (accessed August 8, 2016).

[251] For statistics on Hispanic gangs, see "Demographics: Age of Gang Members," National Gang Center, http://www.nationalgangcenter.gov/Survey-Analysis/Demographics (accessed August 10, 2017).

been emptied of adult men. As we should anticipate, this parental void creates a crisis for the rearing of children who lack a father figure. And so, it is bitterly ironic that wanting to meet the needs of the family often comes at the expense of the most vulnerable: the children they leave behind. Many of these children are ripe for the picking and are swept into the world of drug trafficking, prostitution, and slave rings, adding to the vicious crime gangs at home and exported to other places.[252] While Latinos do seek to keep their families whole, many soon discover that there is no decision made under duress that does not have serious and dark consequences.

Emotional Expression

On a lighter note, "Hispanics are people of the heart," cites a North American Mission Board publication, continuing, "a truth wrapped in cold logic without warmth of life and emotion is not very well-received."[253] Ricardo Lopez of Hispanic Research Inc., however, takes it a bit further, adding, "From the loud moaning of a man who just stubbed his toe, to the exaggerated screams of a mother whose child just took his first step, Latinos excel in the use of sound and facial expressions to convey emotion."[254] What can I say? Hispanics stand guilty as charged!

Take soccer. My mother, now almost ninety years old, acts like a teenager whenever her beloved Mexico is on the field. It is not unusual, as I call and ask how her day went, for her to tell me she was up in the wee hours of the morning watching her beloved *Rayados,* or *Tigeres* of Monterrey, playing a game. I am not a fan of soccer, but I have

---

[252] See http://immigrationinamerica.org/466-drug-trafficking.html (accessed August 10, 2017).

[253] North American Mission Board, *Reaching Hispanics in North America* (Alpharetta, GA: Church Planting Resource Library, 2009), 33, citing Alex. D. Montoya, *Hispanic Ministry in North America* (Grand Rapids, MI: Zondervan, 1987), 18.

[254] See Ricardo López, "Non-Verbal Latino Communication & Social Networking," Green Book Directory, May 6, 2010, http://www.greenbook.org/marketing-research.cfm/non-verbal-latino-communication-and-social-networking (accessed August 15, 2017).

watched a few matches over the years. Honestly, the games are notorious for low scoring, so when someone finally does score a point, the shout "gooooooollllllllll" can seem endless, letting fans release stored-up energy and emotion. The crowds go wild, flags unfurl, patriotism gushes forth, people sing in unison, and my mom—cloistered in her bedroom, separated by hundreds of miles and time zones—joins the celebration, giddy in the excitement of the moment, but only if her team scored.

When Latinos show extravagant emotion, it is not so much that they don't value the importance of phlegmatic logic and reason. They use reason to make important decisions all the time. Yet, there is no "reason," many would argue, why a decision cannot be made with emotional investment; this is why Spanish-language *telenovelas* are so popular. If we ask why emotional expression is so evident among Latinos, I cannot help but point to the baroque environment that nurtures the release of deep emotional feeling. This often happens because whether the facts bear it out or not, Latinos tend to think of important decisions as part of the struggle they have had to endure. For example, buying a modest home for their family is not just an economic decision, or a forgone conclusion. Money for the down payment is hard-won. Often, Hispanics see such major purchases as milestones in their struggle to survive. If they should show what others might see as exaggerated emotion, they just don't get it. For many, strong feelings communicate genuine heartfelt involvement.

Social Attachments

It is safe to say that the corporate mindset also undergirds the attachments Latinos make with business associates, neighbors, and friends. As in other cultures, relationships often lead to more than simply getting together to eat a meal. Often a commonality of religion is taken for granted, and in due time, the strength of the relationship will be tested religiously. True friends know they will likely be asked to attend their friend's children's rites of passage such as a daughter's *quinceañera*, or be asked to be a *padrino* or a *madrina*, godparent, for a newborn child, and so on. The relationship of a godparent, in particular, is taken very seriously.

For Hispanics, relationships that were forged early on have a way of enduring. Personally, it is hard for me to think of my father without also remembering Jesús, affectionately nicknamed *La Borrega*, the lamb, because of his curly hair. My father had many acquaintances, but I grew up thinking Jesús was an uncle. Though he was very close to my father, his passing did not dissolve the tie he had to my family. *La Borrega,* who lives in southern Mexico, made the time to stop over in San Antonio to see Irene, my mother, along with his dear friend's four sons, José Guadalupe, Rodolfo, Angelo, and Alejandro. And though he was traveling more than 2,500 miles by car to visit his own family in Chicago, this elderly man, now in his eighties, found it necessary to reconnect. I am glad he did, for I was reminded again of his love for Rodolfo, my dad. I had never known this, but Jesús was so selfless that he gave (not loaned) my dad a car to drive his young wife back to Mexico, because she could not bear the cold winters in Chicago. It was his generosity that contributed to Alejandro, the youngest son, being born a Mexican.

Dignity

As we might expect, dignity is important across all cultures. One of its aspects is the hope that one will be valued as a human being. For Latinos in general, Mexicans especially, their quest for dignity may however be shaped by perceptions concerning the conquest. In his book *El Laberinto de la Soledad,* Mexican poet laureate Octavio Paz believes Mexicans live with a conflicted memory of *La Malinche,* Hernando Cortez' indigenous mistress, giving birth to the mestizo throngs.[255] According to Paz, Mexico's deep-seated feelings of "inferiority" can be attributed to the spiritual rape and conquest of Mexico. Alfredo Mirandé, however,

[255] Octavio Paz, *El Laberinto de la Soledad,* Mexico: Fondo de Cultura Economica, 1950.

in his *Hombres y Machos,* does not subscribe to Paz' theory that Latin America's painful history is the dominant shaper of her self-identity. Mirandé's research suggests there is no one overriding template. Certainly trustworthiness, honesty, determination to provide for the family, love and loyalty to family and friends, as well as a robust sense of self-reliance, are important shapers of self-worth. But to be fair, the traits Mirandé identifies apply across diverse cultures.

From another perspective, Latino machismo can also have a dark side, which can skew one's understanding of self-respect, particularly when underachievement is often attached to one's essential nature.[256] As to women, one should discard the stereotype of the submissive woman who is subservient to the assertive man. Mirandé shows that qualities such as pride, dignity, courage, perseverance in the face of adversity, and selflessness, often ascribed to males, are also seen as qualities of Latino femininity.[257] The fact is, Hispanic women can be fierce and docile, stubborn and submissive, caring toward others, yet stoic in the face of danger; none of these qualities are mutually exclusive.

Hispanic Corporatism

What are we to make of the Hispanic attitude toward family and, more generally, their sense of togetherness? From a biblical perspective, the importance of community is impossible to overlook. This togetherness, for better or for worse, is seen in the first chapters of Genesis. Sin, as it turns out, is never just an individual problem. When Eve fell into sin, it was inevitable that Adam should also fall. Have you ever asked why? While it is true that God fashioned Eve from one of Adam's ribs, it is just as telling to note Adam's keen sense of discernment. Adam is the one who said of Eve, "This is now bone of my bones, and flesh of my flesh; she shall be called Woman, because she was taken out of Man"

[256] The word *macho* is of Aztec origin and means self-image.
[257] Mirandé, *Hombres y Machos*, 143.

(Gen. 2:23). Generations later, when Genesis was written, the writer interprets Adam's statement and adds, "For this reason a man shall leave his father and his mother and be joined to his wife; and they shall become one flesh" (v. 24). Thus, their children are fated to deal with the tragic consequences. Sin, in fact, is so corporate in its scope that within a few generations, God decides to wipe the whole human family off the face of the earth, leaving one family to survive and repopulate the world.

As biblical history unfolds, this corporate reality is seen in a number of other ways. Yes, individuals stand out for their faithfulness, or their wickedness, but most biblical characters are revealed in the context of their clan, tribe, or people. Jesus, the figure to which the Scriptures point, merits two genealogies linking him to the Jewish patriarchs and to the human race.

Take salvation. The individual's need of redemption is undeniable, but I am concerned that we fail to see just how often the New Testament writers emphasize its communal nature. Peter reminds us that we are each living stones, being built up into a spiritual house of worship (1 Pet. 2:20). Paul speaks of this same corporality when he says we are "fellow citizens with the saints . . . [being] built on the foundation of the apostles and prophets, Christ Jesus Himself being the corner stone, in whom the whole building, being fitted together, is growing into a holy temple in the Lord" (Eph. 2:19–21). The church must never forget its togetherness. Thus, is it any wonder the writer of Hebrews encourages believers not to forsake their assembling together (Heb. 10:24–25)? Vital things happen when God's family gathers—things that cannot happen when we live apart from each other.

Overwhelmingly, the Bible focuses on our eternal togetherness as God's people. While the invitation is certainly extended to us individually (Matt. 11:28; Rev. 22:17), introverts will find life impossible in eternity. Hebrews says that we will arrive at "the city of the living God, the heavenly Jerusalem, and to myriads of angels, to the general assembly and church of the firstborn who are enrolled in heaven" (Heb. 12:22–23). The book of Revelation adds that a great multitude, which no one could count, will be assembled consisting of redeemed people "from every nation and all tribes and peoples and tongues" (Rev. 7:9–10). Given the value the Bible gives to human relationship in all its variations, this writer will not reject something so near to human existence and spiritual life. When we were lost, we were alienated from God and from each other. But in Christ, we have been brought near to him and to each other. One last point: Hispanics tend to carry a community focus with them wherever they attend church. They are likely to think of the church as a family, and make judgments accordingly, based on their view of what a family should be.

Unequal Egalitarianism

While Latinos are known for their strong familial ties, there is nevertheless a sense of organic inequality that characterizes hierarchical society in Latin American countries. Here, the New Testament challenges Latino culture, for it emphasizes equality in at least two dramatic ways. In his letter to the Romans, Paul makes it emphatic that God views us all the same. "[T]here is no distinction," Paul says, "for all have sinned and fall short of the glory of God" (Rom. 3:22–23). Yes, we are all equally guilty of sin. But if we all sin after the common manner, God also offers the promise of salvation to us all, with no one meriting it more than the other. In his epistle to the Galatians, Paul declares:

> For you are all sons of God through faith in Christ Jesus. For all of you who were baptized into Christ have clothed yourselves with Christ. There is neither Jew nor Greek, there is neither slave nor free man, there is neither male nor female; for you are all one in Christ Jesus. And if you belong to Christ, then you are Abraham's offspring, heirs according to promise. (Gal 3:26–29)

As this passage shows, it is because we have been made members of the family of faith that we can no longer sustain the notion that some people merit a more privileged standing before God. God's view of us is filtered through his Son, overcoming the racial, ethnic, gender, or economic prejudices that defines hierarchical society.

In my estimation, Hispanics are challenged with two beliefs that flow from a problem with understanding biblical equality. In the arena of religion, Latinos tend to view certain members of the family, or of their social sphere, as inherently spiritually worthier. Thus, it is not unusual to view grandmothers, wives, aunts, unmarried spinsters as more *sufridas*—more longsuffering, and thus closer to God than the men of the family. Pablo Alberto Deiros notes that when it comes to religion, it is the Latin-American mother who carries the burden, and is seen as the main intercessor for the family.[258] As a result of this popular idea, religious duties are often seen as the domain of the women, their duty being to pray for the family and particularly for the men in their lives. The Bible, of course, nowhere ascribes women a greater godliness by virtue of their gender, and neither does the Catholic Church. That said, this entrenched belief is not likely to dissipate, for as Deiros observes, this characteristic is the "inconsistent manifestation of emotional patterns, which underlie Latino life."[259] The whole thing is wrapped up in the *machismo-hembrismo* relationship throughout Latin America.[260]

A related aspect that flows from seeing women as somehow more adapted to the spiritual needs of the family is its support for Marian devotion throughout the region. As we have noted earlier, virtually every country, whether large or small, has at least one "Virgin Mary" to turn to. This is by design, for among Catholics, Mary, in her assorted manifestations, is always more affectionate and accessible to the cries of her children than God himself. But think of the implication of such

---

[258] Deiros, *Historia del Cristianismo en America Latina,* 186.

[259] Ibid.

[260] Eugene Nida, *Understanding Latin Americans: With Special Reference to Religious Values and Movements* (South Pasadena, CA: William Carey Library, 1974), 67–71. Nida discusses the *machismo-hembrismo* contrast in the area of family and religion.

a hyper-feminine spirituality. If the women in the family have a closer relationship to God, and Mary, the "Mother of God," reaches down from above responding to the cries of her children, the loop is closed, the religious needs of the home are covered, and the male's spirituality becomes optional rather than vital. Additionally, since the Roman Catholic priesthood is totally male and celibate, it leaves men who relish their manly appetites thinking that religious duties are beyond their spiritual abilities and expectations. In our estimation, such beliefs cause many men to practice a more passive faith, rather than one of active involvement.

Of course, from a biblical perspective, the very notion that God is distant and impassive to the cries of his people obliterates the teaching of the Bible. The gospel so wonderfully revealed in the New Testament does not spring up carelessly, but is rooted in the history and promise of that same Old Testament God. Paul understood this when he tied the gospel to its prophetic promises (Rom. 1:2). The author of Hebrews declares that the God who had spoken through the prophets was now speaking through Christ, his Son (Heb. 1:1–2). Peter also links the Old Testament prophets with the glorious salvation revealed in Christ (1 Pet. 1:10–11). We could continue, but the point is clear: Any culture that minimizes the role of men in matters of faith, elevating women to a favored status, must be seriously challenged on its biblical merits.

The Struggle for Survival

Are there other cultural distinctives that are quintessential of the Latino? Here we pause to consider the introduction of a certain animal species, *Bos Taurus* to be specific. Clearly, the part the bull plays in Spain cannot be overlooked. Some scholars believe Phoenician Baal worshipers were the first to introduce the bull to the peninsula. Or it may be that bullfighting was brought into provincial Hispania by Rome as a substitute for, or perhaps to complement, gladiatorial games. Whatever its origins, the bull is a prominent religious figure found in many ancient civilizations. The Sumerian Gilgamesh Epic depicts the killing of the bull of heaven. Upon Moses' delay from Mt. Sinai, the first instinct for rebellious Hebrews coming out of Egypt was to worship a deity in the fashion of a calf, a young bull (Exod. 32:1–8). The cult animal associated with Ba'al worship, and which proved to be the bane of Israel's downfall, was the bull. This powerful beast has had mythical meaning across cultures and, in Spain, the bull became the archetype for all that its people would have to conquer.

There is no doubt that Spaniards revere and respect the raw strength of the *toro.* Bullfighting isn't just a sport like any game that involves a spherical leather object; issues of life and death are always at stake.[261] In Spain and Latin America, bullfighting is metaphorical for man's struggle against the brutal forces of nature. At no time has this struggle been more brutally depicted than when one menacing jet-black beast faced Emilio Muñoz, a thirty-one-year-old *torero,* scheduled to slay the animal.[262] The bull's bloody struggle left such an impression that the Lamborghini automobile manufacturer named a car *Aventador* in homage to this animal's fighting spirit.

Spaniards and Latin Americans make heroes of their bullfighters occasionally of a bull as well); they become legendary, bathed in glory. There isn't a little boy, and even some little girls, that will not aspire to be a *matador.* Young men dream of becoming that skilled slayer of the *toro*—that indomitable force that can "gore" dreams and hopes in an instant, but without which there can also never be any champions. In my youth, I remember hearing of *El Cordovéz,* who was slated to perform at the *Plaza de Toros* in Monterrey, Mexico, providing me the opportunity to see one such hero. Over his thirteen-year long career

---

[261] Judith Noble, Jaime Lacasa, *The Hispanic Way: Aspects of Behavior, Attitudes, and Customs in the Spanish-Speaking World* (Chicago, IL: Passport Books, 1993), 9–13.

[262] The slaying of *Aventador* happened at the *Plaza de Toros* in Zaragoza, Spain, October 15, 1993.

(1959–1972), Manuel Benítez Pérez faced hundreds of bulls, killing a record sixty-four in August of 1965 alone.[263]

Spanish and Latin American history is tragic in many ways, but it is punctuated with heroes, larger-than-life figures like Rodrigo Díaz de Vivar (c. 1043–1099), popularly known as *El Cid.* What is less known is that, to Spaniards, Vivar was *El Campeador*, "outstanding warrior," or "the one who stands in the battlefield." Similarly, Mexico has bathed in glory *los Niños Héroes,* six teenage military cadets who fought and died defending Chapultepec Castle from US forces during the 1847 Mexican-American War. According to legend, in an act of bravery, one cadet, Juan Escutia, wrapped himself in the Mexican national flag and jumped from atop the castle to his death, to keep it from falling into enemy hands. As Alberto Deiros has so aptly noted, "aggressiveness, ferociousness, and belligerence were elements characteristic of the Hispanic spirit. Such attitudes are maintained through the cult of valor and heroism."[264] Of course, winning the victory has its glory, but fighting valiantly to the death earns eternal admiration, all of which brings us to a controversial Latin warrior.

Throughout the 1970s there was no one who more personified the indomitable fighting spirit of Latin Americans than the Panamanian boxer, *manos de piedra* (hands of stone), Roberto Duran. Thus, when this reigning welterweight uttered those now infamous words, "*no mas,*" he set off a firestorm of controversy among Hispanics, which continues today. Did Duran really cower on that 25th day of November 1980? For those who believe he quit for fear of being knocked out, Duran will forever be a disgrace. But most Latinos have arrived at a different opinion. The pugilist waved Sugar Ray Leonard off because Leonard was running around the ring and not really trying to fight him like two

---

263 To be accurate, bullfighting never caught on in all the Latin American countries. Mexico City has the largest bullfighting stadium in the world, seating more than 48,000 people. Today, bullfighting is practiced in Mexico, Colombia, Peru, and Venezuela. It has been banned in Argentina, Cuba, and the Canary Islands.

264 Deiros, *Historia del cristianismo en America Latina,* 260.

warriors on the battlefield.[265] Duran had showed up to fight, not dance, and therein lies the issue. Whether it is bullfighting, boxing, or any other form of hostility, more so than winning, Latinos value the struggle to survive against relentless forces arrayed against them. With respect to bullfighting, I realize that the brutality of killing an animal before a throng of onlookers turns people off. Nevertheless, if bullfighting is bloody, it mirrors the inhumane struggle many Hispanics experience in their fight to survive.

The question to ask, however, is, does the Bible affirm the legitimacy of such a harsh interpretation of life's struggle? In his first epistle to the Corinthians, Paul elaborates on his own experience, and he does not sanitize it. Note the gritty corporal metaphors he uses:

> Therefore I run in such a way, as not without aim; I box in such a way, as not beating the air; but I discipline my body and make it my slave, so that, after I have preached to others, I myself will not be disqualified. (1 Cor. 9:26–27)

Elsewhere, in the epistle to the Galatians, Paul turns to the physical marks on his body (6:17), which he has earned for the sake of the cross. And in 2 Corinthians, he reacts against those who would dare to question his apostleship. Far from pointing to his authoritative epistles, Paul enumerates his traumatic experiences and physical sufferings in detail. "Are they servants of Christ?" he asks.

> I more so; in far more labors, in far more imprisonments, beaten times without number, often in danger of death. Five times I received from the Jews thirty-nine lashes. Three times I was beaten with rods, once I was stoned, three times I was

---

[265] See Frank Lotierzo, "Duran Should Never Again Answer Why He Quit Leonard Rematch," The Sweet Science, October 17, 2013, http://www.thesweetscience.com/feature-articles/17416-duran-should-never-again-answer-why-he-quit-during-rematch-with-leonard (accessed August 29, 2017).

> shipwrecked, a night and a day I have spent in the deep. I have been on frequent journeys, in dangers from rivers, dangers from robbers, dangers from my countrymen, dangers from the Gentiles, dangers in the city, dangers in the wilderness, dangers on the sea, dangers among false brethren; I have been in labor and hardship, through many sleepless nights, in hunger and thirst, often without food, in cold and exposure. (2 Cor. 11:23–27)

There is no getting around it: Death, blood, sacrifice, and struggle are integral to the gospel, seen at the foot of a blood-soaked cross. Like Christ who was destined to be brutally sacrificed (John 1:29, 36; 1 Pet. 1:19), Christians are also admonished to "fight the good fight" (1 Tim. 1:18, 6:12; 2 Tim. 4:7), to endure great conflicts and suffering (Heb. 10:32; 1 Pet. 2:20), and to take up the weapons of spiritual warfare (Eph. 6:2). While some of the language is metaphorical, much of it portends a physical struggle, as faithful martyrs across two millennia would testify.

Superstition, Astrology, Necromancy, etc.

Long before she turned to Christ in faith, my mother was like many Hispanics who turn to superstitious practices as a way of life. One occasion concerned my oldest brother, who came down with a high fever while still a baby. Since it happened so suddenly, my mom's first instinct was to think that someone had probably cast a spell, looking at him with an evil eye (*el ojo*). When her two sisters agreed as to the probable cause, *China,* as nicknamed, took her infant son José to a *curandero*, a witch doctor in the neighborhood. The cure called for the performance of a ritual egg ceremony over the child's body. To date, my mother insists that upon the *curandero's* cure, the fever left my brother almost as quickly as it had come. Some fifteen years later, when my father decided to move the family from Monterrey to San Antonio, she again turned to superstition. Unbeknownst to my father, my mother visited a local *bruja* (witch) to have tarot cards read. The reason: nothing more sinister than a mother's apprehension, wanting to know if things would go well for her family, as we moved from Mexico to the United States.

One telling thing is that my mother was also a devout Roman Catholic. As soon as we arrived in San Antonio, she found the nearest Catholic church and went to the Ash Wednesday mass. My mom, like so many other Hispanics, recited the rosary and prayed to the *Virgen de Guadalupe*, to the saints, and to God for the protection of her husband and family. She sought the comfort of the church and parish priest, yet she saw no inconsistency in turning to superstitious remedies as well. How on Earth can this be?

Perhaps visuals play a part; after all, most superstitions are not totally pagan in their expression. Tied as they are to the church through a long syncretistic process, the rituals and paraphernalia associated with many of its practices come right out of the Church. *Curanderos*, thus, may perform ancient rituals, yet they will also use rosaries, candles with images of Mary or some saint, perform a mass, sprinkle holy water, and even wear clerical vestments. All this has the net effect of confusing people who are biblically uninformed. But is there more?

As is commonly known, parachurch ministries often come into being because of a need, or perceived need, which the local church has failed to address. Sensing the weakness of the church in a specific area, a non-profit will rise to satisfy the need. As history shows, the Catholic Church failed to put forth a persuasive alternative to pre-Columbian and African worldviews. Yet, rather than vanquishing these primitive beliefs through a sound Christ-centered apologetic, the Church did not deem them worthy of serious attention. But the spiritual need that people sensed, and which their animistic beliefs addressed, didn't go away because they were ignored. To the contrary, it was superstition—the counterpart to the evangelical parachurch phenomena—which came forth to fill the void.

Today, superstition is rampant and intensified by its popularity in mass media, which casts it as a harmless game that may work, who knows. Turn on your TV and go to any Spanish-language programming, and it won't be long before an astrologer—often with a sexy, barely clad female assistant—begins giving his or her version of the daily horoscope. Who among Latinos has never heard of Walter Mercado? But he isn't the only one. Today, Alberto Roy, Hector Faisel, Mario Vannucci, David Hernandez, and others flood radio and television, feeding the fascination and devotion many Hispanics have for such beliefs.

Hispanic superstitions are ancient; thus, most Latinos grow up believing that religion and superstitions are two sides of the same coin. Yes, Hispanics believe in an all-powerful God, yet the fact that *curanderos* and *santeros* can also demonstrate what would seem to be miraculous power and insight is proof enough for the need to hedge one's prospects with their wisdom and protections.

From a biblical perspective, spiritual forces are real. When Paul asks about those things that can eat away at our relationship with the risen Christ, he doesn't simply speak of such things as unbelief, or spiritual apathy. He also points to sentient entities that will never register on any scanning device (Rom. 8:31–39). He doesn't just speak about the "what" but of the "who," and the who are angels, principalities, and powers who seek to separate us from the love of God, which is in Christ Jesus.

There is no doubt but that Paul's spiritual purview extends beyond the material world into the unseen realm, but it is there where similarity with Latino superstitious beliefs ends. Unlike so many Hispanics who have no problem turning both to religion and to superstition, Paul keeps to the unqualified avoidance of any connection with superstitions. In the Old Testament, the injunction against dabbling in superstitions is clear and absolute:

> Do not turn to mediums or spiritists; do not seek them out to be defiled by them. I am the Lord your God. (Lev. 19:31; cf. 20:6)

> And beware not to lift up your eyes to heaven and see the sun and the moon and the stars, all the host of heaven, and be drawn away and worship them and serve them, those which the LORD your God has allotted to all the peoples under the whole heaven. (Deut. 4:19)
>
> When you enter the land which the LORD your God gives you, you shall not learn to imitate the detestable things of those nations. There shall not be found among you anyone who makes his son or his daughter pass through the fire, one who uses divination, one who practices witchcraft, or one who interprets omens, or a sorcerer, or one who casts a spell, or a medium, or a spiritist, or one who calls up the dead. (Deut. 18:9–11)

When God says through his prophet, "For You have abandoned Your people, the house of Jacob, because they are filled with influences from the east, and they are soothsayers like the Philistines" (Isa. 2:6), he leaves no doubt but that such practices are foreign to those who claim to have a relationship with the Living God.

Rather than turning to superstitious beliefs for health, happiness, and prosperity, the apostle takes a belligerent, albeit Spirit-driven, attitude against them. Rather than affirming the validity of spiritual wisdom and knowledge, Paul makes known the manifold wisdom of God "to the rulers and the authorities in the heavenly places" (Eph. 3:10). Paul is assured of their defeat through Christ's cross (Col. 2:15). As such, Paul knows he can wage a winning war to bring spiritual forces of darkness under the authority of Christ (2 Cor. 10:3–6). In this struggle, Paul does not fight with his own strength, for he has been fitted with divine armor, which empowers him to stand in victory (Eph. 6:10–17).

At a time when some denominations are embarrassed by the supernatural, relegating the demonic to psychiatric or psychological issues, we can be thankful that most Hispanics know the spiritual world to be real. That said, Hispanic culture is appallingly infused with superstitious and syncretistic beliefs, and is grossly uninformed concerning satanic deception. Hispangelicals will need to commit to a sound doctrine of demonology and be alert, knowing that real satanic forces work to keep the Latino community in spiritual bondage and ignorance.

Fatalism

Any evaluation of the Hispanic mind cannot overlook the subject of fatalism, a tendency to believe that the things that happen in one's life are predetermined, ultimately caused by external forces. For Latinos, depending on their spirituality, or lack thereof, those external forces can be the biblical Judeo-Christian God, or they can be animistic, even ancestral forces that control the unseen world.

One need not be religious to be fatalistic, either. Secular Hispanics can also exhibit a fatalistic attitude when the social structures set in place long ago never seem to change, consigning them and their loved ones to a predetermined future. The point to underscore is the belief that whether through accident of history or by design, those externals are intractable obstacles that keep the individual—indeed, whole classes of people—from achieving any significant progress, despite their best efforts.

Some have questioned whether Latinos are prone to fatalism, and we are safe in asserting that while they do not have a monopoly on it, Latinos are considerable stockholders. That said, the strength of this attitude can vary, with such factors as age, social class, and national origin all playing a role. Certainly, those who have lived in North America are less likely to think so pessimistically, but this is not to say they have no exposure to it. Latino culture itself is a breeding ground for fatalistic language and presuppositions. Thus, even if a person is not a principled fatalist, it can be a convenient red herring when having to account for some failure. *Maldita suerte* (damned luck) is often voiced when some elusive hope fails to materialize. After all is said and done, *que sera, sera*—the fatalistic refrain is popular for a reason.

Does the Bible recognize fatalism? The book of Ecclesiastes describes what most would describe as a fatalistic outlook. In chapter 2:11–15, the preacher notes:

> Thus, I considered all my activities which my hands had done and the labor which I had exerted, and behold all was vanity and striving after wind and there was no profit under the sun.
>
> So I turned to consider wisdom, madness and folly, for what *will* the man *do* who will come after the king except what has already been done? And I saw that wisdom excels folly as light excels darkness. The wise man's eyes are in his head, but the fool walks in darkness. And yet I know that one fate befalls them both. Then I said to myself, "As is the fate of the fool, it will also befall me. Why then have I been extremely wise?" So I said to myself, "This too is vanity."

That this passage is dripping with fatalism there should be no doubt. However, this attitude is a far cry from the fatalistic attitude to which Latinos are prone. Latino fatalism can be very self-absorbed, as Latinos can believe they have been singled out for a perpetual letdown. The preacher, however, describes a truth that all people are consigned to—the young and old, the rich and poor, the wise as well as the foolish. For the preacher, the essence of fatalism, which he acknowledges, is the sure fate of death that awaits us all. Note how he makes this point clear in chapter 3:19–20:

> For the fate of the sons of men and the fate of beasts is the same. As one dies so dies the other; indeed, they all have the same breath and there is no advantage for man over beast, for all is vanity. . . . All came from the dust and all return to the dust.

In considering this statement, we should not fail to notice the preacher's wisdom. Solomon basically reiterates what God had pronounced upon fallen humanity: "For you are dust, and to dust you shall return" (Gen. 3:19). Nevertheless, is there any other condition that speaks to this issue of fate? Isaiah says:

> But you who forsake the LORD, who forget My holy mountain, who set a table for Fortune, and who fill cups with mixed wine for Destiny, I will destine you for the sword, and all of you shall bow down to the slaughter. Because I called, but you did not answer; I spoke, but you did not hear. And you did evil in My sight, and chose that in which I did not delight. (Isa. 65:11–12)

As we can see, the fate that awaits some is not fickle, driven by sheer whim. Rather, it is earned, received for the wickedness of their deeds (e.g., Amos 1–2; Nah. 3; Obad. 1; et al.).

In taking a broader view, we can see that Scripture indeed supports the concept of fatalism, but not as Hispanics and others often think of it. Far from it being applied to one people and not others, far from it being a detrimental fixture, which always results in futility, biblical fatalism is universal and consistent. It is universal because all people die and return to the dust from which they were formed. It is consistent, because all people will carry with them their life's moral record to be judged accordingly. Paul makes this clear:

> The sins of some men are quite evident, going before them to judgment; for others, their sins follow after. (1 Tim. 5:24)

In light of this awful and fateful prospect, the life we live is so fleeting (James 4:14), so temporary (Ps. 89:47), so short (Luke 12:25), that we ought to devote ourselves to those things which truly shape our fate. The wise preacher admonishes all people to "fear God and keep His commandments, because this applies to every person. For God will bring every act to judgment, everything which is hidden, whether it is good or evil" (Eccles. 12:13–14). While politics and world circumstances can certainly circumscribe our temporal prospects, there is nothing that can keep the believer from the love of God if they seek it with all their heart (Rom. 8:31–39).

Hardwired Latinos

While many Americans have been conflicted over the recent trend to take a knee during the playing of the National Anthem at pro football games, or whether to demonstrate a love of country generally, Hispanics who come from Latin America tend to be patriotic to a fault. We can see such displays of patriotism in each one of the twenty Latin American countries, of course, but what is amazing is how they don't check or tone down such exhibitions when they cross into the United States. It was about ten years ago that we saw the American flag trampled to the ground, only to see a Mexican flag raised at a US post office in Maywood, California.[266] And this was no isolated incident. In 2009, a bar owner in Reno, Nevada, was so blatant in his nationalism he hoisted a Mexican flag above the American flag in plain sight for all to see.[267] It happened again in San Diego in 2014, and as recently as September of 2018 the Mexican flag was hoisted defiantly in Brooklyn, Iowa, where Mollie Tibbetts was allegedly murdered by Cristhian Bahena Rivera, an undocumented Mexican citizen.[268] We can be sure that as the Latino population grows, such displays of nationalism will only grow and become more blatant.

As we might expect, such actions can evoke strong emotions from those of us who love the USA, but it should also cause us to seek understanding. After all, this behavior drips with irony, not to mention

---

[266] See "Mexican Flag Flies at U.S. Post Office," WND TV, August 29, 2006, http://www.wnd.com/2006/08/37688 (accessed July 15, 2017).

[267] The incident was originally reported by Channel 2 News in Reno, Nevada, on July 10, 2017.

[268] See Ed Streker, "Mexican Flag Flies Proudly over the town Where Illegal Alien Kills Mollie Tibbetts," American Thinker, September 2, 2018, https://www.americanthinker.com/blog/2018/09/mexican_flag_flies_proudly_over_town_where_illegal_alien_killed_mollie_tibbetts.html (accessed September 21, 2018).

bizarreness, given that most foreign Hispanics have a general disdain for the deplorable way of life back home and the politicians who perpetuate it. In light of such drastic realities, is it not puzzling that those who rely so desperately on America's economic opportunities still feel the instinct to glory in their national pride?

This can be explained, however, when we begin to appreciate a distinct cultural phenomenon, which resonates throughout Latin America. As noted earlier, Howard J. Wiarda reminds us of the "corporatist" and "organic" worldview that most Latinos embrace. In its heyday, Latin America endorsed a social structure that ingrained fierce loyalty. For more than three centuries (1492–1821), the church and state drilled into the Latin American people a belief that, like a human body, they had a blood tie to country and church. Hispanics continue to hold these beliefs deeply, regardless how inept or dysfunctional their leaders may be at any given point in time. It is startling to see the differences between Anglo Americans and Latinos, in the way they tend to promote their native countries. While some Americans feel embarrassment for their country's stunning successes, poor Hispanics glory in a land that has given them little more than a pittance.

Though most of those that come to this country illegally are economically poor, they consider themselves culturally rich, for the one thing that poverty can never take away is their hardwired connection to their native land. In this, I am reminded of a part of a song my mother taught my son to sing: "*Méjico, Méjico, te llevo en el corazón*" (Mexico, Mexico, I carry you in my heart). While my son was born in Waco, Texas, she was doing what comes natural to her, attempting to plant her ideology on foreign soil, in her grandson's young mind. For Latinos, this is a love so deeply ingrained that it crosses the border with them. They owe undying loyalty to their mother country, even if she has failed them. Thus, for many undocumented, Mexico, or Colombia, or Nicaragua, or Peru, or any other country, their land exists wherever they happen to be. For most foreign-born Hispanics, "homeland" is a state of being, not just a country.

So, what does the Bible have to say about such dogged devotion to one's nationality? Generally, people should love and showcase their country with pride. As Israel wandered in the wilderness, the individual tribes were given their own standards to rally the people together. Thus, Numbers 2:2 says:

> The sons of Israel shall camp, each by his own standard, with the banners of their fathers' households; they shall camp around the tent of meeting at a distance.

This verse is significant, for it addresses the Israelites in their desert wandering. While they had not as yet taken possession of the lands each tribe would possess, the tribe needed a symbol to rally around. These standards served them well through their sojourn in the wilderness of Zin. This leads us to maintain that there is nothing inherently wrong with doing all that is possible to gather together as a community of Honduran, or Colombian, or Cuban pilgrims to keep their heritage and national pride alive, while living in a foreign land. We know this happens in some countries as ethnic communities gather to celebrate their own heritage.

That said, disrespecting the host country goes beyond the pale. When Jesus took the Roman coin, he not only acknowledged the sovereignty of the Roman state, but the duty to pay due homage to Rome (Luke 20:25). Similarly, both apostles Paul and Peter recognized the responsibility to honor the existing civil institutions and authorities (Rom. 13:7; 1 Pet. 2:13, 17). Though Paul traveled throughout the empire, at no time did he ever disrespect roman officials, its institutions, or its symbols of authority. Ultimately, people can love their countries and show it, but it is the height of hypocrisy to disrespect the foreign country that shelters them.

Conclusion

In assessing the Hispanic mind, I have tried to focus on those aspects that seem to be common among Latinos, but we confess that there are always exceptions. And, in just about every case, characteristic traits can vary according to age, sex, and the person's personal or family origins. Sometimes people will hold certain traits in check, only to vent them when they find themselves in a crowd, letting the herd mentality take over. While it is unlikely that our cultural profile fits any one person to a T, I am confident that most Hispanics will find something and perhaps many things that resonate with them personally, or with things they have experienced within the Latino community.

From a biblical perspective, all followers of Jesus should know that there is no ethnicity that does not have its troubling traits. Psalm 2 indicts all cultures with willful belligerence:

> Why are the nations in an uproar, and the peoples devising a vain thing? The kings of the earth take their stand, and the rulers take counsel together Against the Lord and against His Anointed, saying, "Let us tear their fetters apart And cast away their cords from us!" (vv. 1–2).

To be sure, all cultures have laudable traits, yet they also tend to tear the fetters and cords of God away, seeking their own self-made path and destiny. Knowing how prone nations can be to rebellion, believers temper their enthusiasm with informed biblical sobriety. Ultimately, all believers should know that we are also citizens of a greater kingdom that will one day permeate the world, whose architect and builder is God (Heb. 11:10).

And what of Hispangelicals, who often feel that they can no longer embrace the culture that birthed them? What of Hispanic evangelicals who pull away from their communities and families for fear of compromising their evangelical faith? For such people, the question of their relationship to the Latino world is a real issue, not merely academic. How do we practice being in the world, yet knowing we are not of our former world (John 15:19)? To parrot H. Richard Niebuhr, should our approach be Christ against culture, Christ of culture, Christ above culture, Christ and culture in paradox, or Christ transforming culture?[269] For myself, my views on Latino culture have weaved through all of Niebuhr's options, evolving and maturing through the span of my life. But, through it all, Hispangelicals have not been redeemed to retreat into the sanctuary of four church walls. Since we never stop being Latinos, an important aspect of our mission is to manifest what redeemed culture could be in a Latino context, and this we will seek to flesh out in the following chapter.

[269] H. Richard Niebuhr, *Christ and Culture* (New York: Harper & Row, 1975).

CHAPTER SEVEN

Then Came the Hispangelical's Challenge

If you aren't in over your head, how do you know how tall you are?

T.S. Eliot[270]

In his study of the Hispanic condition, Ilan Stavans joins in the chorus and agrees with others, confessing that Latinos have certainly been "enchanted with the past," with safeguarding "what is gone."[271] Stavans believes this cultural stasis, however, is not true to the Hispanic world, but is a distortion heaped upon it over centuries of Eurocentric dominance.[272] Nevertheless, this influential writer is comforted in the knowledge that "Hispanics have carried on a solid, ongoing search for an authentic collective identity."[273] Still, after a search that has continued for more than two centuries (ca. 1810–2017), has it yielded results? Most Latino thinkers who sense the magnitude of the issue are less than

[270] Quote widely attributed to T. S. Eliot, source unknown.
[271] Stavans, *The Hispanic Condition,* 215.
[272] Ibid.
[273] Ibid.

optimistic and some have lost hope altogether. Celebrated critic, philologist, and university professor Pedro Henríquez Ureña believed the search was a nonstarter—for everything about Latino culture, including its language, pointed to replication and colonial redundancy rather than to originality.[274] Upon careful review of the leading Latino voices, it would be fair to say that the jury is still out on the success of the search for an authentic Hispanic identity. For a good many philosophers and intellectuals, nothing of any promise appears on the horizon. But have they been looking with total objectivity?

When we began this study, we noted the entrenched ideology that defined the Hispanic world for more than four centuries, and yet it was within the flurry of that ongoing context that the Hispangelical emerged. In the earliest decades of this unprecedented shift, the Latino evangelical could have been dismissed as some quirky aberration, but their growing presence screams for serious reassessment. Hispangelicalism cannot be explained away as some fit of "religious zeal," thereby denying its claims. At some point—and now is the time—Latinos should consider whether something radically new has happened. Is the Hispanic evangelical inextricably tied to the Latino's "circumstance," as thoughtful thinkers have understood it, or does their embrace of the gospel offer an authentic way forward?[275]

No one should harbor naïve beliefs that the Latino circumstance will change on its own. And it is understandable, given the lack of consensus which prevails in the Latino world. Such expectations may be the things that thrill dreamers, but I am convinced that the gospel's power to transform people always happens one-on-one. With each individual,

---

[274] Pedro Henríquez Ureña holds the distinction of being the first Spanish speaker invited to deliver Charles Eliot Norton Lectures at Harvard University in 1940–1941. See *Seis ensayos en busca de nuestra expression* (Buenos Aires: Editorial Babel, 1928).

[275] José Ortega y Gasset coined his now famous saying, "Yo soy yo y mi circunstancia," (I am I and my circumstance) in his *Meditaciones del Quijote*. See *Obras Completas*, Vol. 1 (Madrid: Fundación, 2004), 757.

as we will hope to show in chapter eight, the gospel does not coddle nor commiserate with people because of their lack of a coherent identity. Rather, it goes to the heart of the circumstance which most impinges upon them, subverting the validity of the historical and psychological structures that have plagued the community. Ultimately, Christ's cross and message offer a new and unexpected path, redeeming people, transforming them, making them human billboards of a credible alternate life for others to consider.

Thus, if anyone can show a new way where others have been continually stumped, it is the Hispanic evangelical, who may have been convinced the world was of a certain hue but who now experiences life differently. As Paul declares in Colossians 1:13, believers have entered into a new reality, for God has rescued them "from the domain of darkness," and transferred them "to the kingdom of His beloved Son." Note that Paul does not trot out that old tired dichotomy where darkness and light are pitted as opposite realities, or principles in some endless struggle—a pseudo-worldview that many across the world assume. For Paul, the antidote to arresting life's coercive forces was not found in an ethical-philosophical system. The alternative to "darkness" was to be found in the person of Christ. Far from spoon-feeding them moralistic placebos, the believer is made heir to God's riches of wisdom and knowledge "in Christ" (Rom. 11:33; Col. 1:9, 2:3) and we should ask, why? The question needs to be asked and answered: Does the Hispangelical have access to true knowledge that his kinsmen in the flesh need to hear?

Recovering That Which Christ Came to Save

One of the earliest lessons most Hispanics hear, as they consider the claims of Christ, is that Jesus came to save sinners. But usually, the claim is made in general terms. However, while we believe that Jesus came to save us such as we are (Rom. 5:8), can his saving action be interpreted with greater granulation? Luke says that Jesus came to save "that which was lost" (Luke 19:10),[276] suggesting the recovery of something, not just someone. As such, I can't help but think that salvation isn't just about saving human beings but includes all kinds of things, along with those aspects that make them truly human. A review of the biblical record reveals this to be true for with respect to the objects of his grace, we should note that Christ doesn't just offer some "pie in the sky" salvation. For Zacchaeus, his saving encounter with Christ restored his sense of compassion and honesty (Luke 19:1–10); and for Nicodemus, who surely wrestled with Christ's claims over the course of three to four years, it meant the eventual recovery of courage (John 19:39). Salvation restored the lame man's joyful praise (Acts 3:1–10), and the Samaritan woman had her voice and testimony validated within her community (John 4:7–29). Peter speaks to a harassed, belittled community of believers in the provinces of Asia and encourages them in the knowledge that they are deemed worthy to proclaim the excellences of Christ, who calls people from darkness into his marvelous light (1 Pet. 2:9). In every case people are saved for time and eternity, but their worth to the community is also recovered in a palpable way.

One thing that Christ came to save—to begin to restore in those who would believe in him—was the image of God, which we all bore in the beginning (Gen. 1:26–27; Ps. 8:3–9; 1 Cor. 11:7), but which was fractured through human folly. For his part, the Hispangelical had no idea all that awaited him when he surrendered his life to the Galilean. Perhaps the poor soul turned to Christ in contrition, just hoping to be forgiven. Little did he know that the decision would make him full heir to God's wisdom and knowledge. In rummaging through his

[276] The text is also found in Matthew 18:11, but is likely an interpolation. See Bruce M. Metzger, *A Textual Commentary on the Greek New Testament,* second edition (New York: United Bible Societies, 1994), 37.

unexpected spiritual windfall, he discovered things of inestimable value to him, and also to those around him.

What should the Hispangelical know that his people need to know? Long before the birth of the first *Mestizo*, long before the first *mulato* or *criollo*, indeed, long before the Roman Empire engineered the Spaniard and the Portuguese, God stamped his image upon the core of every human being. If anthropology is right and the human species derived from a common stock, the Bible acknowledged this important fact first. Ethnic diversity is a powerful aspect of our humanity that, from a biblical viewpoint, made it possible for nations and distinct cultures to come into being (Gen. 10–11), but it also had its sinister side. Because it came later, after our moral and spiritual downfall, often our ethnic distinctiveness is that which divides us. But, be of good cheer, for Christ recovers the only thing capable of reconciling the nations: the *imago dei*, common to all human ancestry. It is only Christlikeness that makes the recovery of genuine self-identity possible, displaying it through healed ethnicity (Rev. 22:1–3).

The Challenge of Being a Hispangelical

In our study of Hispangelical beginnings, we pointed out that the evangelical message began making significant inroads into the Latino world when it was couched in its indigenous cultural matrix. While this is true, it is also the case that not everyone sees this with glee. Some ponder whether this means that the culture has to be embraced, such as it is. But even if one does not advocate for the wholesale cultural acceptance, how are critical distinctions and evaluations made and more so, in real time? The issue is not academic, for it concerns how believers will relate to family members, to lifelong friends, to those with whom they work, as well as to those cultural activities in which many find meaning and delight. While some Hispangelicals may never sense the issue quite like it has been framed, it is probably because their context is essentially evangelical; but this is not the case for most Latino believers.

A Blueprint for the Transformed Christian Mind

When the apostle Paul challenges the church at Rome to "not be conformed to this world," we could suppose he was calling for a total break away from one's culture. Furthermore, by boosting them in the "renewing of their mind" with a view to proving God's good, perfect, and acceptable will, Paul would seem to be advocating a move away from the old and on to something new. But, is this Paul's challenge to the church?

As we recount all that Paul has said about God's amazing plan to offer justification and redemption through faith in Christ (Rom. 1–8), we are confronted by a challenge. In Romans 12:3–15:21, Paul describes how a believer's transformation reveals itself in specific cases. But, first, the apostle sets forth a strategy for starting us on our way. Beginning with verses 1–2, Paul lays out the process:

> Therefore I urge you, brethren, by the mercies of God, to present your bodies a living and holy sacrifice, acceptable to God, which is your spiritual service of worship. And do not be conformed to this world, but be transformed by the renewing of your mind, so that you may prove what the will of God is, that which is good and acceptable and perfect.

On considering Paul's admonition, the word "acceptable" is used twice, so we can assume it is central to his teaching concerning acceptability before God. We can further see that Paul says two things. In verse 1, believers are admonished in light of all that he has said (Rom. 1–11), to present themselves as "a living and holy sacrifice, acceptable to God," which is their "spiritual service of worship."[277] This first usage suggests

[277] The word "spiritual" can also be translated "reasonable" as many translations render it (e.g., Modern English Version, New English Translation, International Standard Version, etc.).

this is something every believer is capable of doing and verse 2 gives a twofold process for accomplishing this expectation. First, believers present themselves as living sacrifices by *not conforming to this world* and follow by *being transformed by the renewing of their mind.* Only when Christians embrace this twofold process do they begin to "prove what the will of God is, that which is good and acceptable and perfect."

Not Conforming to This World

A Christian begins growing by *not conforming to this world.* Here we note that the verb "conformed" in verse 2 is technically passive, but conveys an active sense.[278] Christian sanctification begins when the believer no longer conforms to the world, and actively renounces worldly values and behaviors. Paul says as much in some of his other epistles. In Colossians 3:5–11, for example, the apostle challenges followers "to put aside," to "lay aside the old self with its evil practices," before "putting on" the garment of Christian holiness (vv. 12–17). In virtually all his epistles, Paul insists that growth in godliness begins by abandoning sinful behaviors.

While initially the challenge to set aside sinfulness can seem massive, many may assume that God is asking them to disown their culture in whole. However, the Bible nowhere endorses the total renunciation of culture. Paul, for example, made it clear that circumcision had no value in the context of the Christian faith (Gal. 5:2, 6), but that did not mean it was absolutely sinful. As the apostle considered the antagonism Timothy's presence would likely incite among the Jews, he moved to have him circumcised (Acts 16:3). Conversely, Paul had no qualms eating food offered to idols, but he realized his Christian liberty could cause others to sin and so he was willing to set it aside if it might offend someone (1 Cor. 8:1–13).

[278] See Cleon L. Rogers and C. L. Rogers III, "Romans 12:2," *The New Linguistic and Exegetical Key to the Greek New Testament* (Grand Rapids, MI: Zondervan Publishing House, 1998), 339.

Was Paul being inconsistent in rejecting some cultural practices (circumcision), only to practice them, yet accepting some practices (eating meat offered to idols) only to abstain under pressure? Or, were other factors at work as he considered how he would relate to his native culture? Though this work is hardly the place to develop a full-blown ethical approach to the questions raised, I would simply point out that Paul's decisions concerning cultural issues were never driven by a one-size-fits-all approach. Paul was guided by principles he considered inherent to the gospel. Consider the following precepts and maxims he offers:

- All things are lawful for me, but not all things are profitable. All things are lawful for me, but I will not be mastered by anything. (1 Cor. 6:12)
- [L]ove edifies. (1 Cor. 8:1)
- Do not be overcome by evil, but overcome evil with good. (Rom. 12:21)
- Owe nothing to anyone except to love one another; for he who loves his neighbor has fulfilled the law. (Rom. 13:8)
- [T]he kingdom of God is not eating and drinking, but righteousness and peace and joy in the Holy Spirit. (Rom. 14:17)
- So then we pursue the things which make for peace and the building up of one another. (Rom. 14:19)
- The faith which you have, have as your own conviction before God. Happy is he who does not condemn himself in what he approves. (Rom. 14:22)
- [W]hatever is true, whatever is honorable, whatever is right, whatever is pure, whatever is lovely, whatever is of good repute, if there is any excellence and if anything worthy of praise, dwell on these things. (Phil. 4:8)

Sure, the gospel challenges us all to renounce blatant sins, many of which are clearly named. But when it comes to the great variety of issues and challenges we face, it is rarely so cut-and-dried. Life is complicated and we are not likely to find a proof text that speaks directly to every situation that challenges our faith. It is at such moments that we fall back on godly principles to help us work through the issue. Such commands are always operative, but they are also broad and general—seek to edify, love people, pursue peace, do the honorable thing, do that which promotes purity, overcome evil. As such, they do not provide a clear-cut answer—and this seems to me to be intentional. I wonder if we realize how much God honors our own personal decision-making process, but the fact is, he does. If godly maxims, precepts, and commands don't quite work on their own, this is by design. The maxims and commands are generic, but it is the conscience of the believer, which turns them into practical precepts that work when applied.

Believe it: God has equipped us with a redeemed conscience to make his precepts and commands come alive. And so, as important as it is to be Spirit-filled and led, God wants our conscience to work in concert with His Spirit and his revealed truth (Rom. 14:1–9). Furthermore, since we are all maturing at different levels, it is probable that in many cases the decisions we make are not necessarily the same for all believers. But take heed, for in the end, Paul declares, "Happy is he who does not condemn himself in what he approves" (Rom 14:22). Here is truth: As interested as God is in our sanctification making God-honoring decisions, he is just as interested in us acting in accordance with our level of Christian maturity and knowledge at any moment in time (1 Tim. 1:5). When we understand this and realize its implications, there is no singular right action or decision. If you acted with a good conscience, informed by revealed truth (Scripture), Spirit-filled and Spirit-led, your decision, whatever it was, was the right action (Rom. 9:1). Think about it: "David's conscience was bothered because he had cut off the edge of Saul's robe" (1 Sam. 24:5). While some might consider David too sensitive to let something so small bother him, Paul reminds us that, "To the pure, all things are pure; but to those who are defiled and unbelieving, nothing is pure, but both their mind and their conscience are defiled" (Titus 1:15). This example in the life of David shows us just how powerful a redeemed conscience is, able to detect whatever could compromise our faith, or witness.

Hispangelicals, like all believers, will have to navigate the treacherous and lively waters of their culture, and some may choose to decline the challenge all together. I am persuaded that God has equipped us to make honorable decisions and choices regardless of our place along the path of holiness. Remember this, if we don't take up the challenge, then we can never affirm with Paul, "I also do my best to maintain always a blameless conscience both before God and before men" (Acts 24:16; cf. 23:1). Like the apostle, the Hispangelical will likely be a believer in the context of his community. Knowing that he would relate to Jews for life, Paul knew each day would bring some unanticipated challenges, but he was well equipped. We should know this as well.

Transformed by the Renewing of the Mind

If believers were called merely not be conformed to the world, a Christian's life would be little more than reactive, fighting a lifelong battle against the constant allure of the world's enticements. But that is only half the battle—and the lesser half, at that. Already, in the Old Testament, we find that God wants to engage our thinking faculties (e.g., 2 Sam. 7:22; Job 23:6–7; Ps. 16:7; Isa. 1:18; et al.). And in the New Testament, Paul puts forth the positive challenge of *being transformed by the renewing of their mind*. As the following verses reveal, for both Paul and Peter mental engagement was essential:

- Become sober-minded as you ought, and stop sinning; for some have no knowledge of God. I speak this to your shame. (1 Cor. 15:34)
- For those who are according to the flesh set their minds on the things of the flesh, but those who are according to the Spirit, the things of the Spirit. For the mind set on the flesh is death, but the mind set on the Spirit is life and peace. (Rom. 8:5–6)

- Set your mind on the things above, not on the things that are on earth. (Col. 3:2)
- Therefore, prepare your minds for action, keep sober in spirit, fix your hope completely on the grace to be brought to you at the revelation of Jesus Christ. (1 Pet. 1:13)

I must admit that I chose and placed these verses in the order given deliberately. However, I do not believe I have violated the tenor of the Bible concerning the challenge to engage our minds in the furtherance of spiritual sanctification. As you follow the sequence, it suggests that Christians are challenged to think Christianly. Thus, Christian transformation is never thought of as the product of some experience, removed from the problems and challenges of real life. There is a consistent appeal to use rational faculties, to ponder the nature of their relationship with the Savior. This does not mean, of course, that the spiritual element is excluded. In Matthew 16:17, Peter was made aware of just how he arrived at knowledge of the Christ: "because flesh and blood did not reveal this to you, but My Father who is in heaven." The fact is, spiritual guidance and mental engagement are not only not opposed, but work in close harmony.

God expects us to use our minds, even as he illumines our thinking through the Holy Spirit (John 16:13; Rom. 8:5–6). This is possible, not because we happen to believe it. Rather, as Craig Keener notes, "this affirmation does in fact correspond with divine reality, on the level of God's verdict and what he calls the believer to share in affirming."[279] Whereas before, we could only think after the patterns of our fallen mind, now our renewed mind is alive to possibilities that were never really there before, thinking thoughts that conform to who we truly are in Christ.

As we consider the challenge of Romans 12:1–3 seriously, we learn that both the setting-aside of some behaviors and the taking up of others

---

[279] Craig Keener, *The Mind of the Spirit* (Grand Rapids, MI: Baker Academic, 2016), 53.

is not anything completely chiseled in stone. Since we all come to Christ with our own life experiences, God works with us individually and he does it as we think through what must go and what may still remain.

The Possibility of a Hispangelical Legacy

If the Latino world has still not discovered its self-identity, let me say unapologetically, the Hispangelical has the answer! Fortunately, many have realized the greatness of this momentous discovery, and they are poised to impact their world for good. Others, however, are in the process of sorting it all out, praying just how their new faith relates to their community. Does the gospel witness comes at the expense of cultural renunciation?

Hispangelicals should guard against comparing themselves with other evangelicals so that they can see God's vision for their contribution with clarity. Paul said, "But we will not boast beyond *our* measure, but within the measure of the sphere which God apportioned to us as a measure" (2 Cor. 10:12–13). Here is a thought: Rather than mimicking what others have done in the context, we Hispangelicals must discern just what is "the measure of the sphere" to which God has called us and where God would have us realize our potential. Are we one-, two-, or five-talent people? Early in the church's history, God used the Antiochian School to set forth a biblical hermeneutic. The North Africans were instrumental in working through Christian doctrine. Later, it was the Europeans Reformers who brought the church back to the primacy of Scripture over church tradition. God pricked the British to kick-start the modern missionary movement. And in more recent times, the Korean church has been influential in promoting protracted prayer. While I am not saying God excluded the rest of the church from these important developments, I am saying God chose to use these redeemed peoples in a special way.

The truth is, God uses all his people. In this regard, Darren Dochuk has proposed that the Lord has already been using Hispanics to transform evangelicalism in powerful ways. In his "Lausanne '74 and American Evangelicalism's Latin Turn," Dochuk details how God used Hispanic believers in the 1970s to engage in a humbler and more penitent mission, particularly to the underdeveloped world.[280] By doing so, argues Dochuk, Latino theologians Rene Padilla and Samuel Escobar encouraged evangelicalism to reconsider the dichotomy between evangelism and social action, which is sometimes communicated.[281] While I appreciate Dochuk's insights, I ask whether the Hispangelical's legacy lies back in the 1970s and '80s, or whether their work was preparatory. What Padilla and Escobar contributed came from two lowly voices from the hinterlands of South America, and they needed to be heard. But is there more? In my mind, the Latino evangelical is poised to continue contributing, and it just may be in a way totally unexpected.

Then Came the Hispangelical Hunger Artist

In chapter two, "Then Came History," we discussed the lack of a mature Latino identity, which many serious Hispanic thinkers acknowledge. This causes me to ask, is the chronic condition of the Latino their settled fate? Franz Kafka's "Hunger Artist" was exquisite in the art of emaciation, and throngs went to see him at work, but in the end he starves to death with people barely taking note. Is this the fate of the Latino, to hunger after identity, and the world to yawn at the spectacle? If we believe the emergence of the Hispangelical is a mighty work of God's grace, then is he offering to satisfy the need?

In his Sermon on the Mount, Jesus shocks the crowd by elevating moral and spiritual deficits as things to be coveted. Thus, he extols the virtues of spiritual poverty, mourning, gentleness, hunger, mercy, heart purity, peacemaking, persecution and insult (vv. 3–11). Remarkably, in

---

[280] Darren Dochuk, "Lausanne '74 and American Evangelicalism's Latin Turn," in *Turning Points in the History of American Evangelicalism,* eds. Heath W. Carter and Laura Rominger Porter (Grand Rapids, MI: Wm. B. Eerdmans Publishing Co., 2017), 247–286.
[281] Ibid., 265.

each case, those who possess such qualities will be satisfied and blessed, so they are challenged to rejoice. Then follow two similitudes, "salt" and "light" (Matt. 5:13–14). If we resist the temptation to see these as independent traditions, but see them as following intentionally on the heels of the Beatitudes, a clear message comes into focus: The very deficits which people might otherwise resist are how God has equipped them to be salt and light to the world. These qualities, meager as they are, are essential, reflecting the spiritual bankruptcy of a world that has rejected him.

Can those things associated with Latino weakness be used for the kingdom's advancement? Paul gloried in weaknesses (1 Cor. 1:27, 12:22; 2 Cor. 11:30, 12:5–9). Amazingly, even experiences which any sane person would avoid—to be seen as fools, weak, without honor, hungry, thirsty, poorly clothed, homeless, reviled, persecuted, slandered, the scum of the world, the dregs of all things—Paul says made him "a spectacle to the world, both to angels and to men" (1 Cor. 4:9), but not in the sense of Kafka's tragic protagonist—quite the opposite.

If, as Paul proposes, God can use a life under the direst of circumstances, then is there a weakness that cuts across the Hispanic landscape, which God can use for his purposes? Ernesto Mayz Vallenilla, you will remember, reminds us that the Hispanic is someone who is destined "never to truly be already," buttressing an expectancy that is never quite realized. Could this be our beatitude: to identify with a people stunted by history, circumstance, and character, and yet be a spectacle of what a great God can do? Is our calling as salt and light to be such a spectacle?

As I ponder Vallenilla's observations, I cannot help but note that his thoughts sound very much like the "already, not yet" nature of God's kingdom,[282] firing up my imagination. Does the gospel bring new light

[282] George Eldon Ladd, "The Mystery of the Kingdom," in *A Theology of the New Testament* (Grand Rapids, MI: William B. Eerdmans Publishing Co., 1996), 89–102.

with respect to this fundamental Latino weakness? In 1 John 3:2, the apostle John makes a provocative assertion: "Beloved, now we are children of God, and it has not appeared as yet what we will be" (cf. Rom. 5:1–2; 2 Cor. 4:13–17; et al.). John posits the first bold assertion—"now we are children of God"—as a settled fact, to excite believers with his second premise— "it has not yet appeared as yet what we will be." John is not unaware of life's realities, but he knows that the believer's life trajectory is upward, destined for glorious fulfillment based on who we now are, children of God. But, is fulfillment of this promise something that happens only at some distant future? Or is there a real unfolding of this hope in the here and now?

In our estimation, because he is now a child of God, the Hispanic evangelical begins an amazing journey of discovery. As his self-identity in Christ is restored, it helps him see the tragic state of humanity alienated from God (Eph. 4:17–24). His Christian self-identity also helps him recover his self-worth (1 Pet. 1:3–5). From a corporate perspective, Christian self-identity makes it possible for the believer to expand his sphere of service within as a member of God's kingdom (1 Cor. 12:31; Phil. 4:13). If the believer has grown in true knowledge, his sanctification doesn't engender false pride (1 Cor. 4:7; 1 John 2:16; James 4:6) nor belittle those who lack it. God wants believers to display the truth that the lingering effects of anyone's history and experiences can be truly reconciled in Christ.

Let the facts speak for themselves. Unlike the *Hispano* whom Stavans admits is a jumble of chaotic inconsistencies, who has yet to find himself, Hispangelicals have found the true center of life, Christ and Christ alone (John 6:68). And in finding him, they found themselves and their place and purpose in life. As such, the Hispangelical's legacy may be to speak to the anxiety of countless millions of peoples from all nations and tongues—not just Hispanics—who feel that their future never quite arrives. The Hispangelical may still have a future fulfillment, but the life he now lives is a real down payment of that hope, lighting the way for himself and for others to consider.

Hispangelicals and History

The statement "those who forget history are destined to repeat it" suggests that history—everyone's history—has its difficulties and challenges. That said, Hispangelicals should accept their history for what it is, for it is part of what shaped them. Practically, this means that they must stop perceiving their history through rose-colored glasses. Every country has things in their history worthy of praise, but to deny those aspects that some consider better left forgotten only creates problems. If we believe in a God who is the Sovereign Lord of history, we can agree with Paul, who affirmed that "God causes all things to work together for good to those who love God, to those who are called according to His purpose" (Rom. 8:28). The verses that follow (vv. 29–30) remind us that God works through predestination to our effective calling, our justification and, ultimately, our future glorification. The moment we deny anything in our personal or collective past, we put into question the truth that God was aware of it and active through it all.

Additionally, Hispangelicals must come to grips with another critical challenge that comes about because of their history. We earlier turned to Claudio Véliz, who outlined significant differences between the Anglo foxes and the Latino hedgehogs.[283] It is beyond question that Protestants were the product of a momentous revolution that gave birth to religious diversity, and that evangelicalism was one of its offspring. The colonizers, by contrast, created a culture intent on preserving a glorious past, with little appetite or tolerance for change. Thus, evangelicalism springs from a different ideological root than that which nurtured the Hispanic mind. To people invested in the hedgehog mentality, this would seem to pose an insurmountable problem, but I would encourage Hispangelicals to see that we need not abandon the one to embrace the other.

---

[283] Véliz drew his inspiration of the fox and hedgehog comparison from Isaiah Berlin, *The Hedgehog and the Fox* (London: Weidenfeld and Nicholson Ltd., 1953).

The apostle Peter learned an important lesson while staying at the home of Simon the tanner (Acts 10:6–16). Overcome with hunger, Peter received a most challenging ecstatic vision. Seeing a great sheet descending from heaven, he saw the Lord laying a feast before him, but not as he might have expected. Far from kosher, the tablecloth was filled with "all kinds of four-footed animals and crawling creatures of the earth and birds of the air."[284] Upon being commanded to "kill and eat!" Peter recoiled, "By no means, Lord, for I have never eaten anything unholy and unclean." But God would not have it, reminding Peter, "What God has cleansed, no longer consider unholy." Of course, the context suggests Peter should be more open to eating pagan foods, but is that really all? Since this incident is couched within the account of Cornelius' conversion (Acts 10:1–48), it makes it clear that Peter would be challenged to embrace Gentile people and their cultural trappings as well.

Under the banner of grace, Hispangelicals are free to explore the world of the evangelical foxes, and why not? The hedge of separation has been obliterated (Eph. 2:15). By the same token, the redeemed foxes can also appreciate enduring hedgehog values. The beauty of the gospel is that in Christ, cost-benefit calculations make no sense, and zero-sum games are a waste of time. Seriously, in Christ all honest and honorable cultural expressions are to be explored and embraced. As such, the believer of whatever stripe can experience the beauty of redeemed Korean, or African, or European, or near-eastern, or any other ethnicity under the sun, for we are all one in Christ (Gal. 3:12).

Still, while we praise God for the marvelous variety in his kingdom, the Latino, whose identity is now rooted in Christ, begins to reveal just what a Hispanic was always meant to be. The Hispangelical does it by holding on to those cultural values that are worthy of praise (Phil. 4:8). To my knowledge, love of country is not a sin; neither is heartfelt emotional expression and love of family. And, so what if Hispanics like to

---

[284] See also Lev. 11; Deut. 14.

party? Much of Latino culture is commendable, but it must be subject to Christ's lordship.

The Apologetic Burden of the Hispangelical

Still, the Hispangelical is left with formidable challenges. Sometimes, the best thing a Hispangelical can do is to come to grips with a "new normal" for their life and future. At times, and especially when the culture that surrounds them makes life difficult, the Hispangelical is tempted to opt for total retreat—but again, that would be a senseless act of self-mutilation. More seriously, it would communicate the total repudiation of Latino culture, and I can think of no better way to alienate family and community. Instead, I offer the following suggestions.

In my estimation, the Hispangelical's witness is awesome, but they are prone to belittle its power. In a day when movies like *Coco*,[285] or practices like the *Santa Muerte* cult, lift up and glorify the syncretistic worldview of the Latino, the Hispangelical's message can seem tame. This must not happen, for the truth in the gospel is infinitely fascinating to men and angels alike (Eph. 3:10; 1 Pet. 1:12). Here is our challenge. Far from presenting some insipid witness, the Hispangelical must prepare their minds for action on a spiritual plane (1 Pet. 1:13).

However, Hispangelicals, who often tilt to extremes, will need to strike a balance between the views of those who see a demonic spirit working behind every circumstance and secularists who rationalize Satan out of existence. Can the Hispangelical discern when sinister forces are at work, yet also know when the problem stems from a deceitful human

---

[285] The film *Coco* premiered on October 20, 2017 at the Morelia International Film Festival, Morelia, Mexico, and was released in Mexico City the weekend before the *Día de Los Muertos* festivities. The film pulled in $43 million in the month of October. See Tom Huddleston, Jr., "Disney's New Pixar Movie 'Coco' Already Set a Box Office Record," *Fortune*, November 16, 2017, http://fortune.com/2017/11/16/coco-disney-pixar-box-office-mexico (accessed November 22, 2017).

heart? Many romanticize prayer and Bible study, but Paul sees these as implements of war:

> so that we will be able to stand firm against the schemes of the devil. For our struggle is not against flesh and blood, but against the rulers, against the powers, against the world forces of this darkness, against the spiritual forces of wickedness, in the heavenly places. (Eph. 6:11–12)

Pentecostals often lay claim to this ministry, but the broader Hispanic evangelical community should not surrender this ground. Hispangelicals need discernment in this critical area and especially as they are surrounded by a culture that is rife with deception. We should remember that the armor of our spiritual warfare was made for a real spiritual fight.

But the challenge isn't merely from without. Much of the Hispangelical church has been inundated by the dubious gospel of prosperity—a name-it-and-claim-it gospel, a gospel tied to so-called anointed apostles, a gospel that only works if one buys a handkerchief or a vial of holy water—a gospel that is unremittingly me-centered. Hispangelicals need to focus on the core elements of Christ's atoning sacrifice. Paul declared:

> Now I make known to you, brethren, the gospel which I preached to you, which also you received, in which also you stand, by which also you are saved, if you hold fast the word which I preached to you, unless you believed in vain.
>
> For I delivered to you as of first importance what I also received, that Christ died for our sins according to the Scriptures, and that He was buried, and that He was raised on the third day according to the Scriptures. (1 Cor. 15:1–4)

Whatever else Hispangelicals hear, our work is, first and foremost, to preach Christ crucified in atonement for the sins of the lost. In saying this, I am not suggesting that social concern is not important, but if it usurps the primacy of this core message we reject the commission Christ has called us to proclaim (Matt. 28:19–20; Acts 1:8). The fact is, social concern is a vital aspect of a Christian's witness, as James makes clear (James 1:27, 2:14–17, et al.), but it must be expressed holistically, in concert with the gospel, caring for the whole person, body, and soul.

On a more practical level, Hispangelicals also need to understand and practice the priesthood of the believer. From a doctrinal perspective, evangelicals reject the teaching that God guides his people through an ordained priesthood, teaching instead that every believer is a priest before God. Hispangelicals also affirm this doctrine, which demolishes the need for an ecclesiastical hierarchy in matters of faith. However, while they know the teaching, they don't necessarily live it out its implications. The Hispangelical should come to grips with it, for if one is a priest before God, then none of the Christian disciplines can be assigned only to those perceived as somehow being more spiritual. "Anointing," for example, cannot be limited to the "super-spiritual" preacher. Rather, as John notes, anointing is available to all followers of Christ alike (1 John 2:20, 27).

Hispangelical men who understand spiritual priesthood cannot shirk their responsibilities. Those who embrace their priesthood know that they have been redeemed to serve their families, their churches, and their communities. The priesthood of the believer challenges the prevalent notion among Hispangelicals that ministry is the exclusive work of an ordained clergy. Hispangelicals are self-sufficient, ministering grace and the Word wherever they go (1 Pet. 2:5–9). Men and women who understand their priesthood learn to be more responsible to the spiritual needs of their home as well. Rather than being passive recipients, they become active witnesses, evangelists, deacons, Sunday school teachers, fully incorporating into the body of Christ.

Hispangelical Disestablishment

I can't believe I am actually saying this, but thank God for politics, sometimes. One thing that shaped North American evangelicalism's future was its embrace of religious freedom, and it led to a fortunate development. In the wake of disestablishment, many churches awoke to the realization that they could no longer rely on governmental subsidies to keep the doors open. Evangelical churches took it in stride and, as Mark Knoll has noted, these churches found ways to be functional and utilitarian.[286] As Knoll notes, religious disestablishment led to evangelicals putting their spiritual gifts to good use. Far from withering away for lack of governmental subsidies, the evangelical church not only survived but thrived.

As for the Hispangelical community, many have believed that they are incapable of continuing without the support of the more affluent church. But, does perpetual subsidy really help? Here, I am reminded of the church in Jerusalem that in spite of her amazing beginnings, the church never seemed to make it on her own. The church was born poor (Acts 3), and some twenty years later, Paul's collection throughout the Macedonian and Achaean provinces testifies to the continuation of its dependency (2 Cor. 8–9). It is beyond belief but, in time, the Jerusalem church would institutionalize poverty, self-identifying as the Ebionite church,[287] which, as church historian Justo Gonzalez notes, faded "out of history in the fifth century."[288] Perhaps the time has come to challenge Hispangelicals in the economic arena.

---

[286] Knoll, *The Scandal of the Evangelical Mind*, 66.

[287] Carsten Colpe, "The Oldest Jewish-Christian Community," in *Christian Beginnings: Word and Community from Jesus to Post-Apostolic Times*, ed. Jürgen Becker (Louisville: Westminster/John Knox Press, 1993), 91–92. Colpe identifies severe economic stress as leading to the self-designation of the first congregation in Jerusalem as Ebionite, an Aramaic term which means "the poor ones."

[288] Justo González, *The Story of Christianity*, vol.1 (San Francisco: Harper & Row Publishers, 1984), 22.

The adage is true: "Put your money where your mouth is." Latinos are touted as people of great faith, and I know it to be true. But many compartmentalize things, believing they can express faith without it touching their pocketbook. The Bible, of course, reveals that God demands our total surrender, and the Hispanic evangelical community may need to be nudged in that direction with a serious dose of tough love. I am convinced that a sort of disestablishment is called for. Hispanic evangelical churches may need help from time to time, but they should no longer expect a mother church or denomination to subsidize them endlessly. The very thought harkens to the hedgehog mindset, alien to whom we now are in Christ. Our numbers have so increased that expecting to get a regular monthly check from the association, the sponsor church, or the denominational office is not only embarrassing, but diminishes us. So long as Hispanic evangelicals remain dependent, we project ourselves as immature takers with nothing really substantive to offer. It is high time for Hispangelical churches to give generously—nay, sacrificially—to fund the church's efforts to extend the kingdom at home and abroad. So let's exercise our faith in the economic arena—not with a view to enrich ourselves, but to become genuine partners in financing the evangelical cause. Only when we become full partners will the evangelical world take the Hispangelical message seriously.

The Challenge of Latino Hostility

What of the Hispangelical who lives in a nonbelieving home, or works among nonbelieving Hispanics? While many Latino families have embraced the gospel, this is not always true. In many cases, it is only one member of the family who turns initially to Christ, placing the new believer between the proverbial rock and a hard place.

This was the situation in my own case, when I was the first to break away from the family ties to religion and accept Christ as my Savior. My family saw a definite change, and they lost no time attempting to disprove the sincerity of my Christian commitment. Let me give an example: While my family had never prayed at mealtimes, I began to pray before eating—and man, did it create tension in the home. Imagine being surrounded by an alcoholic father and three brothers at the kitchen table, ready to test your resolve. Upon finishing my prayer, I would open my eyes to see my brothers giving me the one-finger salute, and my father shoving a beer in my face. I know it sounds like I was living among Philistines, but from their point of view the guy they saw was worse than an unwelcomed stranger. Hispangelicals who live or work in close proximity to other Latinos will not always find an accepting environment. Since so much of Latino culture is laced with a veneer of traditional religion, anyone who abandons the lifestyle can be seen as a traitor to the faith, no matter how casually they might have practiced it.[289]

So, what is a Hispangelical to do? Peter's first epistle is an excellent source to turn to when believers find themselves in a hostile environment. For Peter's recipients, harassment was an ongoing reality. Note the extent of persecutory language used throughout the letter:

- In this you greatly rejoice, even though now for a little while, if necessary, you have been distressed by various trials. (1 Pet. 1:6)
- Keep your behavior excellent among the Gentiles, so that in the thing in which they slander you as evildoers, they may on account of your good deeds, as they observe them, glorify God. (2:12)
- For what credit is there if, when you sin and are harshly treated, you endure it with patience? But if when you do what is right and suffer for it you patiently endure it, this finds favor with God. (2:20)
- [K]eep a good conscience so that in the thing in which you are slandered, those who revile your good behavior in Christ will be put to shame. (3:16)

[289] Paul E. Sigmund, *Religious Freedom and Evangelization in Latin America,* 52–59.

- Beloved, do not be surprised at the fiery ordeal among you, which comes upon you for your testing. (4:12)
- If you are reviled for the name of Christ, you are blessed, because the Spirit of glory and of God rests upon you. (4:14)

Most commentators who have studied 1 Peter do not believe this language reflects institutional persecution instigated by the Roman state. While the manifestation of the problem Christians are facing is broad, ranging across the provinces of Asia, the problem itself is probably organic, coming from local communities, family, friends and acquaintances who can't seem to understand, much less accept, the person's dramatic change.

First Peter's appraisal comes close to what many Hispangelicals experience from their friends and family whom, to use Peter's own words, "are surprised that you do not run with them into the same excesses of dissipation, and they malign you" (1 Pet. 4:4). Rather than wanting to understand and hear you out, the first instinct is to react unapprovingly against the changes they see. But what does Peter counsel to those who find themselves experiencing such harassment? The apostle knows that harassed believers need more than shallow platitudes for comfort. Note his strong guidance for those who experience such challenges:

- 1 Peter 1:1–2: Peter identifies his recipients as aliens, scattered as a result of the persecution they have endured. The introduction makes it clear that the recipients are the objects of persecution in their own countries, estranged from community.
- 1 Peter 1:3–2:10: Peter builds up the self-esteem of the readers who are being mistreated. They may be despised citizens at home, but they are heirs of glory in God's sight!
- 1 Peter 2:11–3:12: Far from expecting that their harsh treatment exonerates them from having to live a life of holiness and faith, harassed believers are to:
  - exhibit blameless behavior before the world (2:11–12).

- submit to earthly authorities, masters, and spouses (2:13–20; 3:1–7, 8–12).

- 1 Peter 2:21–25: Peter puts forth Jesus as the believer's example of a righteous sufferer.
- 1 Peter 3:13–14: Peter promises that because believers are the people of God, no amount of harassment can ultimately harm them.
- 1 Peter 3:15–4:19: Peter gives a twelvefold theology of righteous suffering:
  1. 3:15–17: Righteous suffering may lead to witnessing opportunities.
  2. 3:18–22: Jesus is our example of one who suffers righteously and is vindicated. The Noah story is given to show how God is able to save the righteous. Thus, Christians can rest knowing their salvation is secure, regardless of what harassment may come.
  3. 4:1: Believers should arm themselves with God's purposes, for suffering will come.
  4. 4:2–6: Believers should resist the temptation to return to the world during times of suffering.
  5. 4:7–11: Believers are to remain steadfast in their faith and godly behavior, in light of Christ's immanent return.
  6. 4:12: Suffering for righteousness' sake should come as no surprise to believers.
  7. 4:13: Suffering should lead to rejoicing in the Lord.
  8. 4:14: Suffering for Christ is evidence of the Holy Spirit's presence in one's life, and confirms the blessing of God.
  9. 4:15–16a: Suffering as a consequence of personal sin should not be confused with suffering for righteousness' sake.
  10. 4:16b: Suffering for Christ should produce a worshipful attitude.

11. 4:17–18: Suffering for Christ will purify the Church and the individual believer.
12. 4:19: Suffering in Christ ought to lead to a greater trust in God.

There is no doubt but that 1 Peter was written to encourage believers to stand firm and endure fiery ordeals as righteous children of God. For myself, I cannot say that my family ever took it to extreme levels, but for a time there was an undercurrent of irreverent mockery. During such times, Peter's counsel helped me to remain strong in my Christian commitment.

To be totally truthful, not all Hispangelicals will have to deal with the challenges I faced, but neither have I faced the truly vexing situations others have encountered. In this, I am reminded of Hebrews 11, which records the many experiences of the faithful. Some became nomads and wanderers, living in holes in the ground (vv. 8–13, 38); others were exiled (vv. 24–27); yet others were mocked, scourged, imprisoned, and put to death (vv. 36–37). Yet, the experiences weren't all troubling, for some of the faithful conquered kingdoms, shut the mouths of lions, quenched the power of fire, and became mighty in war, putting foreign armies to flight (vv. 32–34).

What strikes me about Hebrews 11 is how it reminds me of Charles Dickens' 1859 epic masterpiece *A Tale of Two Cities*. For any Hispangelical who must learn to live within the culture closest to him, it is always like the opening words of Dickens' novel as he describes the time of the French Revolution:

> It was the best of times, it was the worst of times, it was the age of wisdom, it was the age of foolishness, it was the epoch of belief, it was the epoch of incredulity, it was the season of Light, it was the season of darkness, it was the spring of hope, it was the winter of despair, we had everything before us, we had nothing before us, we were all going direct to Heaven, we were all going direct the other way. . . .[290]

[290] Charles Dickens, *A Tale of Two Cities* (London: Dover Publications, 1998), 1.

My experience was something similar. My experiences in church were absolutely thrilling: growing in Christ and establishing Christian friendships; even while my experiences with my parents, two of my brothers, and buddies were dispiriting, most casting me as some kind of fanatic Jesus freak. Happily, I led one of my brothers to faith in Christ; yet, in my cockiness, I attempted to scare my oldest brother into faith by asking him if he knew whether he would go to heaven or hell. The problem was, I asked him as I floored the accelerator of the car, playing chicken with a tractor-trailer. In time, both my mother and father received the gospel, but later, when my oldest brother suffered a life-threatening motorcycle accident and I went to see him at the hospital, he reminded me of my recklessness and threw me out of the room as he cursed Christ. Yes, while God had given me a godly Christian spouse and I had sensed his call to serve him in ministry, two of my brothers, my extended family, and virtually all my friends rejected me. Through it all, Peter's epistle to the provinces of Asia has been a constant source of strength.

Hispangelicals and Politics

Another challenge that Hispangelicals will need to address will be their participation in the political process. While evangelicals, mostly Pentecostal, have created political parties and alliances in Latin America, their support base has not been very strong and their impact has been peripheral to the broad political developments of the region.[291] However, North America is different, for the Hispanic evangelical is growing and all major political parties are looking to count on their support.

For the record, I would say that the Hispangelical's political support should not be expected or bought with the promise of governmental largess. Samuel Rodriguez, president of the National Hispanic Christian

---

[291] See Paul Freston, "Evangelicals and Politics in Latin America," in JSTOR vol. 19, No. 4 (London: Sage Publications, 2002), 271–274; Sigmund, *Religious Freedom and Evangelization in Latin America,* 60–61.

Leadership Conference, noted at their annual meeting in 2016, "We have a problem with the donkey, and we have a problem with the elephant," pointing to the obvious.[292] If the Democrat Party alienates Hispanic evangelicals, who are largely conservative on social issues (e.g., abortion, same-sex marriage), the Republican Party's immigration platform is also very conflictive. The fact is, most Hispanics see abortion as the killing of an innocent child and same-sex marriage as sinful. On the other hand, many Hispanic evangelical congregations across the land have significant percentages of illegal immigrants who attend, come to faith in Christ, and join the church. In some churches, the pastor is an undocumented alien.

When it comes to politics, American-born Hispangelicals find themselves in a quandary. The reality is, both major political parties leave them wanting. So how will they rise to the challenges of their civic duty? I have no doubt that many will tilt in favor of legislation that most benefits them, their pocketbook, and their families. However, they will also favor parties that tackle the international situation, particularly with respect to Cuba, Venezuela, Puerto Rico, and Mexico, to name the countries (and one US territory) most in the news today. Ultimately, it is my sense that vast numbers of Latino evangelicals are pro-Israel, so developments like President Trump's recognition that Jerusalem is the legitimate capital of the Israeli state are broadly applauded. My overall assessment is that Hispangelicals are not monolithically donkeys or elephants, nor libertarians, nor independents. This gives me hope, for the fact that they are not necessarily committed to one party as such may allow God's Word to ultimately influence their vote.

In my estimation, the Hispangelical's politics must be informed by Holy Scripture, which has always been a hallmark of evangelicals. However, in saying this I am not suggesting that Latino believers should

---

292 Kate Linthicum, "Evangelicals Are the Kind of Latinos the GOP Could Be Winning. But Probably Not with Donald Trump," *Los Angeles Times*, May 23, 2016, http://www.latimes.com/politics/la-na-pol-evangelical-latinos-20160523-snap-htmlstory.html (accessed May 3, 2019).

rummage through the Bible to cherry-pick verses that support their political views. The apostle Peter admonishes believers to desire the pure milk of the Word, so as to grow unto salvation (1 Pet. 2:2). But how does that affect our politics? I am convinced that it is only by taking in the Word, reading it, meditating upon it, and committing it to memory that the Word is able to work on us, which is the best thing that can happen whenever we exercise our privilege as citizens of a country.

As I have discussed elsewhere, God accomplishes something miraculous when we are under the work of Holy Scripture. As Hebrews reveals, the written Word is a high-priestly scalpel that cuts deep into the living sacrifice, diagnosing and bringing to light true motives:

> For the word of God is living and active and sharper than any two-edged sword, and piercing as far as the division of soul and spirit, of both joints and marrow, and able to judge the thoughts and intentions of the heart. (Heb. 4:12)

Any cursory reading shows that the written Word begins diagnosing the reader, focusing on their heart motivations. Hispangelicals will certainly vote and run for political office, but before they do, they must settle it that God is the only lobbyist who gets their unqualified attention.

Still, the Word's surgical work, as penetrating and necessary as it is, is really a means to a greater end. As verse 13 reveals, Scripture transfers the person from itself to someone else: "And there is no creature hidden *from His sight*, but all things are open and laid bare *to the eyes of Him with whom we have to do*" (emphasis mine).

As we can note, the written Word, the Bible, brings the surgical subject, the believer, before the presence of the "living Word," Jesus Christ, "with whom we have to do."[293] Evangelicals have sometimes been accused of being book-worshipping Bible-thumpers, but such critics just don't get it. If evangelicals cling to the Bible, it is not because

---

[293] Rudy Gonzalez, *Acceptable* (Bloomington, IN: Crossbooks, 2011), 43–44.

they worship paper and ink. Most evangelicals, and Hispangelicals as well, believe in their hearts that it is through God's inspired Word that they come to know Christ personally.

Hispangelicals can have legitimate political concerns, but we lose our voice if we merely become extensions of the prevailing political discourse. The perennial challenge and opportunity that the Hispangelical will always face is to stand in the presence of his Savior, the risen and glorified Christ (Rev 1:9–20), and to let his thoughts and words be shaped by that encounter. Only then will the Hispangelical have something of value to say to the evangelical community, to the broader Hispanic world, and to the world-at-large.

Conclusion

While I have laid out a challenge to the Hispangelical, the truth compels me to admit that I have probably not even begun to scratch the surface. The issue must remain open-ended, for as the Hispangelical people continue to grow in number, to expand their footprint, so will the nature of the challenges they face change and grow.

Here is a challenge. Some have described North American evangelicalism as milquetoast, and the way it is lived out in suburbia and in bedroom communities across the land may support this view. Many churches, however, defy this characterization, taking on entrenched forces of oppression, preaching a triumphant gospel that offers liberating hope to people in despair. But what of the Hispangelical? Will they succumb to the allure and humiliation of the commonplace?

As Hispangelicals become "mainstream," so will their churches be driven to take on the values of middle America, but it is my belief that those ancient ways will never be totally gone. While it is true that many Latino believers are assimilated within evangelicalism, it is also the case that most are not far removed from a vibrant Latino culture. Additionally, as we have noted, many Hispangelicals are committed to their cultures and express their faith accordingly. This leads to an eventuality.

The Latino evangelical church will need to continue acknowledging and serving in situations common to the Latino context. As such, the greatest challenge they may face will be to embrace their identity in Christ, displaying cultural values worthy of praise, presenting the gospel with cultural sensitivity, thus revealing—by the way they live and worship—the answer to the Latino condition.

CHAPTER EIGHT

Then Came Evangelism and Discipleship

You may break the clods, you may sow your seeds, but what can you do without the rain?

Charles Haddon Spurgeon
Morning and Evening[294]

Introduction

As my wife's family tells it, sometime in the late 1930s, Ellen Cloud, a Methodist missionary on furlough from China, happened to see a little boy with his sister walking along the streets of Clint, Texas. Thinking they might be Chinese, Cloud decided to follow them home. When she knocked on the door, she was greeted by Ignacia Ortega, a Tarahumara Indian, and Manuel Ramirez, a man of Spanish ancestry who had emigrated illegally to the US from Aguascalientes, Mexico. The children were not Chinese as Cloud had thought, but typical *Mestizos.*

[294] Charles Haddon Spurgeon, *Morning and Evening* (Peabody, MA: Hendrickson Publishers, 1991), 35.

Undeterred by the fact that the family turned out not to be Chinese, sister Ellen proceeded to present the gospel to Ignacia and Manuel.

It was not long after that visit that this family headed west to stake their fortunes in California, but had they left the gospel behind? As they traveled, they stopped in Marana, Arizona, to pick pima cotton, hoping to finance their journey, but they never moved on. Now married, the Ramirezes settled in Tucson; and true to the Methodist missionary who had shared the gospel with them, *Nachita* (term of endearment for Ignacia) was used of God to donate property and begin the *Iglesia Metodista Libre*. But that was not all. It became Ignacia's life's mission to reach as many of the people in her *barrio* as she could with the gospel.[295] As for the missionary who had led them to faith in Christ, the family nicknamed her *Nubita* (Little Cloud), remaining a close sister in Christ and friend of the family until her passing.

I tell this story because José Guadalupe, the young boy mistaken for Chinese, also came to Christ, though it would not happen for thirty years. Eventually, however, he would sense the call to vocational ministry, moving his family to attend the then-*Instituto Bautista Bíblico Mejicano* in San Antonio, Texas. But make no mistake: Though late to embrace the Savior, Pastor Ramirez emulated *Nubita* and *Nachita*. Through his efforts, he led many to faith in Christ throughout the 1970s and '80s, and challenged those whom he reached to do the same. It was *Hermano Ramirez* who led a young man named David Reyes to faith—and it was David who led me to Jesus. Six months later, Pastor José Ramirez also became my father-in-law.

As this story suggests, Hispangelicals are not ready-made; they must be reached one by one with the gospel. Because this is so, our membership within evangelicalism should not be assumed. While salvation

---

[295] Belen Gallego, José Guadalupe Ramirez, Maria Angelina Valenzuela, Carolina Ramirez, Virginia L. Gonzalez, interviewed by author, oral recollections, Tucson, Arizona, San Antonio, Texas, 2007, 2017. Mrs. Ellen Cloud served as a deaconess in 1913, 1914. Fourth Missionary Report, Woman's Missionary Council (Nashville: Publishing House of the Methodist Episcopal Church, 1913, 1914), 153.

begins with a personal encounter, generational continuity within a people requires long-range planning.

Thinking strategically, Paul encourages Timothy to deepen the bench by nurturing fruitful believers throughout the four generations that a typical life spans (2 Tim. 2:2).[296] Hispangelicals should do all they can to emulate the strategy. More than ever, Hispanic evangelicals must embrace evangelism and discipleship earnestly, for our challenge is not just to increase our numbers in the pews. As Hispangelical numbers grow, their input must keep pace contributing into every sphere of life where the gospel has something to say. We thank God for so many brethren God has used across the denominational landscape to give birth to the Hispangelical—truly astonishing, given Latin America's historical religious alignment, but there is an implicit destiny in every birth. So let us spread our wings and take to the sky, nurturing successive generations of faithful men and women who will preach the gospel, contribute to the church, and indeed impact the world for good.

Evangelism Hispangelical Style

No doubt, evangelism works best when couched in a people's own circumstance. This is no grand discovery, for others have known the importance of understanding people's cultural context in the presentation of the gospel. Bruno Molina, evangelism associate with the Southern Baptists of Texas Convention, has noted that "to effectively transmit the gospel to any group of people, we should take into account their worldview and unique cultural distinctives while manifesting and articulating the gospel in a way that resonates with them

[296] Assuming Psalm 90:10 as providing a biblical post-flood life-span, the generations of believers would descend from the mid-seventies, to the mid-fifties, to the mid-thirties. The fourth and youngest generation would be in the mid-teens. I hesitate to acknowledge a fifth generation, which would encompass children, who can certainly be saved, but are not otherwise equipped spiritually to engage in the discipleship strategy Paul sets forth.

as authentic."[297] We agree of course, but just how to achieve this ideal in a Latino context is the question.

In his 2012 book, *Center Church*, Timothy J. Keller, senior pastor of Redeemer Presbyterian Church in Manhattan, New York, lays out what he characterizes as a "fruitful" approach to the work of effective outreach.[298] Keller proposes that fruitfulness is the result of a "theological vision" shaped by three concerns, which he puts forth under three labels: 1) Gospel, by which he means a correct understanding and proclamation of the gospel message; 2) City, by which he means an appreciation of the cultural context where the gospel is being proclaimed; and 3) Movement, by which he means an understanding of the church's relationships with its past and with other churches in the community.

I must say, virtually every page of Keller's *Center Church* justifies its cost, and his thoughts on "Gospel" and "Movement" command careful consideration. However, we will limit our focus to his thoughts on "City," which is pertinent to our immediate discussion. Here, Keller offers an approach that is not romantically naïve, nor dismissive of culture: "This is based on the biblical teaching that all cultures have God's grace and natural revelation in them, yet they are also in rebellious idolatry."[299] Thus, Keller encourages the reader both to appreciate cultural impulses in agreement with Scripture,[300] yet also be ready to challenge its "idols," its cultural inconsistencies that don't align with their stated beliefs.[301] But Keller does not look to be a hard-boiled critic. "Having entered a culture and challenged its idols," he stresses, "we should follow through

[297] Bruno Molina, "An Analysis of the Transmission of the Gospel among Transcultural Hispanic Americans" (PhD diss., Southwestern Baptist Theological Seminary, Fort Worth, 2018), 120. I acknowledge a debt of gratitude to Dr. Molina for his dissertation, and the valuable insights it provides in the area of evangelism among Hispanics. Much of what is presented in this chapter is inspired by his work.

[298] Timothy J. Keller, *Center Church* (Grand Rapids, MI: Zondervan, 2012), 120.

[299] Ibid, 24.

[300] Ibid.

[301] Ibid, 123, 125.

by presenting Christ to our listeners as the ultimate source of what they have been seeking."[302]

With a dose of humility Keller does not expect that our own language or experiences are up to the evangelistic task per se. Rather, he encourages readers to become what I would call "cultural polyglots." "The Bible has enough diversity," notes Keller, "to enable us to connect its message to any baseline cultural narrative on the face of the earth."[303] Keller lists and defines five "biblical languages," as follows:

- The language of the battlefield—Christ fought against the powers of sin and death for us. He defeated the powers of evil for us.
- The language of the marketplace—Christ paid the ransom price, the purchase price, to buy us out of our indebtedness. He frees us from enslavement.
- The language of exile—Christ was exiled and cast out so we who deserve to be banished could be brought in. He brings us home.
- The language of the temple—Christ is the sacrifice that purifies us and makes us acceptable to draw near to the holy God. He makes us clean and beautiful.
- The language of the law court—Christ stands before the judge and takes the punishment we deserve. He removes our guilt and makes us righteous.[304]

In reviewing this list, we should not lose sight of Keller's point. While the "languages" make genuine connections to people's cultural situations, they do not endorse the values of a given culture unconditionally. This point is vital. Most often the languages challenge the target culture, revealing how Jesus' atonement "does for us what we cannot do

---

[302] Ibid, 130.
[303] Ibid.
[304] Ibid.

for ourselves."[305] For Keller, "lifting up the substitutionary sacrifice of Christ" within the linguistic range of a biblical language "is the ultimate way to appeal to any culture."[306] While Keller does not elaborate on the languages further, we affirm their value, for each one speaks to an aspect of the Latino condition, as our following thoughts suggest.

The Language of the Battlefield

Concerning the language of the *battlefield*, there is a popular saying among Hispanics, "*¡La vida es una lucha!*" (Life is a battle/struggle!). Unfortunately, this is not just some witty aphorism. Latin American history is written in violence from its inception. And there has hardly been a day in its five-hundred-year history when there hasn't been a war, a conquest, an invasion, a revolution, or a guerilla action somewhere in the region. But what is true regionally is arguably truer for people in general. *The Washington Post* conducted an extensive investigation into violence in Latin America, and found:

> Latin America is home to just 8 percent of the world's population, but 33 percent of its homicides. In fact, just four countries in the region—Brazil, Colombia, Mexico and Venezuela—account for a quarter of all the murders on Earth. Of the 20 countries in the world with the highest murder rates, 17 are Latin American, as are 43 of the top 50 cities.[307]

The findings of *The Washington Post* are unassailable. Latinos know that violence is a horrible and frequent gatecrasher. The question for us is,

---

[305] Ibid., 131.

[306] Ibid.

[307] Amanda Erickson, "Latin America Is the World's Most Violent Region. A New Report Investigates Why," *The Washington Post*, April 25, 2018, https://www.washingtonpost.com/news/worldviews/wp/2018/04/25/latin-america-is-the-worlds-most-violent-region-a-new-report-investigates-why/?utm_term=.c0aa5d3f3009 (accessed June 6, 2018).

with so many Latinos exposed to violence, does the gospel speak to its trauma?

First, it is not difficult to see why battlefield language has been used so successfully by Pentecostals. Most Hispanics, as we have previously shown, have no problem believing in a sinister world that lurks beyond the visible world. Thus, while they might attribute a loved one's drug addiction or death to any number of societal influences or an illness to some physical condition, they can just as readily believe they are in the clutches of diabolical forces dead-set against them. As such, when people credit Satan with destroying their lives (John 10:10), Jesus' militancy against the forces of darkness can be appealing.

For many, it is the language of spiritual warfare (e.g., Rom. 8:31–39; 2 Cor. 10:3–6; Eph. 6:10–20; Col. 1:13, 2:14–15), which gives them the weapons with which to fight. In such a context, substitutionary salvation in Christ is tantamount to offering triumph and victory over *narco-traficantes, pandilleros, bandidos, asesinos, secuestradores, sicarios* and all instruments of demonic forces that threaten death and ruin—literally. When the government is weak and unable to curb the violence as in Mexico and Colombia—indeed, when the government is itself complicit in violence against its citizens, as is the case most recently in Nicaragua—Christ's death, burial, and resurrection confronts and defeats the powers of sin and death at the root cause, the violent and unrepentant human heart.

Nevertheless, we should note that if Latin America is prone to violence, this is also the reflection of a systemic problem. Whether it's driven by machismo, jealousies, or rivalries, whether people feel they have been hexed or bewitched, or turn to pathological religions like the *Santa Muerte* cult, the gospel challenges people on the battlefield of their violent life. And it is only when Christ storms the beaches of our internal killing field, that the gospel achieves its greatest triumph, defeating evil and death within the human heart (2 Cor. 10:1–5; Col. 2:15; et al.).

The Language of the Marketplace

The *marketplace* language, in my estimation, is made to order. Setting aside the fact that from 2010 to 2013 both *Bloomberg* and *Forbes* magazines named Mexican businessman Carlos Slim Helú as the richest person in the world, many Hispanics struggle economically. One historian of Latin America observes:

> So Brazilians and Chileans and Colombians who cannot have a car nevertheless live thoroughly immersed in Western consumer culture and night after night, watch bright television commercials tailored to those able to emulate the lifestyle of the U.S. middle class. It is for this reason, and not just because of proximity and poverty, that so many Latin Americans come to the United States.[308]

But of course, owning a car inevitably becomes just one thing on a long list of must-have items. And so, while North American Latino economic strength continues to increase, so does their appetite for possessions and experiences. Not surprisingly, many Latino families embrace wholeheartedly a "shopper mentality," unaware of its crushing economic boomerang. As a major study reveals, despite holding down multiple jobs, a significant number of Latino households rely on credit cards to pay for basic living expenses.[309] It is ironic that despite having more purchasing power than their *abuelos* could ever imagine, many Hispanics are shackled to endless debt, which their *abuelos* never had. And the question surfaces: Is there an answer for people who have bought the lie that consumerism holds the key to happiness?

Hispanics are a proud people, and most will hold down multiple jobs in an effort to keep the repo man at bay. Nevertheless, many

---

[308] Chasteen, *Born in Blood and Fire*, 16.

[309] Amy Traub, "Credit Card Debt in the Latino Community," Demos, http://www.demos.org/publication/credit-card-debt-latino-community (accessed November 15, 2017).

know they are over their heads, and their economic burdens can open up opportunities. When people understand that despite their material accumulations, recognizing they are spiritually impoverished can be humbling. And it is at this point that Christ, who paid the ransom price to purchase them out of their indebtedness, can be liberating, knowing that no amount of overtime pay can ever meet the need (Ps. 74:2; Jer. 31:11; 1 Pet. 1:18, et al.).

The Language of the Exile

The language of *exile* is powerful for, as we have noted earlier, many Hispanics have experienced the humiliation of having to leave their homes for economic, violent, or political reasons. For many, the brute realities which led to their *diaspora* is a burden hard to bear. But even American-born Latinos can feel disenfranchised. As Molina notes, people can often be made to feel marginalized or exiled when they are viewed as "ethnic" or "other," vis-à-vis the majority culture. The fact is, though people of Hispanic ancestry lived in vast swatches of the US for a hundred years prior to the arrival of their English-speaking neighbors, often they are made to feel foreign.

In the context of such treatment, or perceptions, Latinos should know that Christ—through whom all things on this earth were created, and who is the righteous heir of heaven and Earth—was outright rejected and suffered as an outcast, outside the gate (Heb. 13:12). But rather than being embittered by it, Jesus turned his rejection into something wonderful. Through his cross, Jesus offers reconciliation all who were alienated from God.

Yes, the language of exile holds great appeal, for it has the power to destroy any sense of alienation that the world will heap upon a person. Believers need no longer see themselves as foreigners, but can embrace full citizenship with the saints as part of God's household (Eph. 2:19; Heb. 12:22–24; 1 Pet. 2:9–10; 1 John 1:1–4; et al.).

The Language of the Temple

When we note that, for many Hispanics, pilgrimage is a vital religious rite, any gospel presentation must address this deep-seated belief. Many devout Roman Catholics attach meritorious grace to worshipping at shrines dedicated to Mary, or a saint. Additionally, devout Catholic Latinos make solemn vows to visit a shrine, to purchase an indulgence, to plead for some loved one, including those deceased, whom they believe to be in purgatory.

For those who subscribe to such beliefs, the language of the *temple* can be liberating, for only Christ's substitutionary sacrifice accomplishes what all the shrines and religious pendants in the world can never do. Stephen made it clear that despite the efforts of Israel's ancestors, Moses, Joshua, David, and Solomon, "the Most High does not dwell in houses made by human hands" (Acts 7:48). We can extrapolate from Stephen's words that the language of the temple challenges the validity of any faith necessarily grounded on manmade shrines and artifacts. When it comes to salvation, Christ is the only temple believers need (John 2:20–22). Christ alone purifies us and makes us acceptable before a holy God (Heb. 10:22; James 4:8).

But we must be aware that the language of the temple will definitely challenge many cultural idols. After all, while Latinos revere their religious shrines, when it comes to them personally, cursing, alcoholism, gluttony, a general abuse of the human body is rampant. And so, implicit in the gospel presentation is the challenge many will face when they discover that a believer's body is the sacred temple of the Holy Spirit. For many Latinos, the life of overindulgence and excess is an idol too hard to abandon (1 Cor. 3:16, 6:16; Eph. 2:21; 1 Pet. 2:4–7; et al.).

The Language of the Law Court

For Latinos, any talk of legal issues can bring out strong emotions, for many have been acclimated to believe that anything "official" is by definition corrupt. Throughout Latin America, the police, politicians, bureaucracies, and law courts are viewed with well-deserved suspicion. And though many have fled their countries because of political reprisal and sought sanctuary in North America, their worries about the police or the courts do not necessarily change. Many Latinos are jaded by what would seem to be an unshakable conviction that the legal system, no matter where they happen to live, is somehow always tilted against them.

Obviously, speaking to a community which is predisposed to believe that the legal system is deaf to their cry, the language of the *law court* will get their attention. But will the message be muffled by their life experience? Hawkers of liberation theology will preach that God opts for the poor, but does that mean that the poor are exonerated before a holy God? When the gospel is understood, and despite so much injustice perpetrated against the helpless, the claims of God's law remain leveled upon all humanity. The sinful guilt of all—the rich and the poor, and everyone in between—is presupposed. In coming to the foot of the cross, the person must acknowledge that despite their own victimization, it was their own sinfulness which helped drive the nails into Christ's flesh. Only when that level of honesty is reached is the person ready to hear "the rest of the story." The sinner discovers that Christ became their substitute, receiving the just punishment they rightly deserved (Rom. 5:8; Gal. 2:15–21; 1 Cor. 15:3).

Overall, as we consider these five "languages," we can see that each one offers valuable perspectives to be considered prayerfully. Of course, these perspectives will not apply equally to all Hispanics across the board. Some will have greater power to capture the person's attention, depending on their own experiences, but the point remains: By gaining some genuine understanding of the person we hope to reach, embedding the gospel in a biblical understanding of their issues, whether they be rooted in violence, consumerism, exile and alienation, pilgrimage, legal jeopardy, or any other issue, biblical languages will allow us to present the gospel so as to address their spiritual need with greater relevance (Rom. 5:1, 16; 2 Cor. 3:9; 1 John 2:1; et al.).

While I appreciate Keller's observations with respect to the five biblical languages he identifies, I respectfully add a sixth for consideration: the language of "family." Throughout this book we have made important observations over the role that the nuclear and extended family plays in the life of the Latino. But we have also acknowledged that for many Latinos, those same values are under duress. Are people nevertheless members of the family of God by default, merely for having been born into a "Christian" or a "Roman Catholic" household? Evangelicalism has consistently taught that a person begins life alienated from God and must therefore make a conscious decision to be born again, to be born anew of the Spirit. Christ died on the cross to make such spiritual regeneration possible, so that whosoever believes in him can become a child of God, a member of the family of God (John 1:12–13, 3:16; Rom. 8:16; Gal. 3:26; Eph. 1:5, 2:3; 1 John 3:10; et al.).

Effective Evangelism Strategies

As one might expect, when it comes to sharing the gospel there is no one strategy or model that works across the board. This is to be expected for, as we have noted, the Latino world is complex and diverse. While such complexity might leave a would-be evangelist bewildered, the hope of somehow being "missional" in our outreach only multiplies the challenge.[310] Today, we have no shortage of methods for presenting the gospel. However, I am convinced that whether it is through the giving of a gospel tract like *The Four Spiritual Laws*, a memorized gospel presentation like "Por Fe" or "The Roman Road," using Chronological Bible Storying,[311] small-group studies such as The Alpha Course,

[310] Keller, *Center Church*, chapter 19, "The Search for the Missional Church," 251–263.

[311] For this method see J. O. Terry, *Basic Bible Storying* (Fort Worth, TX: Church Starting Network, 2008).

inviting people to attend *avivamiento* services,[312] or exposing people to Christian broadcasting, there are things that add to the fruitfulness of the outreach. Thus, if Latinos are to be reached, it is usually because other factors are at work.

A Commitment to Prayer—Hispangelicals are convinced that prayer is essential to heartfelt evangelism. As Molina reminds us, "One may infer that what gets prayed about is deemed a priority, and in churches that pray in an intentional and organized manner about transmitting the gospel it happens. One may also infer that since this is a spiritual transaction requiring God to work, that God is pleased to answer the prayers of his people (John 6:44, Eph. 6:19)."[313]

A Commitment to Heartfelt Emotion—Hispangelicals are generally convinced that the gospel must be proclaimed with strong emotion, and with testimonials of people's faith experiences.[314] Latinos do not tend to respond to gospel presentations that are predominantly cold and logical. Rather, they are more apt to consider the gospel if the presentation draws them in emotionally. My own experience tells me that heartfelt testimonies encourage a Hispanic's hope that God is actually active in the life of the person speaking to me.

A Commitment to Hospitality—Hispangelicals recognize the value of hospitality. Christ had repeatedly stayed in the homes of those who were open to his message (e.g., Luke 19:5–6; John 12:1–2; Mark 14:14–16; et al.). Moreover, Jesus set the pattern when he first sent his disciples

---

[312] Most Hispanic evangelicals do not make a clear distinction between services aimed at inner church renewal and services with an evangelistic emphasis. Interview with Rolando Lopez, ethnic church strategist, for the San Antonio Baptist Association, Baptist General Convention of Texas, December, 3, 2017. Lopez, who is a vocational evangelist, notes the continued effectiveness of revival services among Hispanic churches, while they have diminished in the Anglo church.

[313] Molina, *Analysis of the Transmission of the Gospel*, 130.

[314] Ibid., 128. According to Molina's research, 70 percent of the most effective methods of sharing the gospel among Latinos include stories or illustrations used to draw the person in at an emotional level.

out into the field of mission (Matt. 10:11–12). If one wonders why he intentionally sent them out with so little support on hand (vv. 9–10), the expectation that Israel would receive him and his emissaries into their homes with open arms is reasonable.

Similarly, when the church came into being, local congregations were admonished to show hospitality to itinerant preachers and indeed this must have been a broad expectation (e.g., Acts 9:43, 10:6; Peter staying in the home of Simon the tanner). The brief epistle of 3 John focuses specifically on the ministry of hospitality and goes so far as to single out a certain Diotrephes because "he does not receive the brethren" and further, "he forbids those who desire to do so" (3 John 10). The reception of those who spread the word into the homes of the faithful was a strategic function of the early church, and it is no less important in many a Hispanic home.

In all this, one can infer that the Latino's cultural experiences increases their receptivity to the gospel as a result of the trust factor and the welcoming attitude of most Latino families.

A Social Consciousness—There have always been a number of activities that the church has used to nurture evangelism. These would include such activities as Vacation Bible School, neighborhood prayer surveys, social recreation programs, hospital visitation, acts of kindness, tutoring students, food distribution ministries, as well as ministry to single parents and the elderly. As one might surmise, this list is only suggestive; and one should not conclude that doing social ministries brings people to faith automatically. Often, churches can fall into the trap of letting such ministries become ends in themselves, thereby squandering the opportunity to minister to the total person.

In considering its outreach possibilities, the church that is intentional about evangelism must keep Acts 3:1–10 at the forefront of its decisions. The church will discern its own gifts and limitations, hoping to minister to a real need or deficit in the community. But the church will also be convinced that despite its inability to meet all needs, she can follow Peter, who said to the lame man at the beautiful gate: "I do not possess silver and gold, but what I do have I give to you: In the name of Jesus Christ the Nazarene—walk!" (Acts 3:6). The only real and lasting answer to the chronic social conditions that people experience is the life which Christ offers.

A Commitment to Storytelling—Lastly, in any discussion of evangelism, we cannot overlook the impact of storytelling. Latina author Yuyi Morales notes of children's literature:

> The Latino child recognizes himself or herself in the stories, finds in the illustrations things he has at home, sees foods that she eats with her family, cherishes celebrations that his loved ones taught him about, understands habits that exist within her community.[315]

As Morales suggests, the Hispanic world has not merely been the product of their history but as much the product of the telling of their history through stories, ingraining into their life those things that define them. The Hispangelical knows this and knows one other thing: The gospel of Jesus Christ is the greatest story ever told. Christians read the Bible through a Christocentric lens, believing that both the Old and New Testaments attest to Jesus Christ as Savior and Lord. Thus, the Bible's pages are filled with divinely inspired stories that reveal the manifold works (Ps. 104:24), wisdom (Eph. 3:10), and grace (1 Pet. 4:10) of God and, indeed, "the length and width, height and depth" of his love for us (Eph. 3:18). For many Hispangelicals, it is the personal stories that make the grand old story come alive. So, let the Hispangelical continue to cherish those stories learned in the family. But let them also tell of how their story has been enriched and transformed, for having encountered Christ along the path of their life's pilgrimage.

---

[315] Quoted by Jamie Campbell Naidoo, ed., in *Celebrating Cuentos* (Santa Barbara, CA: ABC-CLIO, 2011), xi.

What about Hispangelical Discipleship?

At his birth, Jesus was the Savior of the world (Luke 2:29–32). But even the eternal and only begotten Son of God needed to mature (Luke 2:52). For Jesus, it would take about thirty years before he would begin to flesh out his mission (Luke 3:23). And what of the Hispangelical? At the start of this chapter, I suggested that Hispangelicals need to nurture successive generations of their own who will preach the gospel, contribute to the church at large, and indeed impact the world for good. In pondering this challenge, I am convinced discipleship must be redoubled, for it is only mature Christians who ultimately leave a lasting legacy in their wake.

If the aphorism "demography is destiny" holds then, as Molina notes, the destiny of the evangelical church may well hinge on the degree to which Hispangelicals take discipleship seriously.[316] The *Time* magazine cover of April 15, 2013 touted "The Latino Reformation" and how Hispanic churches are "transforming religion in America."[317] According to the Pew Research Center, "Hispanic Evangelicals not only report higher rates of church attendance than Hispanic Catholics, but also tend to be more engaged in other religious activities including Scripture reading and sharing their faith, compared with other Hispanic religious groups."[318] Of course, what is true of the Hispangelical church in North America is equally true throughout Latin America. This is all good, and it causes me to wonder whether a Latino evangelical's commitment to the basic spiritual disciplines of the Christian faith is God's way of gearing us up for a work that could have tremendous impact. In a previous chapter, I proposed that a Hispangelical's identity in Christ could be

[316] Bruno Molina, oral telephone interview, October 12, 2017.

[317] Elizabeth Diaz, "The Latino Reformation," *Time*, April 15, 2013, cover.

[318] Pew Research Center, "Major New Survey Explores the Shifting Religious Identity of Latinos in the United States" May 7, 2014, http://www.pewforum.org/2014/05/07/major-new-survey-explores-the-shifting-religious-identity-of-latinos-in-the-united-states/ (accessed December 8, 2017).

what the Latino world needs to consider, but could the Hispangelical's contribution extend beyond their own ethnic borders?

Of course, Hispangelicals have never lacked indigenous leaders. Though I never personally studied under a Hispanic throughout my formal schooling, I did receive my first introduction to church history from Justo Gonzalez.[319] It was Josué Grijalva's numerous biblical commentaries which first introduced me to biblical interpretation.[320] I am indebted to Daniel Sanchez for my earliest understanding of missions, and of evangelism from observation and conversations I have had with Rudy Hernandez and Roland Lopez. My appreciation of the pastorate was first formed by my father in-law, Pastor José Ramirez. But may I take a page from Hebrews, for time would fail me to tell about all of God's Hispanic servants who in their own way "conquered kingdoms, performed *acts of* righteousness, obtained promises, shut the mouths of lions, quenched the power of fire, escaped the edge of the sword, from weakness were made strong, became mighty in war, put foreign armies to flight." And yes, I dare not forget faithful Latinas as well, "who received back their dead by resurrection" (Heb. 11:33–35). But, far be it from me to only think in the past tense.

Indeed, I am thrilled to know that God continues to call Hispangelical servant-leaders—whether it is Wilfredo DeJesus or Luis Cortez, who give social justice an evangelical slant; D. A. Horton and Sammy Lopez, Christian apologists to the hip-hop and millennial generations; Guian Paul Gonzalez, who speaks to the world of sports; Ruben Austria and Enricky (Rick) Vasquez, who minister within the criminal justice system; Dinorah B. Méndez and Juan Martinez, who impact the

---

[319] My first church history textbooks in seminary were Justo L. Gonzalez, *The Story of Christianity*, Two Vols. (San Francisco: Harper & Row Publishers, 1984, 1985).

[320] Josué Grijalva wrote a number of abbreviated lay-oriented Old Testament commentaries on Exodus, Hosea, Jeremiah, Isaiah, and Malachi. He also wrote abbreviated New Testament commentaries on Matthew, Mark, John, Acts, Romans, Galatians, Ephesians, Philippians, Hebrews, 1 Peter, and James. All his commentaries were originally printed in San Antonio, Texas, by Munguía Printers.

theological academy; or Juan Florez, who works tirelessly in the small town of Poteet, Texas to help high school dropouts earn their GED. These and countless other leaders embody Christian maturity, taking discipleship to its logical end—changing, transforming, and blessing the world.

Envisioning Hispangelical Revival

A perennial concern among evangelicals is the need for genuine spiritual awakening, and it is intriguing to ponder whether the Hispangelical church could be instrumental in this matter. When we read in 2 Chronicles 7:14 how God challenged Israel to seek revival, its message is direct and to the point: Revival will happen when God's people repent from their iniquity and seek his face in humble prayer. While the Old Testament recipe for revival is not beyond our grasp, so as to have to reach to heaven to find it (echoing Rom. 10:6–8; cf. Deut. 30:12), is there another word that can deepen our understanding of how spiritual renewal might come? Consider the responsibility we have to love God with all our heart, soul, strength, and mind (Matt. 22:37; Luke 10:27). Undertaking that daunting command would certainly stretch our understanding of discipleship, bring spiritual renewal, and in the Hispangelical might manifest itself in the following ways.

The Hispangelical's Mind

For one, the commandment to love God with all our mind (Matt. 22:37) would undercut the popular yet false dichotomy that pits intellect against spirituality among some Latino evangelicals. But let's be clear: This command challenges even the most intellectually gifted, for our powers, however strong they may be, are never enough. When the Bible commands us to love God with *all* our mind, yet knowing we use only a fraction of our mental capability, is this just hyperbole? Or could it be that the redeemed Spirit-filled life unlocks dimensions of our intellect that might otherwise remain dormant?

If we should take Philippians 4:8 seriously, what might redeemed Latino thinkers have to say about truth, virtue, justice, axiology, and ethics? We are called to exercise our powers of concentration, comprehension, and reflection to distill from the verbal and nonverbal tomes of life that which reveals moral excellence and praiseworthiness.[321] Since so much of the Latino's philosophical thinking is aimed at such questions, Hispangelicals should have valuable insights to offer to the evangelical community and beyond.

The Hispangelical's Strength

Second, what of loving God with all our strength? One thing Hispanics are known for is their hard-worker ethic. So what if they take a *siesta*? That is an ancient cultural practice that does not point to laziness, as some may think. To the contrary, it is the *siesta* that gives Hispanics the reinvigorated energy to work long into the evening hours.

Having said that, it is nevertheless a fact of history that Hispanics were subjected over centuries of imperial dominance to do back-breaking labor, which was demeaning and often life-threatening. Thus, there is a well-known sentiment throughout the Spanish-speaking world that says *Nacimos para trabajar como bueyes y mulas* (We were born to work like oxen and mules). Can the Hispangelical find anything redeeming in that painful legacy?

I am convinced that Hispangelicals have much that can be reclaimed for God's glory by virtue of their laborious legacy. The kingdom of God is always in need of hearty laborers (Matt. 9:37–38), and Jesus said, "Do not work for the food which perishes, but for the food which endures to eternal life" (John 6:27). Today, we may have to labor at our jobs, but this should not keep us from asking, "What shall we do so that we

[321] Richard J. Foster, *Celebration of Discipline: The Path to Spiritual Growth,* revised edition (San Francisco: Harper Collins Publishers, 1988), 62–76. My thoughts here are inspired by Foster's discussion of the discipline of study.

may work the works of God?" (John 6:28). Paul considered himself a bondservant (slave) and a fellow-worker with God, who abounded in the work of the Lord (1 Cor. 3:9, 15:58).

In his divine providence, God allowed evil people and circumstances to shape Hispanic endurance for hard labor. Assuming that the work ethic does not evaporate upon regeneration, Molina encourages Hispangelicals to apply their backs to the *missio Dei* (God's mission), resulting in the creation of new and innovative paradigms and practices to colabor with God, aimed at transforming not just individuals but communities and perhaps even stubborn and hurtful societal structures to reflect God's *shalom*.[322] In this way, Hispanic evangelicals could certainly inspire people in every other ethnic group to work tirelessly for the kingdom.

The Hispangelical's Soul

Third, Hispangelicals must also love the Lord their God with all their soul. What can this mean, other than that we are to love God with all that makes us Hispanic? As I have stated elsewhere, God rarely calls us to abandon our cultural context all together. More often, he asks us to forsake those vestigial remnants of the old life and, at the same time, discern its God-honoring virtues and qualities. To quote Molina, "Could Hispanic evangelicals, who are largely *Mestizo*, prism the Spirit of God, thus leading in the area of racial reconciliation *in Christ*?"[323] Additionally, given the Latino fondness to paint life with baroque brushstrokes, Hispangelicals could inspire a revival of godly emotion filled with joy and gladness, bringing godly zeal to the service of the Lord. Hispangelicals might also ignite a renaissance of artistic expression in the evangelical community to the glory of God.

---

[322] Molina, oral telephone interview.

[323] Ibid.

The Hispangelical's Heart

Fourth, and finally, Hispangelicals must love the Lord with all their heart. Since the heart is the inward place of the individual from where "flow the springs of life" (Prov. 4:23), we are safe in affirming that this commandment is all-encompassing. If mind, strength, and soul do not cover it, be assured that loving God with all our heart leaves nothing outside of its domain. Loving God with all our heart implies the abolition of the inherent sickness of the unrepentant human heart (Jer. 17:9). As such, this command becomes a real possibility only for all who are Spirit-led (Rom. 8:1–17). The heart of the redeemed has been reconditioned to desire to know God fully (Jer. 31:33). When a person loves God wholeheartedly, as only one who has known the love of God can, nothing is off the table, nothing is held in reserve.

Conclusion

As I have tried to show, evangelism continues into the Latino world, and a great number of Hispangelicals have surrendered to the disciplines of discipleship. The bench is definitely deepening. Yet in our thankfulness, we should not lose sight of the challenges that longevity itself creates. For the early church, the second century brought both internal and external crises that were only incipient in apostolic times. Gnosticism comes readily to mind, but so does the evolution of the church's ecclesiological structure and, of course, the question of canonicity. Though there is evidence that the New Testament writers dealt with such issues, they were not the burning topics that occupied the ante-Nicene church fathers. Conversely, while the Judaizing issue was red-hot prior to AD 70, it became much less significant thereafter. In light of all this, one lesson that history teaches is that the passage of time brings with it challenges that are not often detected on the horizon.

Alas, who's to say what is passing, chronic, or just beginning for the Hispanic evangelical? Will Pentecostalism continue to dominate the

Hispangelical ranks? Or will Hispanic evangelicals proliferate equally throughout the evangelical community? Will the allure of the prosperity gospel continue to prevail, or will this also pass? Will our message be idiosyncratic, focused exclusively on our own struggles, or will we have a relevant message to the broader evangelical community? Finally, and perhaps most urgent, given our longstanding cultural association with religious syncretism, how will the Hispangelical world respond to its challenges moving forward? May we have the wisdom to see the opportunities and challenges that are on the horizon, even as the Hispangelical clock grows from minutes to hours.

Conclusion

What Comes Now?

Often, Latinos can't help but revert to form. Recently John Leguizamo, a Colombian-born, Brooklyn-reared movie star, produced a Broadway spectacle, *Latin History for Morons,* using Latin figures from the past—Spanish conquistador Francisco Pizarro (1471–1541), Mexican revolutionary Pancho Villa (1878–1923), and Mexican Marxist artist Frida Kahlo (1907–1954)—to provide the visuals for its promotion.[324] With humor and irreverence, Leguizamo hopes to educate non-Hispanic audiences to the three thousand years of Mesoamerican and Latino contribution to the making of America. So far so good, but, then came something predictable.

Seizing the moment, Jorge Ramos, who was interviewing Leguizamo, brought up a theme of his, *Reconquista,* suggesting that perhaps *Latin History for Morons* was Leguizamo's way to further Latino cultural reclamation of the United States. Leguizamo smiled and heartily agreed.[325] And in doing so, I couldn't help but note that Leopoldo Zea's analysis of the Latin American mind is still spot-on. True to everything that makes

[324] John Leguizamo, "Latin History for Morons," https://latinhistorybroadway.com (accessed November 28, 2017).

[325] See *Real America with Jorge Ramos,* a five-episode series by Fusion TV, particularly the second episode, which aired Tuesday, November 28, 2017. See also Matt Fernandez, "Jorge Ramos to Launch 'Real America' Series on Fusion," *Variety,* http://variety.com/2017/tv/news/jorge-ramos-real-america-1202611336/ (accessed November 28, 2017).

them Latinos, Ramos and Leguizamo promote this drive to install Latino culture in the United States using borrowed Iberian history, for apparently their own native Latin-American history offers no support.

Doesn't Jorge Ramos know that the *Reconquista* was something totally Spanish, and in actuality should work logically against Hispanic hopes for cultural reclamation? Don't Latinos know that the Spanish Catholic conquerors who came across the Atlantic did to the inhabitants of the "New World" what the Muslim Moors had attempted to do when they crossed the Mediterranean to invade Iberia? Moreover, where the Moors only partially succeeded over the course of eight centuries (711–1492), the Spaniards accomplished the feat within fifty years (1492–1540s).[326] Seriously, the only historically faithful *Reconquista* scenario would be for the indigenous peoples of Latin America to rise up against all Iberian influences and reinstate pre-Columbian culture in all its glory; this is not likely to happen. Like so many historical events, the Spanish *Reconquista* might prove an interesting study, but to suggest that Latin Americans identify with it is nonsense.[327] It is tantamount to expect that native American tribes would embrace O'Sullivan's concept of American manifest destiny with enthusiasm! Don't Latinos know that their real challenges have nothing to do with gaining squatters' rights on US soil? After all, they continue to evacuate their own native soil in droves.

And why? The real issue is internal, a matter of the mind and heart, dealing decisively with resistant ideas, beliefs, and behaviors that have thwarted the Latino people across time. Alas, these two modern-day Hispanics are not so modern after all. Prone to anachronistic reasoning,

---

[326] Wiarda, *The Soul of Latin America*, 86.

[327] On this issue, Mexico's newly elected president Andrés Manuel López Obrador would seem not to be "down" for the *Reconquista*. In a recent letter to Spanish King Felipe VI and Pope Francis, President "AMLO" has called on them to apologize for the "abuses" of Spanish colonialism over the course of three hundred years. See "Mexico Demands Spain Apologize for the Colonial Abuse of Indigenous People," *The Guardian*, March 25, 2019, https://www.theguardian.com/world/2019/mar/25/mexico-demands-spain-apology-colonialism-obrador (accessed May 4, 2019).

turning to borrowed history—for there is apparently no indigenous history that works—both Ramos and Leguizamo are Exhibit A of the issue we have been discussing.

Thus, lest you failed to notice, just about every chapter has been couched in a historical perspective, and for good reason. While there are many students of Latin America who insist that historical realities no longer hold sway in the twenty-first century, we know better than to buy into such silly notions.[328] Why does a doctor need to know one's medical history, when what we need is a cure from some present illness?

Again, why is NASA investing billions of dollars to develop and place into orbit the James Webb Space Telescope? As you may know, its purpose is to peer into the sky, hoping to observe the furthest reaches of space. But let's be clear on what astronomers hope to study: NASA hopes to expand our ability to capture the earliest moments in the formation of the universe.[329] All of this begs the question: Are these astronomers who cast a vision for the future of space exploration actually closet romantics absorbed with meaningless history? Or, is it that knowing something about the earliest moments of our universe provides valuable insight for questions that remain unanswered, even at this late date? Seriously, take just about any human endeavor, from farming to philosophizing, and you will discover that historical perspective is integral to its understanding and application.

That said, my best reason for being unabashedly concerned with history is that the Bible itself is historical through and through. If you take the first chapter of Genesis and the last chapter of the Apocalypse, we are treated to the beginning and the end of human history. The Bible, as we know, contains many genres, but as is broadly accepted, its message is couched within a historical narrative and framework. If we read the Psalms, for example, we also have external and internal information that

---

[328] See for example the "McOndo Group," a society of prominent literary figures who advocate for moving away from the folklorism which has prevailed in the past. See Prevost and Vanden, *Latin America: An Introduction*, 182–183.

[329] James Webb Space Telescope, https://www.jwst.nasa.gov (accessed September 15, 2017).

helps us evaluate the historical time when they were penned. The same can be said for the Proverbs and the Prophets. One of the most painstaking exercises of the biblical theologian is assigning a historical setting to a biblical text. While we may not agree on conclusions reached, we agree that placing that text within a particular timeframe is necessary, and only possible because of the text's historical indicators.

The same is true for the New Testament. The four Gospels depict the historical birth and ministry of the Messiah. The book of Acts chronicles the birth and earliest developments of Christianity and the church. Paul's epistles are situational, which is to say they address specific historical conditions. The general epistles, though they are not necessarily written to deal with a situation at a specific church, nevertheless address historical realities like the harassing and persecution of believers (1 Peter), heresy (1 John), apostasy (Hebrews), interpersonal relationships (2, 3 John), and so on. Finally, the Apocalypse is notoriously difficult to interpret, but whether you approach it from preterist lens, a dispensational perspective, or even an amillennial symbolic point of view, we are all in agreement that its message says something about history, human history, and its ultimate consummation.

Thus, I conclude by encouraging the continual study of Latin American history. I am convinced that it is time well invested, for three important reasons. First, it only makes sense that we would want to know the essential history of people that border us to the south. Of course, the same could be said of our northern neighbors. But Canadians are not projected to grow to one hundred and fifty million in the United States by mid-century. So, learning more about Mexico and Latin America, in general, just makes good sense.

Second, Latin American history is five hundred twenty years old, surpassing US history by more than a century. However, if we also take into consideration pre-Colombian influences, many of which still thrive, that time span lengthens to multiple millennia. More significantly, part of that history was played out on lands that now constitute many of our states west of the Mississippi, and of course, Florida on the southeastern coast. It is no mere coincidence that so many US cities are named "San," "Santa," or something else reflecting a strong Roman Catholic and Spanish colonial tradition. The definite article "Los" as in Los Angeles, California; Los Alamos, New Mexico; or Los Fresnos, Texas, along with others, reveals the definite intent of the founding Spaniards to give the communities they were founding an explicit stamp and heritage.

This brings us to the third and most important point: The history of Latin America bears little resemblance to United States history. There are precious few touchpoints, and this fact alone makes it vital to gain necessary insight and perspective. It is always tempting to draw comparisons, and some of that might actually be necessary.[330] But Latin America, and by extension its children, needs to be understood on its own terms. Studying Latin American history may help us better to walk in its shoes and, hopefully, sensitize us to feel something of the struggle Latinos have endured across time.

But, then came the Hispangelicals. I have no doubt that they are a new creation in Christ, but are they being transformed by the renewing of their mind? Overall, our aim in studying history is to gain a knowledge of the past necessary for understanding something of the Hispanic and Hispangelical today. Note that I say "something," for historical facts alone are insufficient to provide satisfying answers. But, knowing important historical developments and understanding their ongoing significance is always a good way to begin broadening our knowledge of a people. Certainly, it will help us understand the Hispanic experience. But equally so, it will also help us to appreciate the challenges Hispangelicals face as they bear witness to their own context and the evangelical community.

---

[330] Randall Hansis, *The Latin Americans: Understanding Their Legacy* (Boston: McGraw-Hill, 1997), xiv. Hansis argues that North Americans need to understand their history in order to understand Latin American history better.

After reviewing broad Hispanic aspirations in our introductory remarks, I proposed that the Hispangelical should have to respond to two questions specifically:

> *Where do Hispangelicals stand and what do they have to say about it?*
> *Do Hispangelicals have the insight to present the gospel in a way that it addresses and answers the aspirations and hopes of the people?*

Some time back, I remember being told that people should never ask a question that they themselves cannot answer. And so, for the record, allow me to answer the questions, at least for myself.

First: *Where do Hispangelicals stand, and what do they have to say about it?* Some time back, Kalman H. Silvert, professor of Latin American politics and culture-at-large, chided Uruguayan novelist José Enrique Rodó for what he considered to be his naïve critique of American culture. Coming from underdeveloped countries, Silvert believed that Rodó and other Latino thinkers lacked the intellectual depth and background to critique a country as progressive and sophisticated as the United States.[331] Silvert observed that even the ideas they used to deliver their critique were borrowed, undercutting the importance of their reflections. "When it comes time for him [Rodó] to return what has been borrowed with the interest of his country's special cultural point of view," Silvert concluded, "he finds that nobody is listening because what he has to say is either not significant or not fresh in a different cultural context."[332]

On its face, Silvert's observation is brutal, but could his critique also apply to Hispanic evangelicals? Do they have anything vital to say to

[331] Kalman H. Silvert, *The Conflict Society: Reaction and Revolution in Latin America* (New York: Harper & Collins, 1966), 141. For Silvert's bio, see https://pabook.libraries.psu.edu/silvert__kalman (accessed October 15, 2017).
[332] Silvert, *The Conflict Society*, 142.

the broader evangelical community? Or, is their voice so idiosyncratic it is discounted as cultural, fun to hear—like the mariachi band playing in the restaurant—but forgotten once the meal is finished and the bill is paid?

To begin with, Silvert should not get away with thinking that his thoughts were truly original, while the Latino's were pillaged from other cultures. As is well known, all cultures have pillaged ideas, and the European were no exception. The Judeo-Christian worldview—from which Silvert drew—also emanated from the confluence of Macedonian and Middle Eastern thought. Excise Greek philosophy and the influence of Hebrew and Christian sources, and Europe is left with brute paganism. In critiquing Latino thinkers as unoriginal, Silvert was critiquing himself, and indeed the whole of the Greco-Roman world!

Nevertheless, with respect to the Hispangelical, must our contribution come at the expense of self-evisceration? Hispanic evangelicals must guard against the seduction of thinking they can become someone they are not. For myself, coming to faith in Christ never forced me to abandon my ethnicity, my culture, my family. At my core, I am a citizen of God's kingdom—and since his kingdom is earthly as much as it is heavenly, I am free to be a redeemed Hispano, saved by grace through faith in Christ. Like Paul, I am not conscious of anything against myself (1 Cor. 4:4); so even as I strive to achieve Christlikeness, I will be true to who I am.

Hispanic evangelicals stand where God has placed us, but he hasn't placed us anywhere to be monoliths. Hispangelicals, like all believers, are pilgrims. So we move forward, confident that the Lord, who began a good work in us, "will perfect it until the day of Christ Jesus" (Phil. 1:6).

Second, *do Hispangelicals have the insight to present the gospel in a way that it addresses and answers the aspirations and hopes of the people?* I have served Hispangelical churches for more than forty years, and it is my opinion that we have not really lived up to this challenge. If we have fallen short, it is because so often we cannot see beyond our circumstance, undercutting the responsibility we now have to the broader evangelical community. In saying this, I do not set myself up as an example, for I have also fallen short of letting the gospel reach its full depth of authority. But, as God gives me insight, I will strive to preach a gospel that addresses the fundamental problems that humanity-at-large experiences. That said, do not fault me if on occasion I address my kinsmen directly. Saint Paul did it when he devoted three chapters in his epistle to the Romans to the "Israel question" (Rom. 9–11). Peter did it when he spoke directly to the Jews (Acts 2, 4:11–26). Stephen did it when he addressed the dysfunctions of the Jews throughout history (Acts 8). I will do no less, for God has called us first to speak to our own.

Some time back, my wife and I were invited to a party. The hosts had all the guests play a game, which involved going into a room where the hosts had placed a tablet with the beginnings of a story already written. The aim was for each subsequent couple to pick up the story where the previous couple had left it and add their own paragraph, thus advancing the plot. As the party began to wind down, the story was brought out and read for all to hear. As we might imagine, there were interesting twists, hilarious experiences, sad moments, and even things that didn't make sense for while every couple could read what previous couples had written, some failed to pick up the thread. Alas, every couple that wrote could not know what those who would follow would write. Interestingly, the story was left open-ended, with some issues in the narrative left unresolved. As I think back on that experience, I am convinced that the whole exercise was a mirroring of evangelical history to the moment.

And so, Hispangelicals have come to the tablet of evangelical history with pen in hand. How will their paragraph read? Will their contribution be awkward, unconnected? Will they turn inward, myopically speaking only of their circumstance, or will they interpret their context in such a way that it enlightens the greater movement of which they are now a part? As Hispanic evangelicals increase, will they embrace maturity fully, taking on all the responsibilities that are concomitant with it?

I end with the writer of Hebrews, who saw some troubling issues with those to whom he wrote, but concluded through it all:

> But, beloved, we are convinced of better things concerning you, and things that accompany salvation, though we are speaking in this way. (Heb. 6:9)

May God be pleased to look kindly upon Hispangelicals, and to endow us with "all things that accompany salvation."

Selected Bibliography

Books

Almirudis, Hiram. *Episodios de mi vida y la Iglesia de Dios que yo conocí.* Leon Valley, TX: Self-published, 2013.

Anderson, Charles W. *Politics and Economic Change in Latin America: The Governing of Restless Nations.* Princeton, NJ: D. van Nostrand, 1967.

Andrews, Andy. *The Noticer Returns.* Nashville: W Publishing Group, 2013.

Arekion, Glenn. *The Power of Praying in Tongues: Unleashing the Supernatural Dimension in You.* Pescara, Italy: Destiny Image Europe, 2010.

Arias, Mortimer. "El Protestantismo," *Presencia* [La Paz, Bolivia], August 6, 1975.

Axtell, James. *The Invasion Within: The Contest of Cultures in Colonial North America.* New York: Oxford University Press, 1985.

Baird, William. *History of New Testament Research.* Vol. 1. Minneapolis: Fortress Press, 1992.

Batalla, Guillermo Bonfil. *Mexico Profundo: Reclaiming a Civilization.* Austin: University of Texas Press, 1996.

Becker, Jürgen, ed. *Christian Beginnings: Word and Community from Jesus to Post-Apostolic Times.* Louisville: Westminster/John Knox Press, 1993.

Berger, Peter L., and Thomas Luckmann. *The Social Construction of Reality: A Treatise in the Sociology of Knowledge.* New York: 1966.

Beller, Jacob. *Jews in Latin America.* New York: Jonathan David Co., 1969.

Berlin, Isaiah. *The Hedgehog and the Fox.* London: 1953.

Bowden, Henry Warner. *American Indians and Christian Missions.* Chicago: University of Chicago Press, 1981.

Bradbury, Ray. *Fahrenheit 451.* New York: Ballantine Publishing Group, 1953.

Braithwaite, William Stanley, ed. *The Book of Georgian Verse.* New York: Brentano's, 1909.

Brenner, Michael. *A Short History of the Jews.* Princeton, NJ: Princeton University Press, 2010.

Brisco, Thomas. *Holman Bible Atlas.* Nashville: Broadman & Holman Publishers, 1998.

Buelow, George J. ed., *"A" History of Baroque Music.* Bloomington: Indiana University Press, 2004.

Burgess, Stanley M., and Eduard M. Van der Maas, eds. *New International Dictionary of Pentecostal and Charismatic Movements, revised edition.* Grand Rapids: Zondervan, 2002.

Campbell, Ted A. *Methodist Doctrine: The Essentials.* Nashville: Abingdon Press, 2011.

Carter, Heath W., and Laura Rominger Porter, eds. *Turning Points in the History of American Evangelicalism.* Grand Rapids, MI: Wm. B. Eerdmans Publishing Co., 2017.

Carrasco, David. *Religions of Mesoamerica.* San Francisco: Harper & Row, 1990.

Castillo, Ana, ed. *Goddess of the Americas, La Diosa de las Americas.* New York: Riverhead Books, 1996.

Catholic Conference, United States. *Catechism of the Catholic Church.* Libreria Editrice Vaticana, 1994.

Cene, Leoncillo Veguilla. *Cinco Formas de Sincretismo Religioso en Cuba.* Master's thesis for Seminario Teologico Bautista "R.A. Ocania," Habana, Cuba, 1997.

Cervantes, Richard. *A Guide for Conducting Cultural Assessment of Latino and Hispanic Clients.* Bayamon, PR: Universidad Central del Caribe, 2017.

Chasteen, John Charles. *Born in Blood & Fire: A Concise History of Latin America.* New York: W. W. Norton & Company, 2006.

Comte, Isidore Auguste Marie François Xavier. A *General View of Positivism*, Project Gutenberg, http://www.gutenberg.org/ebooks/53799.

Conrad, Geoffrey W. *Religion and Empire.* Cambridge: Cambridge University Press, 1984.

Cousins, Norman. "Introduction: The Need for Continuity," *American Library Association Bulletin.* October 1954.

Crumrine, M. Ross, Alan Morinis eds. *Pilgrimage in Latin America.* Westport, CT: Greenwood Press, 1991.

Deiros, Pablo Alberto. *Historia del Cristianismo en América Latina.* Buenos Aires: Fraternidad Teológica Latinoamericana, 1992.

Dickens, Charles. *A Tale of Two Cities.* London: Dover Publications, 1998.

Elizondo, Virgilio, A. F. Deck, and T. Matovina, eds. *The Treasure of Guadalupe.* New York: Rowman & Littlefield Publishers, 2006.

Erickson, Millard, J. *The Evangelical Left.* Grand Rapids, MI: Baker Books, 1997.

Evans, Craig A., and S. E. Porter. *Dictionary of New Testament Background.* Downers Grove, IL: InterVarsity Press, 2000.

Farrer, Austin. *Faith and Speculation: An Essay in Philosophical Theology.* Edinburgh: T. & T. Clark LTD., 1967.

Foster, Richard J. *Celebration of Discipline: The Path to Spiritual Growth, revised edition.* San Francisco: Harper Collins Publishers, 1988.

Friedman, George. *The Next 100 Years: A Forecast for the 21st Century.* New York: Anchor Books, 2009.

Patrik Fridlund and Mika Vähäkangas, eds. *Philosophical and Theological Responses to Syncretism.* Leiden/Boston: Brill Academic Publishers, 2017.

Garcia, Jorge G. E., ed. *Latin American Philosophy in the Twentieth Century: Man, Values, and the Search for Philosophical Identity.* Buffalo, NY: Prometheus Books, 1986.

Gardner, Helen, Fred S. Kleiner, and Christin J. Mamiya. *Gardner's Art through the Ages.* Belmont, CA: Thomson/Wadsworth, 2005.

Gerstner, John H. *The Evangelicals: What They Believe, Who They Are, Where They Are Changing.* Nashville: Abingdon, 1975.

Giddens, Anthony, ed. *Positivism and Sociology.* London: Heinemann Educational Publishers, 1974.

Graham, Gordon. *The Shape of the Past.* Oxford: Oxford University Press, 1997.

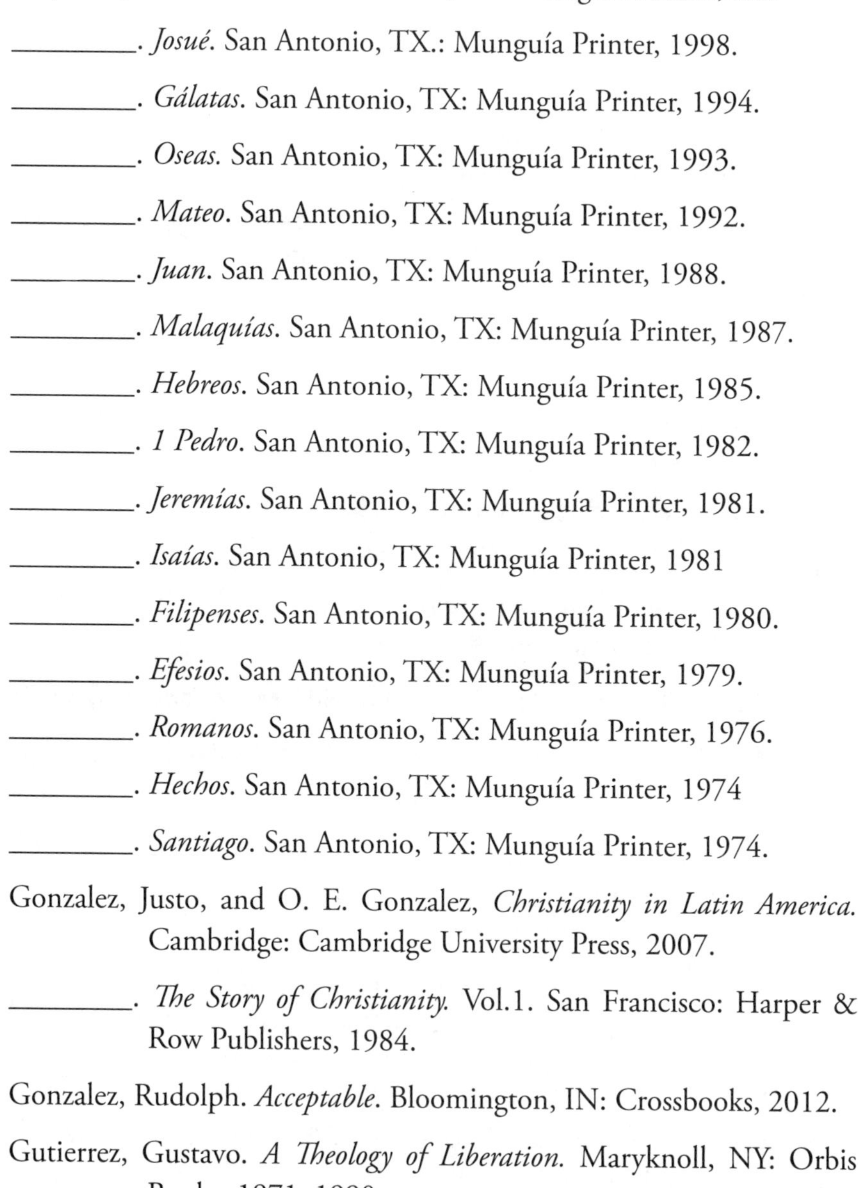

Grijalva, Josué. *Éxodos*. San Antonio, TX: Munguía Printer, n.d.

________. *Josué*. San Antonio, TX.: Munguía Printer, 1998.

________. *Gálatas*. San Antonio, TX: Munguía Printer, 1994.

________. *Oseas*. San Antonio, TX: Munguía Printer, 1993.

________. *Mateo*. San Antonio, TX: Munguía Printer, 1992.

________. *Juan*. San Antonio, TX: Munguía Printer, 1988.

________. *Malaquías*. San Antonio, TX: Munguía Printer, 1987.

________. *Hebreos*. San Antonio, TX: Munguía Printer, 1985.

________. *1 Pedro*. San Antonio, TX: Munguía Printer, 1982.

________. *Jeremías*. San Antonio, TX: Munguía Printer, 1981.

________. *Isaías*. San Antonio, TX: Munguía Printer, 1981

________. *Filipenses*. San Antonio, TX: Munguía Printer, 1980.

________. *Efesios*. San Antonio, TX: Munguía Printer, 1979.

________. *Romanos*. San Antonio, TX: Munguía Printer, 1976.

________. *Hechos*. San Antonio, TX: Munguía Printer, 1974

________. *Santiago*. San Antonio, TX: Munguía Printer, 1974.

Gonzalez, Justo, and O. E. Gonzalez, *Christianity in Latin America*. Cambridge: Cambridge University Press, 2007.

________. *The Story of Christianity.* Vol.1. San Francisco: Harper & Row Publishers, 1984.

Gonzalez, Rudolph. *Acceptable*. Bloomington, IN: Crossbooks, 2012.

Gutierrez, Gustavo. *A Theology of Liberation.* Maryknoll, NY: Orbis Books, 1971, 1990.

Hale, Charles A. *Mexican Liberalism in the Age of Mora, 1821–1853.* New Haven, CT: Yale University Press, 1968.

Hall, Marcia B., and Tracy E. Cooper, eds. *The Sensuous in the Counter Reformation Church,* Cambridge: Cambridge University Press, 2013.

Hanke, Lewis. *Aristotle and the American Indians.* Bloomington: Indiana University Press, 1970.

Hansis, Randall. *The Latin Americans: Understanding Their Legacy.* New York: McGraw-Hill Publishers, 1997.

Hermes, Rafael. *Origen e Historia del Mariachi*, segunda edicion. Editorial Katun, S.A. Republica de Colombia, 1983.

Jenkins, Philip. *The Next Christendom: The Coming of Global Christianity.* Oxford: Oxford University Press, 2002.

Keefe, Susan E., and Amado M. Padilla. *Chicano Ethnicity*. Notre Dame, IN: University of Notre Dame Press, 1987.

Keener, Craig. *The Mind of the Spirit.* Grand Rapids, MI: Baker Academic, 2016.

Keller, Timothy J. *Center Church*. Grand Rapids, MI: Zondervan, 2012.

Knoll, Mark A. *The Scandal of the Evangelical Mind.* Grand Rapids, MI: Wm. B. Eerdmans, 1994.

________. *The Rise of Evangelicalism: The Age of Edwards, Whitefield, and the Wesleys: A History of Evangelicalism.* Downers Grove, IL: InterVarsity Press, 2004.

Ladd, George Eldon. *A Theology of the New Testament.* Grand Rapids, MI: William B. Eerdmans Publishing Co., 1996.

Lastaria, Jose Victoranio. *Recuerdos Literarios*. Santiago, Chile, 1885.

León-Portilla, Miguel. *Aztec Thought and Culture.* Norman: University of Oklahoma Press, 1963.

Luna, Félix. *Grandes protagonistas de la historia argentina: Juan Manuel de Rosas*. Buenos Aires: Grupo Editorial Planeta, 2004.

Lynch, John. *New Worlds: A Religious History of Latin America*. New Haven, CT: Yale University Press, 2012.

Manschreck, Clyde L. ed. *A History of Christianity.* Vol. 2. Grand Rapids, MI: Baker Book House, 1964.

Martin, David. *Tongues of Fire: The Explosion of Protestantism in Latin America.* Oxford: Blackwell Publishers, 1990.

________. *Pentecostalism: The World Their Parish.* Malden, MA.: Blackwell, 2002.

Martyna, Brożyńska, Krzysztof Kowal, Anna Lis, and Michał Szymczak. *5xWhys. Method First Handbook*. Lódz, Poland: 2K Consulting, 2016.

Mayer-Serra, Carlos Elizondo. *Por eso estamos como estamos. La economía política de un crecimiento mediocre*. México City: Debate Editorial, 2011.

Mayz Vallenilla, Ernesto. *El Problema de América, Cuadernos de Cultura Latinoamericana.* Mexico City: Universidad Nacional Autónoma Mexicana, 1994.

Metzger, Bruce M. *A Textual Commentary on the Greek New Testament.* 2nd ed. New York: United Bible Societies, 1994.

Mirandé, Alfredo. *Hombres y Machos: Masculinity and Latino Culture.* Riverside: University of California Press, 1998.

Molina, Bruno. "An Analysis of the Transmission of the Gospel among Transcultural Hispanic Americans." PhD diss., Southwestern Baptist Theological Seminary, Fort Worth, TX, 2018.

Montoya, Alex. D. *Hispanic Ministry in North America.* Grand Rapids: Zondervan, 1987.

Mora, Jose Luis. *Obras Sueltas de Jose Luis Mora, Ciudadano mejicano: Revista Politica,* Sydney, Australia: Wentworth Press, 2018.

Naidoo, Jamie Campbell, ed. *Celebrating Cuentos*. Santa Barbara, CA: ABC-CLIO, 2011.

Nida, Eugene. *Understanding Latin Americans: With Special Reference to Religious Values and Movements*. South Pasadena, CA: William Carey Library, 1974.

Niebuhr, H. Richard. *Christ and Culture*. New York: Harper & Row, 1975.

Noble, Judith, Jaime Lacasa. *The Hispanic Way: Aspects of Behavior, Attitudes, and Customs in the Spanish-Speaking World*. Chicago: Passport Books, 1993.

North American Mission Board, ed. *Reaching Hispanics in North America*. Alpharetta, GA: Church Planting Resource Library, 2009.

Núñez, Emilio A. *Liberation Theology*. Chicago: Moody Press, 1985.

O'Malley, John W., Gauvin A. Bailey, Steven J. Harris, and T. Frank Kennedy, eds. *The Jesuits II: Cultures, Sciences, and the Arts, 1540–1773*. Toronto: University of Toronto Press, 2006.

O'Meara, Thomas F. "Baroque Catholicism," *The HarperCollins Encyclopedia of Catholicism*. San Francisco: Harper Collins, 1989.

Ortega y Gasset, José. *Meditaciones del Quijote*, Obras Completas, Vol. 1. Madrid: Fundación, 2004.

Payne, Douglas W. *Storm Watch: Democracy in the Western Hemisphere into the Next Century*. Washington, DC: Center for Strategic and International Studies, 1998.

Paz, Octavio. *El Laberinto de la Soledad*. Mexico: Fondo de Cultura Economica, 1950.

Pedraja, Luis G. *Teología: An Introduction to Hispanic Theology*. Nashville: Abingdon Press, 2003.

Perowne, Stewart. *The Life and Times of Herod the Great*. Phoenix Mill: Sutton Publishing Ltd., 1956, 2003.

Platt, David. *Follow Me.* Carol Stream, IL: Tyndale House Publishers, 2013.

Prevost, Gary, and H. E. Vanden, *Latin America: An Introduction.* Oxford: Oxford University Press, 2010.

Raat, W. Dirk, ed. *Mexico: From Independence to Revolution, 1810–1910.* Lincoln: University of Nebraska Press, 1982.

Ramos, Jorge. *The Latino Wave.* New York: HarperCollins Publishers/ Rayo, 2004.

Resnick, Seymour. *1001 Most Useful Spanish Words.* Mineola, NY: Dover Publications, 1996.

Rodó, Jose Enrique. *Ariel.* Middlesex: Echo Library, 2008.

Rodriguez, Daniel A. *A Future for the Latino Church.* Downers Grove, IL: InterVarsity Press, 2011.

Rogers, C.L. Rogers III. *The New Linguistic and Exegetical Key to the Greek New Testament.* Grand Rapids, MI: Zondervan Publishing House, 1998.

Sánchez Cardenas, Julio A. *La religión de los Orichas: Creencias y ceremonias de un culto afro-caribeño.* Carolina, PR: Esmaco Printers Corp., 1978, 1997.

Sanders, J. Oswald. *Spiritual Leadership.* Chicago: Moody Press, 1994.

Schiffman, Laurence H. *From Text to Tradition: A History of Judaism in Second Temple and Rabbinic Times.* Brooklyn, NY: Ktav Publishers, 1991.

Sigmund, Paul E., ed. *Religious Freedom and Evangelization in Latin America.* Maryknoll, NY: Orbis Books, 1999.

Silvert, Kalman H. *The Conflict Society: Reaction and Revolution in Latin America.* New York: Harper & Collins, 1966.

Spurgeon, Charles, H. *Morning and Evening.* Peabody, MA: Hendrickson Publishers, 1991.

Stavans, Ilan. *The Hispanic Condition: The Power of a People.* New York: Rayo, 1995, 2001.

Stoll, David. *Is Latin America Turning Protestant?* Berkeley: University of California Press, 1990.

Sweeney, Douglas A. *The American Evangelical Story.* Grand Rapids, MI: Baker Academic, 2005.

Terry, J. O. *Basic Bible Storying.* Fort Worth, TX: Church Starting Network, 2008.

Trompf, G. W. *The Idea of Historical Recurrence in Western Thought, from Antiquity to the Reformation.* Berkeley: University of California Press, 1979.

Ugarate, Ruben Vargas. *Historia del culto de María en Iberoamérica: y de sus imágenes y santuarios más celebrados.* Madrid: Editorial Huarpes, 1947.

Ureña, Pedro Henríquez. *Seis ensayos en busca de nuestra expression.* Buenos Aires: Editorial Babel, 1928.

Van Baalen, Jan Karel. *The Chaos of the Cults.* Grand Rapids, MI: Wm. B. Eerdmans, 1942, 1962.

Vargas, Manuel. "On the Value of Philosophy: The Latin American Case," *Comparative Philosophy,* Vol. 1, No. 1 (2010).

Vasconcelos, José. *La Raza Cósmica.* México, D.F.: Espasa-Calpe, S.A., 1992.

Véliz, Claudio. *The New World of the Gothic Fox.* Berkeley/Los Angeles/London: University of California Press, 1994.

Verduin, Leonard. *The Reformers and Their Stepchildren.* Sarasota, FL: The Christian Hymnary Publishers, 1964.

Vought, Dale V. *Like a Flickering Flame: A History of Protestant Missions in Spain.* Sevilla: Publidisa Publishers, 2001.

Wakefield, Steve. *Carpentier's Baroque Fiction: Returning Medusa's Gaze.* Woodbridge, Suffolk: Tamesis, 2004.

Waterworth, J. *The Council of Trent: The Canons and Decrees of the Sacred and Ecumenical Council of Trent.* London: Dolman Publishers, 1848.

Wiarda, Howard. J. *The Soul of Latin America.* New Haven, CT: Yale University Press, 2001.

Womans Missionary Council. *Fourth Missionary Report.* Nashville: Publishing House of the Methodist Episcopal Church, 1913, 1914.

Zea, Leopoldo. *Essays on Philosophy and History.* Jorge J. E. Garcia, ed. Buffalo, NY: Prometheus Books, 1986.

________. *The Latin-American Mind.* Translation by James H. Abbott and Lowell Dunham. Norman: University of Oklahoma Press, 1963.

Journal, Magazine Articles

Diaz, Elizabeth. "The Latino Reformation," *Time*, April 15, 2013.

Freston, Paul. "Evangelicals and Politics in Latin America," JSTOR, Vol. 19, No. 4 (2002), 271–274.

Garcia, Jorge G. E. "Importance of the History of Ideas in Latin America: Zea's Positivism in Mexico," *Journal of the History of Ideas,* Vol. 36, No. 1 (Jan.-March 1975).

Gehrz, Chris. "Recalibrating the 'Evangelical Paradigm,'" *Patheos,* July 13, 2017.

Irving, David R. M. "Latin American Baroque," *Early Music,* Vol. 39, No. 2 (May 2011).

Masci, David. "Why Has Pentecostalism Grown So Dramatically in Latin America?" Pew Research Center, November 14, 2014.

Turner, David L. "Matthew 21:43 and the Future of Israel," *Bibliotheca Sacra* 159, No. 633 (Jan–Mar 2002).

Widmer, Randolph J. "The Rise, Fall, and Transformation of Native American Cultures in the Southeastern United States." *Reviews in Anthropology* 39, No. 2 (2010).

Electronic Sources

Anderson, Allen. "The Origins of Pentecostalism and its Global Spread in the Early Twentieth Century." Graduate Institute for Theology and Religion, University of Birmingham (2004). http://www.ocms.ac.uk/docs/Allan%20Anderson%20lecture20041005.pdf.

Beliefnet News, "Why Are U.S. Hispanic Catholics Joining Pentecostal, Evangelical Churches?" Beliefnet (2011). https://www.beliefnet.com/columnists/news/2011/10/why-are-u-s-hispanics-choosing-to-leave-the-catholic-church.php.

Boehme, Ron. "The Fourth Wave." US Renewal. http://www.usrenewal.org/the-fourth-wave.

Buchanan, William. "We Shall Overwhelm: Deciphering Bureau of Labor Statistics Data on Hispanic Workers," The Social Contract (2013). http://www.thesocialcontract.com/pdf/twenty-two/tsc_20_2_ w_buchanan.pdf.

Copeland, Kenneth. "Five Benefits of Praying in Tongues." Kenneth Copeland Ministries. http://www.kcm.org/real-help/prayer/apply/5-benefits-praying-tongues.

Croughuell, Thomas. "What Every Catholic Needs to Know about Saints—Our Friends in High Places." OVS News Weekly (2011). https://www.osv.com/OSVNewsweekly/Story/TabId/2672/ArtMID/13567/ArticleID/10325/

What-every-Catholic-needs-to-know-about-saints--Our-friends-in-high-places.aspx.

Daily Mail. "More Than a Third of Americans Think Hispanics Are Illegal Immigrants . . . and Films and TV Are to Blame." Daily Mail (2012). http://www.dailymail.co.uk/news/article-2202444/More-THIRD-Americans-think-Hispanics-illegal-immigrants--films-TV-blame.html#ixzz26MW2WI7m.

Erickson, Amanda. "Latin America Is the World's Most Violent Region. A New Report Investigates Why." *The Washington Post*, April 25, 2018. https://www.washingtonpost.com/ news/worldviews/wp/2018/04/25/latin-america-is-the-worlds-most-violent-region-a-new-report-investigates-why/?utm_term=.c0aa5d3f3009.

Ethics and Religious Liberty Commission. http://erlc.com.

Fernandez, Matt. "Jorge Ramos to Launch 'Real America' Fusion Series." Fusion (2017). http://variety.com/2017/tv/news/jorge-ramos-real-america-1202611336.

Generación Ñ. http://generation-ntv.com.

Goddard Space Flight Center. https://www.jwst.nasa.gov.

Guardian. "Mexico Demands Spain Apologize for the colonial abuse of indigenous people." March 25, 2019. https://www.theguardian.com/world/2019/mar/25/mexico-demands-spain-apology-colonialism-obrador.

Hagin, Kenneth. "Seven Reasons Why Every Believer Should Speak in Tongues." Kenneth Hagin Ministries. .http://www.rhema.org/index.php?option=com_content&view=article&id=1053:seven-reasons-why-every-believer-should-speak-in-tongues&Itemid=145.

Hawkins, Benjamin. "Fields Ripe for Harvest in Hispanic Population." Southwestern Baptist Theological Seminary (2012). https://

swbts.edu/news/releases/fields-ripe-harvest-hispanic-population-sanchez-says.

Hayward, Steven F. "How Is 'Liberation Theology' Still a Thing?" *Forbes* (2015) https://www.forbes.com/sites/stevenhayward/2015/05/10/how-is-liberation-theology-still-a-thing.

Hernandez, Edwin I. "Latino/a Research: An Educational and Ministerial Profile of Latino/a Seminarians." Latino Research @ND (2007). https://latinostudies.nd.edu/assets/ 95307/original/lr_nd_v4n4finalweb.pdf.

Holy Rosary, "Benefits of the Rosary," http://www.theholyrosary.org/rosarybenefits.

Huddleston, Tom. "Disney's New Pixar Movie 'Coco' Already Set a Box Office Record," *Fortune*, November 16, 2017, http://fortune.com/2017/11/16/coco-disney-pixar-box-office-mexico.

Kunerth, Jeff. "Hispanics Flock to Pentecostal Churches." *Orlando Sentinel*, January 2, 2010. http://www.orlandosentinel.com/features/os-hispanic-pentecostals_3-20100101-story.html.

Kwon, Lilian. "Pentecostal Impact Is Growing in Latin America." *The Christian Post* (2006). http://www.christianpost.com/news/pentecostal-impact-growing-in-latin-america-23067/#KjvoYC1KkzRs6sZo.99.

Leguizamo, John. "Latin History for Morons." (2018). https://latinhistorybroadway.com.

Linthicum, Kate. "Evangelicals Are the Kind of Latinos the GOP Could Be Winning. But Not with Donald Trump." *Los Angeles Times*, May 23, 2016. http://www.latimes.com/politics/la-na-polevangelical-latinos-20160523-snap-htmlstory.html.

Lopez, Ricardo. "Nonverbal Latino Communication and Social Networking." Green Book Directory (2009). http://www.

greenbook.org/marketing-research.cfm/non-verbal-latino-communication-and-social-networking.

Los Cojolites. "Alma y Colores de Mexico." YouTube video, 5:20, posted October 6, 2014. https://www.youtube.com/watch?v=aavRzHta1YM.

Lotierzo, Frank. "Duran should never again answer why he quit rematch with Leonard." The Sweet Science, October 17, 2013. http://www.thesweetscience.com/feature-articles/17416-duran-should-never-again-answer-why-he-quit-during-rematch-with-leonard.

Lukins, Julian. "Professor Proves Pentecostalism and Scholarship Can Coexist." *Charisma* (2010). http://www.charismamag.com/site-archives/570-news/featured-news/11969-a-professor-with-spirit.

Mann, Benjamin. "Wisconsin Chapel Approved as First US Marian Apparition Site." Catholic News Agency (2010). https://www.catholicnewsagency.com/news/wisconsin-chapel-approved-as-first-us-marian-apparition-site.

Mena, Veronica. "Twenty Marian Devotions by Country in Latin America." The Catholic Company, July 10, 2015. https://www.catholic-company.com/getfed/20-marian-devotions-latin-america.

Misra, Tanvi. "The U.S. Hispanic Population Is Disproportionately Young." Citylab (2016). https://www.citylab.com/life/2016/04/six-out-of-ten-latinos-are-millennials-or-younger-pew-research-center-study/479010.

National Gang Center. "National Youth Gang Survey Analysis." NGC (2011). http://www.nationalgangcenter.gov/Survey-Analysis/Demographics.

New Advent. "Syncretism." New Advent (2018). http://www.newadvent.org/cathen/14383c.htm.

Pew Research Center. "'When Labels Don't Fit,' Hispanics and Their Views of Identity" (2012). http://www.pewhispanic.org/files/2012/04/Hispanic-Identity.pdf.

________. "Changing Faiths: Latinos and the Transformation of American Religion" (2007). http://www.pewhispanic.org/2007/04/25/changing-faiths-latinos-and-the-transformation-of-american-religion.

________. "Major New Survey Explores the Shifting Religious Identity of Latinos in the United States" (2014). http://www.pewforum.org/2014/05/07/major-new-survey-explores-the-shifting-religious-identity-of-latinos-in-the-united-states.

Ramos, Jorge. Biography. https://www.jorgeramos.com/en/biography.

Rampell, Catherine. "Mapping Unwed Motherhood." *The New York Times*, May 2, 2013. http://economix.blogs.nytimes.com/2013/05/02/mapping-unwed-motherhood/?_r=0.

Sabogal, Fabio. "Hispanic Familism and Acculturation: What Changes and What Doesn't?" *Hispanic Journal of Behavioral Sciences* (1987). https://journals.sagepub.com/doi/abs/10.1177/07399863870094003.

Stetzer, Ed. "Avoiding the Pitfalls of Syncretism." *Christianity Today* (2014). http://www.christianitytoday.com/edstetzer/2014/june/avoiding-pitfall-of-syncretism.html.

Straker, Ed. "Mexican Flag Flies Proudly over the Town Where Illegal Alien Kills Mollie Tibbetts." American Thinker (2018). https://www.americanthinker.com/blog/2018/09/mexican_ flag_flies_proudly_over_town_where_illegal_alien_killed_mollie_tibbetts.html.

Traub, Amy. "Credit Card Debt in the Latino Community." Demos (2014). http://www.demos.org/publication/credit-card-debt-latino-community.

Tucker, Duncan. "Santa Muerte: The Rise of Mexico's 'Death Saint.'" *BBC News* (2017). https://www.bbc.com/news/world-latin-america-41804243.

University of California Residence Policy and Guidelines (2018). http://ucop.edu/general-counsel/_files/ed-affairs/uc-residence-policy.pdf.

US Census Bureau. "Projections of the Size and Composition of the U.S. Population: 2014 to 2060" (2015). http://www.census.gov/content/dam/Census/library/ publications/demo/p25-1143.pdf.

US Government Publishing Office, "Comprehensive Immigration Reform: Faith-Based Perspectives," https://www.govinfo.gov/content/pkg/CHRG-111shrg56073/html/CHRG-111shrg56073.htm.

Youth Policy.org. "Latin America & The Caribbean: Youth Facts." http://www.youthpolicy.org/mappings/regionalyouthscenes/latinamerica/facts.

Vélez Rodriguez, Ricardo. "La Filosofía en Latinoamérica y los Problemas de la Originalidad y del Método," Universidad Federal de Juiz de Fora, Brasil. http://www.ecsbdefesa.com.br/defesa/fts/FLPOM.pdf.

Walsh, Brian. "Marian Apparitions in the Americas." Eternal Word Television Network. http://www.ewtn.com/library/mary/marian.htm.

Weiskittel, John K. "Voodoo You Trust? John Paul II Betrayal in Benin." Novus Ordo Watch (1993). http://novusordowatch.org/voodoo-you-trust-weiskittel.

Western Union. "Send Money to Latin American with Western Union." https://www.westernunion.com/au/en/send-money-to-latin-america.html.

WND.com, "Mexican Flag Flies at U.S. Post Office" (2006). http://www.wnd.com/2006/08/37688.

Ancient Sources

Aristotle, *Politics,* Book V. Edited by Carnes Lord, second edition. Chicago: University of Chicago Press, 2013.

Francisco Suárez, *De Legibus,* Book 8. In *Routledge Encyclopedia of Philosophy*, rep.routledge.com.

Horace, *Epistle I*, Book II. In *Horace: The Odes*, ed. J. D. McClatchy. Princeton, NJ: Princeton University Press, 2002.

Marcus Aurelius, *Meditations,* Book V. United Kingdom: Penguin Books, 2005.

Plato, *The Republic.* Trans. R. E. Allen. New Haven, CT: Yale University Press, 2006.

Television Sources

Jon Garrido News Network, January 12, 2010, Hispanic8.com. Garrido reports that 85 percent of all US Hispanic Protestants identify themselves as Pentecostals, approximately 6.2 million people.

NBC, *Meet the Press,* with host Chuck Todd interviewing Democrat House Minority Leader, Nancy Pelosi, April 23, 2017.

Musical Compositions

"*Ódiame*," composed in 1959 by Peruvian Rafael Otero Lopez (1921–1997). Lyrics inspired by a sonnet written by Federico Barreto, "*El último ruego*" (The Last Plea). Lyrics at https://www.lyrics.com/lyric/34006432/La+Santa+Cecilia/Ódiame.

"La Copa Rota," composed and written in 1966 by Puerto Rican Benito de Jesus (1912–2010). Lyrics at https://genius.com/Jose-feliciano-la-copa-rota-lyrics.

Los Intocables, *"Por Eso Estamos Como Estamos,"* by Eduardo López, released 2009, track 12 on *Intocable—Classic*, Sony Music Latin. Lyrics at https://www.letras.com/los-apson/por-eso-estamos-como-estamos.

Oral Interviews

Gallego, Belen, José Guadalupe Ramirez, Maria Angelina Valenzuela, Carolina Ramirez, and Virginia L. Gonzalez, interviewed by author, oral recollections, Tucson, Arizona, summer 2007; San Antonio, Texas, November 2017.

Lopez, Rolando. Ethnic church strategist for the San Antonio Baptist Association, Baptist General Convention of Texas, December 3, 2017.

Molina, Bruno. Evangelism associate with the Southern Baptists of Texas Convention, telephone interview, October 12, 2017.